Phil:

Just thought it was safe to

LONG DRIVE THROUGH A SHORT WAR

declare another war!!

Peter

12/5/04.

J. Fox

LONG DRIVE THROUGH A SHORT WAR

Reporting on the Iraq War

Peter Wilson

Hardie Grant Books

To Pilita, with thanks.
For putting up with my being in Iraq.
And just for putting up with me.

Published in 2004
by Hardie Grant Books
12 Claremont Street
South Yarra, Victoria 3141, Australia
www.hardiegrant.com.au

National Library of Australia Cataloguing-in-Publication Data:

Wilson, Peter.
    Long drive through a short war: reporting on the Iraq War.
    ISBN 1 74066 143 5.
    1. Wilson, Peter – Journeys – Iraq. 2. Iraq War, 2003.
    3. Iraq – Description and travel. I. Title.
956.70443

Edited by Sally Moss, ConText

Photography by John Feder, with additional photographs
from Stuart Clarke and Stewart Innes
Cover design by Klarissa Pfisterer & Hamish Freeman
Typeset by Pauline Haas, Girl's Own Graphics
Printed and bound in Australia by Griffin Press

10 9 8 7 6 5 4 3 2 1

On the cover:
A family flees the siege of Basra. One hundred metres before
Mohammed Mohsin reached us he hoisted his tired son onto
his shoulders so the family could hasten their pace.

CONTENTS

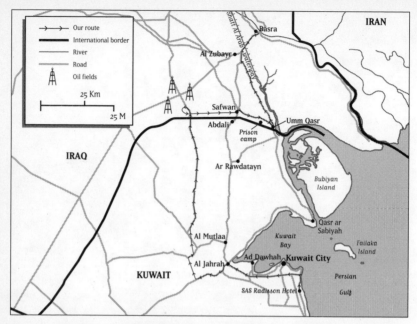

Northern Kuwait and Southern Iraq

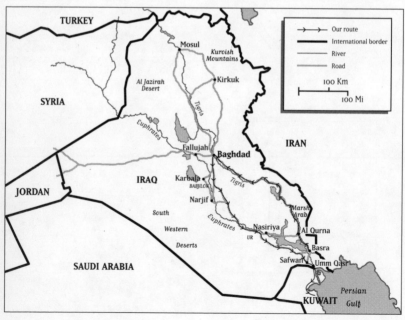

Iraq

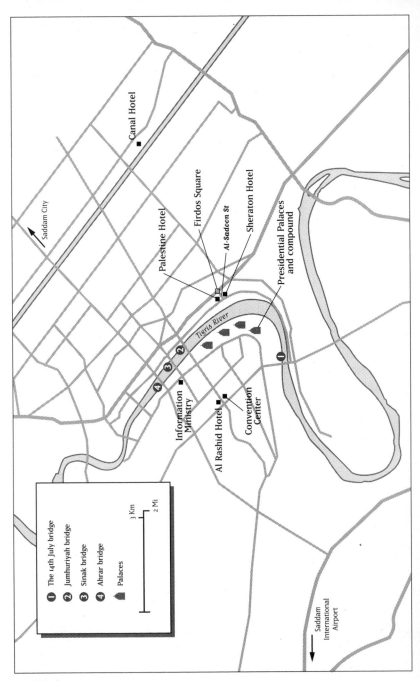

Baghdad

1

WHICH WAY TO THE FRONT?

'OK, so who here has ever been taken captive or held against their will?'

Our instructor, a tough little veteran of the British Marines, peered at me and two dozen other journalists who had come along for a military survival course, an idiot's guide to coping with twenty-first century warfare.

It was early February 2003, only weeks before the outbreak of war in the deserts of Iraq, and we had gathered in Heckfield Place, an eighteenth-century mansion in the damp English countryside, to spend a week learning how to stay alive while covering that war.

That day's exercise had involved being grabbed by surprise, having bags tied over our heads, then being shoved around in a forest for a while. Now that we had wiped the mud off our clothes, we were discussing coping strategies and being asked whether anything like that had happened to us before.

I had never been a prisoner; neither had the photographer sitting next to me, the *Chicago Tribune*'s Terrence James. But an American television producer said he had once been held for several hours at a checkpoint in Africa. A German cameraman managed to come up with an entire day when he had been held in an Israeli police station. Then the instructor turned to Ahmad Al-Rikabi, a pudgy Iraqi-born journalist from the US Government-funded Radio Free Europe. He had been detained only once, he said almost apologetically, when he'd been dragged into a car from a street in Lebanon and thrown into a darkened room.

'After about a month it started to get to me,' he added.

Heads swivelled in his direction. Terrence turned to me, nodding his head knowingly.

'Yeah,' he whispered, 'I *hate* it when that happens.'

The worst thing, Ahmad continued, was listening to people being tortured in the room next to his. 'After a while, you start to wish it is you being tortured rather than having to listen to it day and night,' he said.

'No,' I said to Terrence, 'I'm pretty confident I'd rather listen to it.'

We were joking because the course material had become increasingly grim. We had been lectured on the dangers of chemical weapons, booby traps and heat fatigue. Vivid simulations – complete with fake blood – of what to do if a colleague has an arm blown off in front you, or how to react to a landmine and a mortar explosion, were not exactly my thing. No one in my family has ever seen anything resembling military action, and my schoolboy career in the Australian Army cadets ended when it was discovered that not only could I not carry my own kit bag on a ten-kilometre march through the bush, I couldn't lift the thing off the ground.

I don't read war books and I am afraid of guns. I did once own a slug gun but I never actually hit anything. But our employers – and their insurers – had ordered us here because of the rising toll of journalists in places like the Balkans and Afghanistan.

My fellow students were mostly men around my age – I had just turned forty-two. Some had flown in from America or from cities in Europe and the Middle East. Quite a few, like me, were London-based foreign correspondents.

I was nervous about going to Iraq because of the enormous number of things I did not know about high-tech warfare and because of what I did know about simple, low-tech violence.

London, where I had been working as the *The Australian* news-paper's Europe correspondent for the previous year, was my third foreign posting. I had spent half my twenties in Tokyo and my mid-thirties in Washington, and I had seen some horrible things. In Haiti I saw people who had just been hacked to death with machetes. A week before coming to Heckfield Place for this 'Hostile Environment' course I had been in Gaza, where I saw a young Palestinian whose face had just been literally blown off by an Israeli machine gun.

As we sat around in the bar having a beer with our instructors that night there wasn't a lot of excitement over what was to come. The talk was about when the war was most likely to start, where one could get the best deal on a chemical weapons suit, and whether it would be best to try to get into Iraq from Jordan or from Kuwait.

The one thing we didn't talk about was the topic many of my friends were debating back in London and Sydney – namely, whether the war should take place at all.

Personally, I was deeply ambivalent. I was worried by Washington's presumption of the right to decide which governments were entitled to hold weapons of mass destruction and I considered the claims about Saddam's links to al-Qaeda to be spurious. On the other hand, I knew that tens of thousands of people had already died under Saddam Hussein and that his fall would be no bad thing.

I thought Iraq's tragedies could be traced back not just to Saddam's 1990 invasion of Kuwait or his rise in the 1970s but as far as the 1930s, when colonial Britain pulled out of the newly crafted nation without establishing a functioning democracy, leaving a succession of minority leaders from the Sunni Muslim minority who resorted to ever more violent means to oppress their people. It wasn't much of a position, but then I didn't feel it was my job to always take a position. Not because I had no opinions but because I was a reporter.

My career began on the *Sun News-Pictorial* in Melbourne in 1979 and I had spent the past decade on *The Australian*, Rupert Murdoch's national daily. Those I have always admired most in journalism are the men and women who do their best to report as fairly as possible about what is happening and leave it to the readers to form their own opinions.

My goal in Iraq would be to report on what the war meant for the Iraqi people, based on what I could witness myself. But like many of the hundreds of journalists around the world then getting ready for the war, I had no idea just how I was going to do that, if at all. As I took a train home to London at week's end I was focused on two things: getting a visa to Iraq and buying all the equipment I would need for a trip that could last weeks or even months.

*

Those correspondents who were permanently based in the Middle East or exclusively covered the 'war on terror' had been preparing for months or even years for the coming war. My preparations were a lot shorter as I had a brief that covered dozens of countries and took me through a succession of steep learning curves – a German election today, an Irish sports event tomorrow . . .

Getting my Iraqi visa proved impossible. The Iraqi Embassy in London insisted that as an Australian citizen I would have to apply to their embassy in Canberra. That meant sending off an application and hoping my colleagues in *The Australian*'s Canberra bureau would find time to do the required lobbying on my behalf. In the end, a few Canberra reporters managed to get visas for themselves but my application got nowhere. The shopping trip was always going to be much easier.

When Evelyn Waugh wrote his great satire on war reporting, *Scoop*, he based part of its main character, William Boot of *The Beast*, on Bill Deedes, one of the reporters with whom he covered Italy's 1935–36 invasion of Abyssinia (Ethiopia). As Deedes tells it in a book he published in 2003, when he was told to go to war he went out and bought three tropical suits, riding breeches for winter and summer, bush shirts, quinine pills, slabs of black chocolate, a camp bed, a sleeping bag, and long boots 'to deter mosquitoes at sundown'. Altogether his gear weighed about 270 kilograms and had to be carried in several suitcases and a large cedar trunk with a zinc lining 'to keep ants at bay'.

My shopping expedition seven decades later was just four kilometres from Deedes' preferred Regent Street vendors, but it produced a rather different haul. I went to camping stores looking for clothes that could cope with the hot days and cold nights of the desert. The wardrobe of choice being packed by journalists on several continents was expensive, lightweight, mountain-climbing clothes. I came away with a pair of grey pants with legs that unzipped to become shorts, a pair of lightweight beige jeans, a super-light fleece sweater that rolled into a small ball and an unattractive but almost weightless waterproof jacket.

The preferred accessories were light camping items, some pills that were supposed to make water safe to drink, and a tough, black backpack to protect a laptop computer.

All up, with a few T-shirts and other basics, it weighed less than ten kilos and fitted easily into a sports bag. If that was all I had to take to Iraq, I would have been happy. Sadly, I also had to find room for a chemical weapons suit, my laptop, a satellite phone, a gas mask, a helmet and, worst of all, the terrifically heavy flak jacket that a previous correspondent had left behind in the London office. Thankfully, he was roughly my size. This lot weighed another thirty kilos and had to be squeezed into a large case.

I was lucky to be advised on that shopping expedition by my partner, Pilita Clark, who understood what I would be doing in Iraq, and why. Pilita is also an experienced journalist and has worked mostly for a rival paper, the *Sydney Morning Herald*, but was just about to start work on a new international affairs magazine at the *Financial Times*. Her change of jobs was a relief, as it wasn't always easy having a partner who was also a competitor. In Washington, where we were both correspondents for our respective papers, I used to say that if she ever left town without saying why, I hoped she was having an affair; otherwise she was onto a big story that would make me look stupid.

I didn't take Pilita on the last leg of my shopping trip, to a local chemist. The Hostile Environment instructors had shown us how to put together an emergency first aid kit. This was not Boy Scout first aid about tying neat bandages and tourniquets but ugly, primitive stuff – what to do if colleagues had gaping holes in their sides, or their guts were spilling out. They told us to buy big hunks of gauze to shove into large wounds, scissors strong enough to cut through clothes and plenty of heavy-duty bandages. I got the lot and it made a gruesome sight, packed in among my new fleecy sweater and socks.

The pay office in London issued me with US$10,000 in cash, which I hid in various pieces of clothing, including inside a normal-looking belt which unzipped along the seam to conceal about $4000.

One thing that did not occur to me was to buy maps of Iraq. I assumed they would be easy to find once I got to the Middle East. A miscalculation.

*

Right up to a couple of weeks before the war I was not sure just how I would cover it.

In early March it was decided that *The Australian* would 'pool' or share its coverage with other capital city papers owned by News Ltd, such as Sydney's *Daily Telegraph*, Brisbane's *Courier-Mail* and Melbourne's *Herald Sun*. Everything I wrote would go to those papers as well as *The Australian*. I had argued that *The Australian* should provide its own coverage because it sells in all those cities alongside its 'sister' papers but it was obviously cheaper to share resources.

News Ltd's main rivals, the Fairfax papers, also pooled their coverage, sending reporters and photographers from the company's two main papers, the *Age* in Melbourne and the *Sydney Morning Herald*, whose work appeared in both papers.

At first, it seemed that only one other News Ltd reporter would be sent to cover the war with me: Ian McPhedran, the head of the News Ltd Canberra bureau which produced stories for all of the company's papers – except for *The Australian*, as it had its own team of reporters. If you were only going to send one, McPhedran was a good choice. A tall, bluff forty-five year old, he was one of the country's leading defence reporter. He had been on a few dangerous assignments over the years, including East Timor's fight for independence in 1999, but because of his defence contacts, it was originally decided he should go to Doha, capital of the small Gulf nation of Qatar, where American, British and Australian officials would be holding the main media briefings. In the first Gulf War in 1991, these military briefings made a star out of the US commander 'Stormin' Norman Schwarzkopf and provided most of the main news stories, or front page 'splashes'. Still, everyone knew that it could be a very dull place to be, so far away from the real action.

Now that I had missed out on a visa we changed our plans. Ian had managed to get a visa from the Iraqi Embassy in Canberra, so he was redirected to Baghdad, where Saddam Hussein was vowing to fight the invading armies to his death. Baghdad was where most journalists wanted to be when the war reached its climax but it would have its drawbacks.

Iraqi Information Ministry 'minders' would control the foreign journalists' movement and prevent open contact with ordinary Iraqis. Reporting from Baghdad would probably involve spending much of the war confined to a hotel room as the story unfolded else-where. Reporters might be unable to send stories at crucial periods, either because of US scrambling of satellite links or because Iraq might try to close down communications. And of course Baghdad could end up being quite a dangerous place.

US bombers and missiles would be targeting government facili-ties rather than any hotel a journalist might stay in, but this was the same US military that had accidentally bombed the Chinese Embassy in Belgrade in 1999. And if Saddam's regime did collapse there might be some sort of retaliation against Western reporters by the Iraqi military or gangs of civilians.

The Pentagon had decided that it had lost the 'press war' in Vietnam by allowing journalists to move about too freely, and in the first Gulf War by refusing to let the press have any access at all to its forces in the war zone. For this war the military strategists decided to revert to something more like the World War II model of media management, inviting 600 correspondents to be formally attached to US forces and another 150 or so to go along with British forces. The practice, known as 'embedding', was one option available to me.

This time around the embedded journalists would not be given uniforms or honorary ranks they carried in World War II, and the US and British military would not impose censorship apart from stop-ping reports that gave away potentially dangerous information such as the exact location of a unit. But journalists would eat, sleep and travel with 'their' units from the start of the war. They would have no control over their own movements and it would be a matter of luck whether their unit ended up storming Saddam's palaces or sit-ting in the desert digging latrines. Embedded journalists would not have translators to allow them to talk to Iraqis, and in any case they could hardly expect to have useful discussions with locals while tag-ging along with a US tank unit.

I was determined to resist this way of covering the war, as it would mean reporting on the soldiers' war rather than the people's war. Instead I decided to try to get into Iraq by driving in from Kuwait in the south, the launching pad for the US and British attacks. That would be the most high-risk strategy, as self-propelled journalists might spend the whole war stopped at the border by Coalition forces, and could come under fire in the middle of an unpredictable conflict. But by following along in a four-wheel-drive vehicle, once the Coalition forces had crossed the border one might be able to cover the war itself and enter 'liberated' towns and cities well before the Coalition reached Baghdad.

The north of Iraq was already effectively out of Saddam's control. A decade of patrols by US and British warplanes had imposed a 'no fly zone' on the Iraq Government and allowed the local Kurdish population to assert its autonomy. That meant the most important early fighting would be in the south, where the prime target would be the country's second-largest city, Basra. Barely an hour's drive from Kuwait, Basra would need to be the Coalition's first big conquest, after seizing the rich oil fields just over the border from Kuwait.

Coalition spokesmen were promising that independent news crews – dubbed 'unilaterals' by the Pentagon – would not be hampered by Coalition forces but neither would they be helped or protected like the embedded journalists.

Now that Ian was going to Baghdad, a third reporter, 37-year-old Rory Callinan, would go to Qatar to cover the briefings at the biggest US base in the region, Camp As-Saliyah on the edge of the capital, Doha. I didn't know Rory, but he had reported in East Timor and Afghanistan and was well regarded by his paper, the *Brisbane Courier-Mail*.

Northern Iraq would be covered by Catherine Taylor, a Beirut-based freelance journalist who used to work for *The Australian* in Sydney. Her war did not start well. She desperately needed money from head office in Sydney to pay her expenses and allow her to move around but when the first cash transfer was made, the bank forms required the sender to explain the purpose of the transfer. Somebody in Sydney wrote 'Money for Iraq War', a description that set alarm bells ringing in the international banking system and left Catherine cashless, and stranded, for some time.

One week into March we had come up with a reasonable war plan. Rory would write the daily splashes from Doha. Ian would add eye-witness or 'colour' stories and news from Baghdad. Catherine would file on news from the north and, with luck, I just might get into southern Iraq and follow the advance north. But there were serious question marks over all of our roles. Ian might not be able to file. Catherine's ability to move around in northern Iraq was not guaranteed, and nobody knew what sort of news would come from Doha. My contribution was even less certain; it would be either exclusive material or an utter waste of time and money. There was every chance that I might not get across the border, and there was no way of knowing what conditions would lie ahead if I did.

The idea of travelling alone was not appealing and, as it turned out, did not eventuate. Just as I was booking my air ticket, I discovered that somebody else had managed to get a visa in Canberra and would be coming to cover the war with me. His name was John Feder, the chief photographer in Ian McPhedran's Canberra bureau. McPhedran, naturally, wanted John to go to Baghdad with him, but the group's executives ruled that Feder should not go to Baghdad. They decided that Ian's reports could be illustrated by photos from wire agencies and freelancers who were already in Baghdad.

McPhedran was less than happy as he planned to concentrate on writing about the people and situations he saw in Baghdad, rather than pulling together broader reports with information from wire agencies and Internet news sources. That meant his work would be greatly enhanced by matching photos, and he also believed it would be safer to be part of a two-man team.

I was delighted. We had never met but I was acutely aware that good photos would enrich my stories, especially when my priority was to report on how the war was affecting civilians. John and I arranged to meet in Doha, the main base for the Coalition forces, including the Australians. Rory Callinan would not be getting there for a week or so, and it seemed a reasonable place to do our first stories before heading to Kuwait. We would then fly to Kuwait, pick up a translator and head for the Iraqi border. That was the plan anyway.

John Feder

*

On Friday, 7 March Pilita flew off to Holland for a long-arranged weekend with friends, meaning there were no emotional farewells when I left the next day. Aboard my plane I noticed an awful lot of men – and just a few women – aged thirty-five to forty-five, all carrying hardy backpacks and wearing what looked like brand-new mountain-climbing clothes.

The flight arrived after midnight in Doha, a clean, heavily land-scaped waterfront city full of air-conditioned shopping centres and obvious wealth. I took a room at a mid-range Rydges hotel, which is where John Feder arrived two nights later.

At breakfast in the hotel we shook hands and eyed each other. He was a slim man, with dark hair, who didn't look his forty years. We had done our research on each other and I had heard that he was an unusually nice guy, a good person to be with if you had to spend a lot of time living in somebody's pocket. I knew my reputation would have made him slightly more apprehensive. Before being posted to London, I had spent four years as the news editor, then deputy editor of my paper, positions in which I became known, euphemistically, as a tough boss. John was friendly but guarded.

I had been aware of John's work for some time – he used to work for *The Australian* before he was seconded to the News Ltd bureau in Canberra – and I knew that as well as being an experienced photographer he had done several difficult assignments. He had spent five months in East Timor, a gruelling assignment for which most reporters and photographers had to be turned over on relatively quick rotations.

Over the next few days, as we worked together on a few stories around Qatar and spoke over lunch, I found that John was no fool-hardy war photographer. He was particularly worried about his mother, Julia, and the stress this assignment would cause her. His father, Bruno, had died six months earlier and John did not even want to think about the effect it would have on his mother if he got into serious trouble. Like me, he was nervous, mainly about getting the story but also about the danger involved in the war. Just four weeks earlier he and his girlfriend, Nadine, had shifted into a new house in Canberra and acquired a dog, Floyd. Life was good, and the last thing he was interested in doing was taking any silly risks. I found this deeply reassuring. I did not want to be with somebody too stupid to feel fear or too macho to admit it. We would spend our first four days together in Doha, trying to report on Australia's contribution to the Iraq War. This proved surprisingly difficult.

Early one morning, we made the half-hour taxi ride to Camp As-Saliyah, where the Australian military had set up its headquarters with the US and British command centres. The Coalition troops rarely ventured off the base, a sprawling complex of warehouses ringed by barbed wire and prison-like security. The desert, a flat expanse of limestone, gravel and super-fine sand, started at the edge of the camp. The troops slept in large tents inside the warehouses but nothing could keep out the sand, which hung like a yellow fog of dust inside their quarters.

It was here that, for the first time, we ran into the Australian military's remarkably secretive approach to the media. We wanted to do some profiles on Australian soldiers getting ready for war but were briskly told there would be no access to anyone with a combat role. We would be allowed to interview some headquarters staff here at the base, but even then we could not publish their surnames or the names of their home towns, nor even tell the public where that soldier was based in the Middle East.

When asked why we could not report that troops were in Qatar, the Australian military spokesmen claimed it was because of the Qatari Government's domestic political concerns, insisting that Qatar did not want its own people to know that the enormous foreign base on the edge of Doha actually had foreign troops in it.

In fact, the unelected Emir of Qatar had been much more open than the Australians, allowing the local press to report on the presence of the US, British and Australian troops in their midst, even tolerating prominent photographs of the base. We had been forbidden from taking such photos.

The Americans were more open than the Australians and when I told a senior British officer about these restrictions, he laughed, saying the British military encouraged the sort of profiles we were trying to write – what they called 'hometown hero' stories. Little wonder that the Australian military has to spend increasing amounts of public money advertising to meet its recruiting targets.

The Australians eventually wheeled out their commander in the Gulf, Brigadier Maurie McNarn, for a brief press conference in the afternoon, just before midnight, eastern Australian time – making it almost impossible for anyone to meet their deadlines back home.

John and I were the only ones who tried to make the late editions of that night's papers, and we ended up with a large front-page spread in *The Australian*. It was no earth-shattering scoop but we were pleased just to be 'on the scoreboard'. We decided to head for Kuwait on Thursday 13 March. It was obvious by now that the war would start within days and it was time to start thinking about how we were going to get into southern Iraq.

*

Our first two hours in Kuwait City went badly.

Every four-wheel-drive vehicle in the country had been booked for weeks and we had been advised to turn up and try to find one when we were there. The best we could manage at the airport was a new-ish sedan.

I got behind the wheel to start what would obviously be a long and unique road trip. If all went well we would be driving through Mesopotamia, the ancient land where man literally invented the wheel. We knew that deserts, sand storms and a fast-moving war would test our professional skills, our personalities and perhaps our courage. Excited, we headed out of the airport onto a brightly lit modern highway for the brief run to our hotel . . . and immediately got lost.

The ten-minute drive became a ninety-minute tour of desert highways dotted with Arabic road signs. At one point we came across a police checkpoint which, according to John's confident reading of the map, did not exist. The two policemen were surprised to see us and hugely amused when we told them we were looking for the Radisson Hotel. They sent us back in the direction we'd just come from, and in the rear-view mirror, I could see them laughing uproariously.

By the time we reached the hotel, each of us was convinced he had been lumbered with the world's worst navigator. I didn't tell John about the nickname Pilita invented for me many years ago, shortly after our first road trip together in the United States. Whenever we are in a car she calls me Vasco da Gama – and she doesn't mean it as a compliment.

Early the next morning we set about trying to find some sort of four-wheel drive and to equip ourselves for an expedition into Iraq. Kuwait City, the only real city in the country, is like an endless, flat, gravel car park. Wide highways dominate the landscape, lined with smashed cars which hint at the local road safety standards. The only penalty for speeding here is a fine – no loss of licence – and that is not much of a disincentive in such a wealthy country.

We knew that tens of thousands of US and British troops were out in the desert to our north, getting ready to fight, but there were almost none on the streets of Kuwait City, where life seemed curiously calm. As we toured the city's hire car offices and began buying camping supplies, most of the Kuwaitis we met were remarkably confident that the Americans would sort out Saddam without too much trouble. The Kuwaiti Government was claiming to have ensured that virtually everybody had a gas mask but we soon realised this was far from the truth. Not that anyone seemed to care.

While other Arab states were unhappily resigned to war, Kuwait was wildly enthusiastic, eagerly awaiting the demise of their old foe Saddam, whose invasion of their country in 1990 was rarely forgotten. Billboards around the capital and signs on the sides of buses reminded Kuwaitis of the 600-odd compatriots still missing after Iraq's attack. They were almost certainly dead but were referred to in Kuwait as POW/MIAs (Prisoners of War or Missing in Action) – the same acronyms still used in the United States to describe those who went missing in the Vietnam War.

Eventually, the manager of the car hire office in our hotel announced triumphantly that he had just got his hands on a brand-new white Mitsubishi Outlander. It was a big improvement on our sedan so we signed up straight away. We soon realised that our grand new vehicle was the sort of 4WD better suited to suburban shopping than to trekking into the desert. It was little more than a beefed-up station wagon, with not much engine power and little carrying space to speak of. In fact, we were embarrassed to park it next to the big macho jeeps of the better-prepared news teams staying in the hotel. While they would be strapping two dozen big metal jerry cans on top of their trucks, we would be parked in their shadow tying six plastic containers onto the roof of our wagon.

John had arrived without a flak jacket or helmet and when Rory Callinan reached Qatar on Sunday 16 March, I called him to say we needed his jacket more than he did. Rory's vest was not big enough for his bulky frame – 187 centimetres tall and weighing 93 kilos – and was a better fit for John but Rory was understandably less than keen to give it up, as that would make it harder for him to eventually get permission to find his own way into Iraq. But he did the right thing, getting Fairfax photographer Kate Geraghty to bring it with her when she flew to Kuwait to visit an Australian war ship.

On Tuesday 18 March, President Bush gave Saddam forty-eight hours to capitulate or face attack and the Pentagon began advising all foreign journalists to leave Iraq. Ian McPhedran had no intention of leaving. He had managed to get into Baghdad from Jordan on one of the last commercial flights entering the Iraqi capital before its airport closed. That meant that he and Paul McGeough of Fairfax were the only two Australian reporters left in the capital.

Paul and his wife Pam Williams had spent New Year's Eve at our place in London only a couple of months earlier and even then he was well prepared for Iraq. When he was sacked as editor of the *Sydney Morning Herald* in 2000, the blow had been softened by his appointment to the new position of 'reporter at large', based in New York. This was the journalistic equivalent of dying and going to heaven, and *still* getting your name in the paper. The posting was obviously expensive, but it had proved an astute investment for Fairfax. Freed of the normal duties of a New York correspondent, McGeough had been able to concentrate on the war in Afghanistan and the build-up to conflict in Iraq, producing a coherent and first-rate body of work for the Fairfax papers on the 'war on terror'.

Fairfax's photographer Jason South had left Baghdad, and so had people from Australia's public broadcaster, the ABC, and its largest commercial network, Nine. The major American television networks, ABC, CBS and NBC withdrew their crews. Fox had been expelled a month earlier, and CNN, the other major all-news network, would be kicked out by the Iraqis at the end of the week 'for spreading propaganda'. The British networks were staying put, however, and while the exodus from Baghdad continued, in Kuwait City more than a thousand journalists were anxiously getting ready to try to cross the border into Iraq. Hundreds more were camped in the Jordanian capital of Amman, a six-hour drive west of Baghdad, hoping that they could eventually get into Iraq from there.

By Wednesday 19 March, the eve of Bush's deadline for war, British Airways had stopped flying into Kuwait, but there was still no sense of panic in Kuwait City, except among the journalists trying to figure out how to get into Iraq. In fact the British Government had planned two charter flights out on that day but one was cancelled because of low demand.

At precisely 5.34 a.m. on Thursday 20 March, the Coalition launched its attack on Baghdad, with 900-kilogram precision-guided bombs dropped from F-117 Nighthawk stealth fighter-bombers and more than forty cruise missiles fired from six US Navy vessels in the Mediterranean, the Red Sea and the Persian Gulf. More than sixty thousand troops charged over the border from Kuwait.

The Iraqis responded by lobbing a few missiles into Kuwait. One landed near Jahra, Kuwait's second largest city twenty kilometres west of Kuwait City. Nobody was injured but the relaxed public mood in Kuwait City was jolted. Cars began streaming south out of the capital. The roads quickly became clogged and the phone system started to crack under heavy traffic.

Our shopping expeditions became more urgent. We hadn't brought along any of the camping gear we were going to need if we ever got to the desert, thinking we could buy it here, but Kuwait is not exactly a haven for camping, hiking or other outdoor hobbies, and the gear proved hard to find. After several days we finally found what seemed to be the only camp stove in Kuwait City but the shop assistants refused to sell it because they had no others in stock and they wanted to keep it as a display item. We asked to see the floor manager but got nowhere, so we made a series of visits, on each occasion demanding to see a more senior manager. Eventually we found ourselves upstairs in a large office pleading our case to a senior executive. He couldn't believe he was being troubled over such a trivial matter and brusquely ordered his minions to sell the foreigners their stupid stove.

While we were getting organised, the Kuwaitis had sealed off the main highway north towards Iraq at a police checkpoint in a place called Al Mutlaa, eighty kilometres short of the border. We realised too late that we should have camped out near the border before the Coalition first attacked. A few reporters had been right

Hundreds of news crews were trying to get across the border into Iraq in rented 4WDs with do-it-yourself 'press' markings. About one in ten succeeded.

next to the border and had already followed the Coalition troops into Iraq.

One crew who made it over on Friday, the second day of hostilities, was from Britain's ITN network, led by one of Britain's most experienced war correspondents, Terry Lloyd. Lloyd had been the first reporter to reach the Kurdish town of Halabja in 1988 after Saddam had attacked it with chemicals, killing five thousand people, and for this war he had rejected an embedded role in favour of travelling independently.

We had bumped into him and his crew earlier in the week in Kuwait City, and compared notes about where we were all heading. We agreed that the aim was to head towards Basra as soon as it seemed safe. Like most media crews the ITN team had used sticking tape to spell out 'TV' on the sides and roof of their vehicles. John and I hadn't done this yet, as we thought we might need to sneak over the border unidentified. In any case, the 'TV' labels would turn out to be of no use to Terry Lloyd and his crew.

By Saturday dramatic TV footage was coming from embeds inside Iraq, and there were already some reports from unilaterals. John and I were getting horribly frustrated as we still couldn't see how we were going to get near the border, let alone across it.

The British and US military had their own media officers in Kuwait, and CNN and the BBC had been given access to northern Kuwait. But the Australian military's media officers had been slow to react and were still back in Qatar. One US spokesman, a Lieutenant-Colonel Cox, admitted to me that they were not particularly interested in helping the Australian media. When I argued that the participation of Australian soldiers should entitle the Australian public and media to some access he said we actually had the same status as journalists from 'countries like Hong Kong, Sweden, France and Germany'.

'Our leaders are less concerned about reinforcing the partners we already have and more concerned about extending the Coalition.'

I quickly relayed that comment to the senior Australian military spokesman in the region, Colonel Mark 'Pup' Elliot, back in Qatar, but I did not get a call back.

The numbers were looking pretty grim for us. We were among 2074 journalists registered with the US military in Kuwait, some 529 of whom were embeds. That left 1545, most of whom were now trying to get across the border. Eventually fewer than ten per cent would succeed. The only part of Iraq where news crews were moving around relatively easily was in the north.

We heard from the foreign desk in Sydney that Catherine Taylor was now near the Iranian border. Late on Saturday morning she ran into the ABC's reporter Eric Campbell and freelance cameraman Paul Moran and told them she was heading to a village where there had been US and Kurdish attacks on Ansar al-Islam, a militant Islamic group which opposed both Saddam and the US. Campbell and Moran decided they had better go to the same village. Both had new-born babies and were determined to be as careful as possible, but no amount of caution could guarantee anybody's safety in this war zone.

At 2.15 p.m. Moran was filming Kurdish fighters near a check-point outside the village when a taxi driven by an Ansar al-Islam fanatic pulled up beside him and exploded. Moran, thirty-nine, was killed instantly and Campbell was injured. Moran would be reported as the first foreign journalist to die covering the war – but others had already beaten him to that horrible distinction just over the border from Kuwait.

Shortly before the ABC's tragedy, Terry Lloyd and his crew were driving in their two 4WDs towards Basra after sending their first report from Iraq. Heading straight for Basra did not turn out to be such a great idea. According to the crew's Belgian cameraman, Daniel Demoustier, they sailed past the advance Coalition forces to confront two vehicles of Iraqi soldiers who apparently wanted to surrender.

Demoustier, who was driving the lead 4WD with Lloyd beside him, turned around and raced back towards the Coalition lines but the Iraqis followed closely, giving a thumbs-up signal to show they were friendly. They were then fired on by Coalition tanks, according to Demoustier, and the Iraqis returned fire. Demoustier ducked for cover below his dashboard, and just before the 4WD crashed into a ditch he saw that Lloyd was missing and his door was open. Demoustier found cover in a ditch and was later picked up by a news crew that had been travelling at a more cautious pace. The two men in the other ITN vehicle, cameraman Fred Nerac and translator Hussein Osman, were no doubt killed but their bodies were not found. An investigation by ITN would find that Lloyd had been hit by one bullet, and was picked up with Iraqi survivors by a local businessman driving a minibus. Lloyd was still conscious and uttered a few words when he was put in the van but ITN believes he was already fatally wounded. Before the minibus could reach hospital it was hit by a second US attack, possibly from a helicopter. The British reporter was wounded again and, according to ITN, 'ten minutes later when the minibus reached the hospital in Basra he was no longer alive'.

That night in my room in Kuwait, John and I watched the television reports stating that Lloyd and two members of his crew were missing. We were trying to relax with our first drink in a week. Alcohol is banned in Kuwait but we had managed to find someone to sell us some home-made Thai whisky. We talked about the impact it would have on our families if anything did happen to us. I mentioned that a close friend from Melbourne, Paul Stewart, had lost a brother who was a member of a news crew killed in East Timor in 1975. It turned out that Paul was also a mate of John's. With a shared friend and a few drinks under his belt John opened up. He could not figure out, he said, why I had a reputation as such a hard bastard. We were still stuck in Kuwait, but at least we were bonding.

*

The next day, Sunday, was a work day in Kuwait, and we spent the morning trying to get official permission to pass the police roadblock at Al Mutlaa. Much of our time in Kuwait City had been spent trying to get a series of official passes that we were repeatedly told we would need in order to get near the border. Now John had heard that we needed yet another pass, this one from the Ministry of Defence's ominous-sounding Department of Public Relations and Moral Guidance. In its car park a well-muscled, dark-featured man stopped to swap information after updating his press pass in the ministry.

Stewart Innes was a half-British, half-Lebanese thirty-seven year old who normally worked as a trade consultant for the Canadian Embassy in Kuwait. Like most other embassies it had closed because of the looming war, and Stewart had decided to look for work with the media as a translator and 'fixer', or organiser, as much for the adventure as for the tax-free US dollars. He was charming, he spoke perfect Arabic and he appeared to be enterprising, making it clear he knew his way around the local bureaucracy.

Stewart looked as if he could be an excellent interpreter, which interested me as I had spent some time looking for one in Kuwait, to no avail. The bigger, richer TV crews had driven up the price of translator–fixers to US$500 a day, well above our budget. I was starting to think that it might be wiser to find someone in Iraq, if we ever got there. Someone from Kuwait might find it harder to cross the border, and even harder to work in Iraq, given recent relations between the two countries. In any case, Stewart said he had already found work with a couple of foreign TV crews from New Zealand,

Stewart Innes on the roof of Saddam's grandest place – later the headquarters of the occupation administration – as fires burn in central Baghdad. John Feder

France and Germany. We exchanged cards and he said he might have a friend who could work for me. We drove our separate ways, promising to keep each other informed if one of us found a way in.

John and I decided to head to the police post on the highway where the press were being turned around. Other reporters warned us that a crew from the London *Sun* had earlier tried to drive on but had been chased down and stripped of their media credentials. We didn't plan on 'doing a runner' but we did get out and try to talk our way through. An unusually friendly Kuwaiti policeman got chatting with us, and when his boss was out of earshot he quietly suggested that we take a desert road to the border, insisting it would be easy to reach Iraq that way. If he was right, we might be on our way.

He told us to go back a few kilometres towards Kuwait City, then turn right and head west towards Saudi Arabia. We would eventually see a road leading to the right towards an airfield, and if we kept going past the airfield we could find our way north to the border. Excited, we drove off and rang our new friend, Stewart, to tell him what we had learned. He said we should be careful because there were landmines and bandits up those roads but he was intrigued by what we were up to.

Soon after turning west we did come across a road to the right but we decided it was too close to be the one the policeman had described, so we kept driving. It had been the correct turn-off and a couple of hours later we reached the Saudi border. We drove back in darkness, determined to try again the next day.

ITN had confirmed that Terry Lloyd was dead; Fred Nerac and Hussein Osman were still missing and the network was withdrawing its remaining independent team from southern Iraq. The British military cited the tragedy as another reason why independent journalists should stay out of southern Iraq.

'We have a set-up where we have reporters embedded,' a spokesman told reporters.

'And in those circumstances the military is clearly effecting a degree of responsibility for their welfare. For those outside of that system clearly this is a hugely, hugely dangerous environment and media organisations have to be aware of that and have to take responsibility for their personnel.

'There's very little we can do if journalists are outside of our network and operating on their own basis ... Our advice would be don't go there.'

We then learned that Lloyd's crew was not the only one to have found itself in trouble. A US Army spokesman, Colonel Guy Chiefs, said the military had begun receiving calls from journalists in Iraq who were 'under fire, screaming for help'.

The next day, Monday 24 March, we headed back in search of that tantalising desert route to the north that we had missed the previous day. We quickly found ourselves driving in reasonably heavy US military traffic on an unmade road. Sure enough, the road did lead to a US airbase so we took another rough road to the right to avoid the airbase checkpoint.

The landscape was dead flat and the road we were on seemed to be going in a straight line. We passed a series of US military camps, their tents surrounded by barbed wire perimeters and newly excavated earthworks. The flow of military traffic continued and we tried to avoid eye contact with the drivers of the trucks that barrelled past in their own clouds of sand. We were driving along in our cumbersome flak jackets, with my helmet at the ready to make us look more 'military'.

The big question was whether we were actually heading north. All we had been able to find was a photocopy of a map of Kuwait, which had little detail of these desert roads, and a rough copy of a map of southern Iraq. As John drove, I pulled out my Thuraya satellite phone for the first time and started flipping through its instruction manual to try to work out how to use its Global Positioning System. By stopping on the road, sticking the phone out the window and pressing a button for its GPS function, I soon got the coordinates of our latitude and longitude. After driving on for another ten minutes, we stopped and took another reading, then plotted the two sets of coordinates on the map to find that we were indeed heading due north, parallel to the highway twenty kilometres further east. There was no such road on our map but we kept this up, figuring that if we were not stopped by the military we would eventually run into the border.

The conversation turned to our supplies. When we put together what each of us had bought on our shopping trips we realised we only had enough food for a week and it was almost all dried noodles. There was no way of knowing how long we might be in Iraq or what sort of conditions we were heading into, so this was clearly a problem. Ten minutes later we saw a large square object sitting beside the road ahead of us. We stopped next to it to find that a whole pallet of US military ration packs, or Meals Ready to Eat (MREs) had literally fallen off the back of a truck. Bingo.

Having resigned ourselves to living on dried noodles we now stood laughing as we sorted through our loot – meals of roast beef, curried chicken, jambalaya and a dozen other dishes. They came with self-heating satchels, desserts, drink powders and what the Americans call snacks and candies. We threw three boxes of twelve into the back of our cramped 4WD, regretting that we could not fit any more.

After a few more kilometres the roadside was lined with broken cardboard boxes of plastic water bottles which had fallen off another truck. We stopped and picked some up. What would be next – beer?

Half an hour later we could see plumes of smoke on the horizon from oil rigs that had been set alight by the retreating Iraqis. Soon after that we reached our first border checkpoint, which our rough map suggested would lead to a Demilitarised Zone of several kilometres before another set of checkpoints on the Iraqi side. We nodded our way through the first checkpoint without stopping, got briefly lost in the DMZ and were redirected by a Kuwaiti soldier at a second checkpoint to a larger border crossing a couple of kilometres to the east. Several Kuwaiti soldiers were manning that gate and when we identified ourselves they refused to let us pass. A British sergeant was going to let us through until a British officer arrived to side with the Kuwaitis and turn us around.

We drove east along the border to the little town of Safwan, where we failed to talk a Kuwaiti border guard into letting us through, then continued almost to the water at port Umm Qasr, a port which is the only other town on the border. The entire border was lined with barbed wire and large defensive earthworks called berms. We could see the breaches where the Coalition tanks had rolled through but all were now guarded.

We had no choice but to head back to Kuwait City. It had been another frustrating day but we felt we were making progress. Back

An oil rig blazes in southern Iraq. This was the first thing we saw when we crossed the border from Kuwait, and the Kuwaitis battling the fire warned us that Iraqi fighters still roamed the area at night. John Feder

at the Radisson we saw a British military spokesman announce to CNN 'We have taken Umm Qasr'. The same conquest had already been announced more than once and there were still reports that the town was far from pacified.

'We are referring to it as militarily secure,' he said, conceding with a nice touch of understatement that 'there are still some people in there who are not entirely friendly'. Southern Iraq, meanwhile, was 'largely under control' and Basra had been surrounded by British forces, the British spokesman said, but the British did not want to get drawn into that city until necessary.

Most of the 'embeds' on television were reporting on the power and speed of the US military thrust north towards Baghdad and broadcasting pictures of Iraqi villagers giving joyous welcomes to the GIs. The picture coming from the 'unilaterals' was gloomier. Raids by Saddam loyalists meant that even the southern oilfields were no longer safe and the smiling welcomes seemed to have disappeared when the first US tanks had passed on to the north. An aid worker in Kuwait City told us that Coalition officials had cancelled a promised trip to Safwan because even that small outpost right on the border was still not safe after dark.

The next morning, Tuesday 25 March, Stewart dropped by our hotel. He was impressed by our efforts in the desert, as the TV crews he had hooked up with were showing no such initiative. He had also fallen out with them because they wouldn't provide him with a flak jacket for Iraq. We said that was outrageous and told him that if he joined us we would buy him one.

A few hours later the deal was done. We would pay him US$100 a day while we were in Kuwait and US$300 a day inside Iraq. It paid off straight away. Stewart had contacts who could get us a real 4WD – a large blue Pajero. When he delivered it later that afternoon, John and I felt like we had left our toy car behind to join the adults. Kuwaiti insurance did not cover any vehicle entering Iraq and there was no point pretending we were staying in Kuwait. The hire firms knew why journalists wanted all their 4WDs, so we had to give a credit card imprint of US$30,000, which went onto John's corporate card.

For a total of about $2000 we bought a camouflage-patterned flak jacket for Stewart, who had his own gas mask, and sand-coloured helmets for him and John. Stewart's jacket was a lot lighter and offered less protection than ours, which had ceramic plates, but it was the best available in Kuwait.

In my room that night John pushed me to try to get across the border again the following day. I felt we would be wasting our time driving around the desert again unless we had some reason to believe we could cross the border. My inclination was to spend a day reporting on the situation in Kuwait so I would at least get something into the paper. But John was adamant.

'Every day we spend in Kuwait is a wasted day,' he fumed. 'So if we do spend the day driving around in circles and not getting over the border what have we lost? Nothing!'

I eventually agreed. The Iraqi Government, meanwhile, was making much of the continued resistance in Umm Qasr. If 'little Umm Qasr' was still fighting, declared the Information Minister, Mohammed Saeed al-Sahhaf (who would soon be known everywhere as 'Comical Ali' for his ridiculously upbeat assessments of Iraqi resistance), how would the Coalition fare when it tried to enter a real city like Basra or Baghdad?

Comical Ali's opponents had their own credibility problems. The Coalition spokesmen were already exaggerating their progress in southern Iraq and in 'taking out' Saddam and his top associates, and tonight they announced that an uprising had supposedly broken out in Basra. Just before the prime-time television news in London, the British forces around Basra claimed to have witnessed 'a popular uprising' which the British deputy commander, Major-General Peter Wall, said was 'just the sort of encouraging indication we have been looking for'. The Arabic news network Al-Jazeera, the only non-Iraqi media outlet with a reporter in Basra, said there was no sign of any uprising at all. They were right, and Coalition officials later conceded to me privately that the uprising claim was a deliberate lie aimed at encouraging the real thing.

After dinner we headed to the Hilton where Chip Cummins, a *Wall Street Journal* reporter I had met on my Hostile Environment course, gave us two large maps of Iraq to photocopy. He had been in a convoy of mostly American journalists that had been helped across the border by US contacts the previous afternoon. What they found, he said, 'was nothing like the optimistic picture you get from CNN'. 'Even in Safwan people were really antagonistic, they surrounded our cars screaming at us and waving sticks. It was scary and really unpleasant.'

Things had got even worse after dark. British troops had warned them that armed Iraqis were driving around specifically looking for journalists to kill because they were 'soft' targets, but Coalition forces refused even to let the unilateral reporters camp near them, saying their presence would endanger the Coalition forces. Chip's convoy ended up spending a frightened night on the move before coming straight back across the border in the morning.

The fact that the Coalition forces were making no effort to protect unilateral journalists, and the unsettling news that Iraqis may have been hunting press vehicles made us hold off on putting the 'TV' markings on the Pajero. But the next day, we were determined to get ourselves into Iraq.

A Qatari watches the Al-Jazeera news network in a TV store in Doha. John Feder took this shot to illustrate a story about the Arabic network, whose coverage angered both sides of the war.

2

OVER THE BORDER

Journalist Philip Knightley once observed that Australia has an unusually strong tradition of war journalism, calculating that for its size Australia produced more World War II correspondents than any other country. He asked his friend the journalist Murray Sayle why that might be, and during a visit to the Royal Military Academy at Sandhurst, Sayle put the question to a British Army general.

'Why do Australians make such good war correspondents?' the general repeated. 'Because, dear boy, they're so very good at camping!'

John and I were now undermining the general's assumption that all Australians can cope well roughing it in the field. Somehow I had been stuck with a photographer who was more comfortable chatting in an inner-city café than pitching a tent or fixing a car. He was as useless as me. Thankfully, Stewart was more competent in 'men's skills'. He could tie a knot, for instance, having spent a summer long ago working on yachts in the Mediterranean.

We spent the morning of Wednesday 26 March kitting out the Pajero a lot more professionally than the rather pathetic effort John and I had made with our first 4WD. We got $160 worth of sturdy roof-racks fitted and found metal jerry cans so we could carry a lot more petrol and water on the roof. The more delicate equipment went comfortably into the back compartment, leaving the rear passenger seat empty for John and his cameras along with our flak jackets, a few bottles of water and something to nibble on. Nobody argued when Stewart announced that he wanted to drive, and from then on I sat next to him.

We headed out in the afternoon along the track we had found past the airfield, this time knowing where we were going. Stewart soon became a bit too confident, going so fast over a bump in the road that the roof rack lifted up and slammed down twenty centimetres forward, denting the roof and several side panels.

An hour north we came across a large, slow US convoy and fell in behind to patiently tag along. Two other media cars had already done the same thing. The dozen soldiers in the convoy's last vehicle, a canvas-topped truck, knew what we were up to and laughed at our audacity while insisting with hand signals that the media 'followers' kept back at least ten metres.

At the first checkpoint all three tag-alongs were waved through with the convoy. The other two media cars thought we were now over the border and broke away to accelerate north, not realising that they would be unable to leave the DMZ. We had made the same mistake two days earlier so we stuck to the convoy, which took several turns before eventually reaching the decisive crossing. Just as we were about to reach a British soldier manning the final checkpoint, a 4WD with 'Kuwait Oil Company' written on its doors cut in front of us.

The soldier stopped it and demanded to see the driver's papers. That meant we were also likely to be checked and turned around. We had already been self-conscious about the fact that we did not exactly fit the khaki colour scheme of the convoy, thanks to our deep blue Pajero and glimpses of John's purple suitcase showing through the blue tarp on the roof. Now we were even more nervous as we sat silently while the soldier interrogated the driver in front of us. In one last act of bravado, I told the others to act annoyed, then I caught the guard's eye by waving my hands and pointed angrily to the disappearing convoy. Interrupting his conversation with the KOC driver he looked around to see the three of us gesturing impatiently in our helmets and flak jackets. He nodded an apology for holding us up and waved us around the other 4WD, then went back to questioning its driver. We roared by, shaking our heads angrily at the impertinence of this delay.

We were through! A few seconds later the elation was replaced by another thought. 'Shit, we're through. Now what?'

Passing that border and its earth fortifications left us feeling suddenly naked. We also realised that, as it was already 3.30 p.m., darkness was just three hours away and we had no idea of where we could safely spend the night. From this moment on we would be winging it, making a hundred quick decisions a day about logistics and safety on top of our journalism.

One road went straight to the right, due east along the Kuwaiti border to Safwan about twenty-five kilometres away, while several other roads headed north deeper into the oilfields. From what we had heard Safwan was not exactly a friendly spot, and we were surrounded by land so flat that it was impossible to find a secluded camping spot.

A few kilometres to our left a sabotaged oil rig was blazing and several 4WDs and fire-fighting trucks were clustered around it. We drove over and got a friendly reception from the Kuwait Oil Company fire-fighters, who were openly enjoying the job of putting out the fire.

'These are the ones we have fun with,' said Ali Asad, in balaclava and overalls to shield him from the heat of the fire. 'Normally we just do tank fires and little things but these are a challenge.'

They chatted to us for a while and let John take photos of the burning well, which threw out enough heat to be uncomfortable from a hundred metres. Their leader, Aisa Bu Yabes, said it should take only a couple of weeks to put out the burning wells and pumping stations but he was not sure because Iraqi resistance meant it was still not safe to inspect the whole oilfield. We were less than thrilled to hear that truckloads of armed Iraqis roamed through the oilfields each night.

'It is still hostile here – we leave before dark every day,' Yabes said.

I called the editor of *The Australian*, Michael Stutchbury – Sydney was eight hours ahead of Iraq so it was about midnight for him – to tell him we had finally made it into Iraq. He was excited but urged caution. We are old friends and he joked that if we got hurt he would face severe retribution not just from Pilita but from his wife Deb and sons Alex and Harry.

Looking back into Kuwait, the border was protected by an anti-tank trench that was several metres deep and ten metres wide, then an open patch of ground and a high earth mound. That mound was broken every few hundred metres by an observation post and occasionally by a tank pointing its gun into Iraq. As we drove east along the border most of the Kuwaiti soldiers at the observation posts returned our waves and we decided it might be safest to camp near one of those observation posts.

A few kilometres along the border we stopped next to one of the posts. Stewart got out and called out in Arabic to check that he wasn't entering a minefield. Then he walked to a more comfortable yelling distance with his hands in the air and asked if we could stay where we were for the night. The answer was no – by crossing the border we had entered a banned military zone, a soldier yelled back, and somebody was coming to get us to bring us back into Kuwait. Stewart shouted that we would keep driving and cross back at the next checkpoint, which we had no intention of doing.

As we drove on we came across an Iraqi farm boy tending a few goats next to his family's tomato crop and small dirt hut. We stopped for a quick chat. His name was Saad and he was fifteen, he said. His bare feet were so wide that they could never have seen shoes. This was our first interview with a liberated Iraqi but we were rather more excited about it than he was. He did not smile once and all he would say about the war, before asking for food and cigarettes, was that he was not happy that the Americans had invaded.

Safwan was as miserable as we had heard. As we drove along its thinly built-up main street an aid convoy from the Kuwaiti Red Crescent was packing up after distributing food and water. The convoy was accompanied by an armed escort and two busloads of journalists who had been graced by the US military with a brief chance to enter Iraq safely. The British writer Christopher Hitchens turned one of these fleeting visits, literally 150 metres over the border, into a full-length first-person article in *Vanity Fair* about his experience of the mood of war-time Iraq.

We got out to chat with Australians Geoff Parry and Robin Brown, a reporter and a cameraman with Australia's Channel Seven, who were accompanying the convoy, then asked a few basic questions of locals, who were more interested in carrying home their new boxes of food.

Like Umm Qasr, this border crossing had long been a harsh, poor place favoured by smugglers and thieves. These towns had received little of the wealth that passed through them; and that was before a decade of UN sanctions choked off most trade and made

Crash course in camping. Stewart wonders what he has got himself into as I try to boil a billy with Kuwait's last available camp stove. This is our first camping spot beside the road outside Umm Qasr and I was wondering what the buses were doing there. They had been used to transport Iraqi prisoners. John Feder

life tougher. Even the children seemed lean and scarred by poor diets. A group of teenage boys became more aggressive in their demands for water and cigarettes, eventually trying to force open the Pajero's back door.

The light was already starting to fade and we decided to head for Umm Qasr, another twenty kilometres to the east. The Coalition had been insisting for days that it held the town, and a group of Australian Navy divers were inside its port trying to clear it of mines so it seemed our best bet for a safe night. There was little conversation and plenty of urgency as we drove on through a terrain looking much like the world of Mad Max. The light from burning oil wells disappearing behind us was replaced by the flames atop distant oil refineries ahead of us. Layers of sand high in the atmosphere had turned the sky brown and the sun orange. Electricity poles leaned at crazy angles and mangy dogs picked through flat, low farm fields dotted with dilapidated mud-brick farm houses.

Just before 6 p.m., with the light fading, two armed figures ran onto the road in front of us, pointing their weapons straight at us and waving us down. They had chosen their spot well as we had nowhere to turn or escape. We were totally in their control and seriously scared. Only when the car had stopped could we see that they were British Royal Marines. As they frisked us on the roadside then searched the car for weapons we laughed almost hysterically with relief.

'Mate, nobody has ever been as pleased to see you as we are right now,' I told the corporal, who nodded tolerantly as he continued searching me.

They said Umm Qasr was just a few kilometres ahead but it was not safe after dark and in any case we were about to breach a curfew imposed by the Coalition. The good news was that we could stay by the side of the road another couple of hundred metres on from their dug-out. We could make out several empty buses parked along the road, and a little huddle of four or five media 4WDs parked next to them. We pulled in beside the last of those 4WDs. The other journalists were quiet and tense as they hastened, in the last glimpses of light, to prepare meals, pack up satellite phones and bed down for the night inside their vehicles.

We quickly did the same. Stewart and I put up the tent behind the car while John downloaded from his digital camera to his laptop computer the photos he had taken during the drive. He had shots of the oil rig fire-fighters, Saad, the street scenes in Safwan and the desolate landscape east of there. This was the first test of John's

John uses his satellite phone and antenna to transmit photos from between the tent and the Pajero on the edge of the road outside Umm Qasr. Transmitting was always a tense time. Stewart Innes

favourite new toy, an 'inverter' he had bought from an electronics store in Canberra. Plugged into a cigarette lighter, it inverted the DC power of a car battery into an AC current for ordinary appliances. Combined with a four-plug powerboard it meant we could power or recharge our mobiles and satellite phones, two laptop computers, his cameras and a camp light.

Because we had travelled along the border we were just a few kilometres from Kuwait, close enough for our mobile phones to work on Kuwait's normal land-based system. Another ten kilometres or so north and we would be out of range and would then need to rely on the two satellite phone systems we had between us.

One was my hand-held Thuraya, which uses a satellite dedicated to that part of the Middle East. Saddam's regime had outlawed Thurayas, frowning on any form of independent communication and considering them military equipment. The GPS function could be particularly useful on a battlefield, although we had heard ominous stories about the signals of such devices being picked up by US military equipment and attracting missiles.

Our other sat phone was John's larger M4, a more powerful device roughly the size of a laptop computer, which could send the larger loads of information needed to transmit photographs. It had its own fold-out antenna and a compass to help point it at the right satellite. Photographers working in the field tend to spend much of their nervous energy grappling with these sat phones and antennae, so John was enormously relieved when his laptop, mobile and antenna all spoke to each other to allow a successful first transmission from Iraq.

With a camping light shining dimly in the back of the Pajero we huddled around to eat our first MREs. By pouring water into a self-heating plastic pouch we produced a chemical reaction that generated heat. A second sealed bag containing food was then placed inside the heating pouch, and a few minutes later dinner was ready.

We were now concentrating on the fussy concerns of camping, savouring trivial joys like finding a clean cup or a coffee satchel or a chocolate bar. Stewart produced a Swiss pocket knife which we realised was our only decent blade. It impressed John and me awfully and soon became our most valuable tool. While cold water was enough to heat the MREs, thankfully our hard-won camp stove produced hot water for coffee and washing the sand and dust off our faces. Despite the cold and dark, we were just starting to relax and exchange information with the French TV crew parked next to us when a mortar exploded somewhere between us and the border. What followed was remarkable.

A second mortar exploded, then gunfire could be heard to the east in Umm Qasr, which we realised was closer than we thought. Next came the high-pitched cheers of a large number of men, coming not from the town but from what we thought was empty desert straight across the road from where we were parked. A white flare went up and we could see a cluster of about a dozen large white tents a kilometre or so away, inside a barbed wire compound. It was a large prison camp. The empty buses lining the road next to us had been used to transport about three thousand captured Iraqi soldiers there. The mortar had triggered shooting from Saddam loyalists inside Umm Qasr, which in turn had set off the cheering in the prison camp.

Just after 8 p.m. a journalist from Agence France Presse ventured over to the British soldiers to ask what was going on. He returned a few minutes later to say they believed there was a good chance that they – and we – would be attacked during the night. If so we should not run into the low dunes behind our cars, as there were minefields and trenches back there and any attack would probably come from those trenches. This news of a minefield was something of a shock as we had already taken turns to wander twenty metres into the dark with a handful of toilet paper.

Instead of running that way, the British soldiers had said, we should cross the road towards their dug-out and the prison camp, as they had cleared that side for landmines and there were some natural ditches in which we could hide.

'Oh, but remember,' the French reporter added. 'That means we will be running towards the British so we have to yell out "Commando, I'm coming!" and come one at a time. They will be watching with night goggles for any movement and if we don't yell that out or if we come in a large group they say they will shoot us.'

He smiled apologetically for having almost forgotten this rather important detail, before moving on to pass the instructions to the other cars of journalists. We nodded slowly and thanked him as if these were normal bedtime instructions. We did not talk to each other as we walked to the back of our car but I noticed that John and Stewart, like me, were quietly practising saying 'Commando, I'm coming! Commando, I'm coming!'

Before long the crump of distant artillery started to come from the north, the direction of Basra, accompanied by an occasional dull flash of light on the horizon like a small false dawn.

At 10.30 p.m. one of the Marines ran crouching out of the dark, saying they had received a warning of a chemical gas attack. That sent an already tense group of journalists diving into the back of their cars to dig out gas masks and make sure that their protective suits were handy.

By now it was breakfast time in Sydney so I called Stutchbury to say I would be sending, or 'filing', a description of what we had seen to go with John's photos. I sat in the front seat writing my story out longhand in the large cardboard-bound notebook I would carry throughout the war. I had decided that, for now, dictating over my land-based mobile phone to a copytaker in Australia would be simpler than using my laptop computer. John was in the tent, testing whether it was possible to sleep in a bullet-proof vest. Given the cold, and the possibility of late-night dashes across the road, we all stayed fully dressed with our flak jackets on inside our sleeping bags. My sleeping bag was up to my waist as I sat in the car scribbling away.

Stewart opted to sleep in the driver's seat beside me and managed to do just that, despite the light being on and my slow and quite loud dictation by phone, with my shoulder just a few centimetres from his.

At times I turned off the interior light and wrote by the light of a torch or plugged the camping light into the powerboard. But the drain on the car battery – especially when I was using the laptop – meant I still had to turn the engine on occasionally to keep the battery charged. Even that did not drive Stewart out of the car, although it did wake him. This had been his first real day of working in the media and he wanted to hear my story being dictated.

Stewart was finding the whole media experience fascinating and was constantly asking questions of John and me about what we were doing and why. Sitting in the glow of the dashboard that night, and on other nights to come, I would occasionally mumble to myself when stuck for a word or phrase, or if I was working on a laptop I might mutter a troublesome sentence to myself to try to get it right. Without opening his eyes Stewart, supposedly asleep next to me, would quickly suggest a solution. He might have been up for twenty hours and lying 'asleep' for an hour but he was actually soaking up, and processing, everything he heard. Apart from wanting to hear how our day would seem to the readers, he was also interested in how reports were put together and what I had found valuable in the day's interviews and research.

Stewart had also begun asking John technical questions about photography. John is not one for going on about artistic composition or lens speeds but he was happy enough to answer questions for Stewart, who had brought his own camera along to document his adventure. He had been asked by the Canadian ambassador to put together a slide show to explain what he got up to during the war, and at times he became a bit of a war tourist, demanding that we take his photo in front of a shattered tank or a damaged portrait of Saddam.

I finished writing my story about 2 a.m., then called a copytaker in Australia and read it out over the phone. I had had about three hours' sleep when the sunlight through the windscreen woke me. I looked up to see a group of young Iraqi men walking past the front of the car away from Umm Qasr, their leader carrying a white flag. Stretching my cramped legs beside the car I could see another group coming towards us, with two or three more waving white flags. I called John, who crawled out of the tent and got a couple of shots of them walking by. Stewart spoke to them in Arabic about the conditions in Umm Qasr. They said they were port workers who had been stranded in the town for days because of the fighting and were now heading home to Safwan or farm houses dotted through the area.

John set up his satellite phone again to send off these new images, and I called the copytaker back to add a final paragraph to my story explaining the photos of the dawn parade behind white flags. The British troops searched the young men for weapons, then let them pass.

Our breakfast was dried noodles and coffee. Given that I am largely bald, I always keep my hair very short but I had shaved my head just before we set off from Kuwait, making my morning wash a lot easier. After splashing a few handfuls of water on our faces we packed up our gear and decided to go the last few kilometres into town.

The other media cars headed off with their own plans, two or three of them agreeing to travel together for safety. Everybody swapped experiences of roads and security conditions as other journalists were among the few sources of information that could really be trusted. Most reporters had already learned not to rely on the over-bullish claims from embedded journalists and Coalition spokesmen of warm welcomes and pacified towns. A Kuwaiti fixer for a Spanish television team told us that some media crews had got into the port at Umm Qasr and were camping there with mine-clearing divers from Australia, Britain and the US who were clearing mines from the port. Our first priority was to find somewhere safe to stay that night and the port seemed the best option.

As the road entered Umm Qasr it was lined every twenty-five metres or so with sparsely leaved trees. To the right of the road was about 150 metres of flat, empty land, then the residential part of the town – street after street of low mud-brick homes behind high brick walls. The streets were reasonably busy with people, and children near the road ran towards us as we approached, sticking out their hands and calling for water. On the left of the road were a closed petrol station and what looked like a few factories and run-down workshops.

Umm Qasr had obviously never been a pretty place but a decade of sanctions had tipped it well and truly into ugliness. The roads were unsealed, rubbish lay around the streets and the whole place had a dusty, dirty feel. We drove past the town and down to the port district, finding ourselves after about two kilometres at a major gateway to the oldest part of the docks. Instead of nestling in a harbour the port stretched for a couple of kilometres along a river bank, with newer facilities in a long sprawling complex to our left.

Next to the gates of the old port was a two-metre high mosaic of Saddam Hussein. A few tiles had been shot out of his face, and the words 'Fox Raiders – 2nd Battalion, 1st US Marine Division' had been spray-painted across it.

Two young Marines guarding the gate told us we could not enter without the approval of somebody inside the port. The problem of course was that unless they let us in we could not reach the Australian divers to get such approval, and the Marines said they could not leave their post to get a message to the divers. We waited for more than an hour as the Marines radioed their superiors for instructions but the final answer was that one of the Australian divers had to meet us at the gates before we could be admitted.

The Marines conceded the Catch 22 nature of this little dilemma but had nothing else to offer: 'We're just following orders, sir.'

They told us that the one large building we had passed, a former hotel and port administration centre on a square at the edge of town, had been taken over by the British as their local headquarters, so we tried our luck there. After another lengthy wait at its front gates we again got nowhere. Lieutenant-Colonel Ben Curry, a spokesman for Britain's 3rd Commando Brigade, grudgingly came out to speak to us but was belligerence personified. All we wanted was to get a message to the Australian divers but without even opening the gate Curry said that as we were not embedded he had 'no remit to help us at all'.

Waiting alongside us were three middle-aged Iraqi men who had come to complain to the British that they were being harassed by members of the Ba'ath Party, the Arab nationalist organisation that had produced Saddam Hussein and been the political vehicle of his dictatorship, dominating almost every aspect of Iraqi public life.

They refused to give their names but had still shown some bravery by approaching these gates in full daylight. About fifteen local men skulked on the far side of the square, watching closely to see who went near the British base.

'We want the soldiers to come into the town and get Saddam's people,' one of the three men told Stewart, who was translating his first real interview for me. 'They want to cause trouble and uproar – they are trying to make us revolt so the Coalition will hit back and hit our families and start bigger trouble.' Plenty of party members were still armed and living in the town, emerging at night to stir up trouble, they said.

'Everyone knows who they are but none have been caught.'

After a few minutes an interpreter for the British Army who identified himself only as Abdul came out of the gates to meet them. As he emerged, one of the men who had been watching from across the square walked straight up to within two or three metres to listen ostentatiously to the conversation. A wiry man of about thirty, he wore a bright pink parka and a pinched, sullen expression. The three men refused to speak until he left, which he only did when Abdul told him to move away.

The three men then gave Abdul five names of local Ba'ath Party leaders, all of which he said he recognised.

'If you knock on any door in Umm Qasr,' one of the three men told us after Abdul had left, 'people will tell you they don't want Saddam Hussein but they are scared to do anything. People have always only been able to get work, education, anything if they are members of the Ba'ath Party and everyone is sick of it.'

At this point three more men pulled up on bicycles to listen to our conversation, prompting the first trio to change the topic for a little while, then walk away.

It was now 11.10 a.m. in Iraq. I took a mobile phone call from *The Australian* in Sydney, where it was 7.10 p.m. It was a speaker-phone call from the final editorial conference which puts the front page together each night. They were happy with the photos and story we had filed but had decided they also wanted a front-page story and photos from inside Umm Qasr.

Attention was focussing on the town because it was Iraq's only deep-sea port and therefore the only entry point for the aid ships waiting to deliver supplies to southern Iraq. Its unexpected resistance had held up those shipments, making the town a showcase of the mixed Iraqi attitudes to the Coalition forces and a symbol of the Iraqi Government's battle for survival.

Iraqi ministers were urging the rest of the nation to be inspired by the bravery of 'little Umm Qasr', and the ugly little town was suddenly being discussed in political capitals around the world.

'Umm Qasr is a city similar to Southampton,' UK Defence Minister Geoff Hoon told the House of Commons that week, while explaining that it was one of the most important towns in the whole country.

'He's either never been to Southampton, or he's never been to Umm Qasr,' a British soldier in the town told the BBC. Another soldier reportedly agreed: 'There's no beer, no prostitutes and people are shooting at us. It's more like Portsmouth.'

The only problem with this new request from Sydney was that we had just fifty minutes to find and file the words and photos for the first edition. We jumped in the Pajero and drove along a few streets taking photos of the town and trying to get our bearings, stopping for a few words with a British sergeant who was leading a foot patrol along a largely deserted street.

'We have been in town for two or three days doing what we do best – quietening things down,' he said. 'Belfast on a warm day,' was his joking description of how he and his men had found their work in Umm Qasr.

'We own the port and the town isn't too bad now. One patrol ran into a couple of guys with AK-47s last night but we're getting on top of things.' The surprising thing about the previous night's mortars, he said, was that they seemed to have come from right on the Kuwaiti border, the very first territory seized by the Coalition.

A few hundred metres from the British headquarters we found the vandalised Ba'ath Party office. Two large holes had been blown in a wall and looters had ransacked the shattered furniture and filing cabinets. John went in one direction taking photographs while Stewart and I picked our way through other offices, talking to the dozen or so locals who had been attracted by our presence. I picked up one file, which was a young woman's party membership record. It had her photograph and details about her family, her own party membership and her work career. I folded it into my notebook thinking it might be interesting to have translated in a quieter moment.

After a few minutes we met outside and spoke to more locals. John and I were amused when a middle-aged man in a loose checked shirt responded to the news that we were Australian with a big smile of recognition and the exclamation: 'Ahhh, John Howard!'

Australia was the third-biggest military contributor of troops to the Coalition, behind the US and the UK, but we had never really thought of our prime minister as a household name in places like this. The conversation quickly became more serious.

'If the Americans go, we are all dead,' the man in the checked shirt said. 'They [the Saddam loyalists] know who we are and we know who they are. We are safe while the Americans are here but if they leave, my family and everyone else will be too scared to stay.'

As others jostled to have their say the conversation became the first of dozens that would be dominated by the resentment of ordinary people at the shortage of basic services, especially water, that the Americans had vowed to protect.

'America has promised us food, democracy, medicine, water ... everything,' said a 36-year-old father of four. 'So far we have nothing. Kuwaiti radio says they have delivered 44,000 meals to Umm Qasr but we have not seen any of it.'

In the coming weeks I would become convinced that the Coalition's mishandling of these early days fuelled many of the problems that would subsequently plague the occupation. The US military's own field manuals on civil affairs and the legal framework of battle zones make it clear that every metre captured by an army becomes its legal responsibility and that the needs of the local population should be addressed immediately. That was simply not done in Iraq, and much of the potential goodwill of the Iraqi people was lost. There was a window of several weeks in which ordinary Iraqis were prepared to give the Coalition the benefit of the doubt, but the attitudes of many were eventually hardened by the lack of water, power and policing.

By now we had only about twenty-five minutes to deliver a story that had still not been written and photos that needed to be downloaded into a computer, selected, captioned, and transmitted by sat phone.

As we raced out of town John took some final shots through his side window, including one of a woman and her children sitting against the front wall of their home. John had spotted the scene at the last moment and yelled to Stewart to ease up. He hardly had a chance to slow down but the family was lined up so perfectly that it looked like a posed photo.

To avoid the crowds that gathered every time the car stopped we raced back to the one isolated spot where we felt safe – our camping spot of the previous night, a few kilometres out of town. I was dictating a story to a copytaker before we arrived, and when we did pull up John flew into his equipment, throwing together the three parts of the antenna and various cables. Fifteen minutes later we had both met our deadline of 8 p.m. Sydney time.

We relaxed for a few minutes, feeling as if we had done a hard day's work. In fact it was barely noon, so we drove back into town to see what we could find for the next day's papers. Stewart began translating some of the signs – one of the port complexes, we learned, was called the 'Mother of All Battles Quays'.

At the west end of town, where the homes seemed to be newer and larger, Arabic graffiti in red paint extolled that street's loyalties with 'Yes, yes, yes to the great leader Saddam', while just a few blocks to the east a shift in political geography was shown in graffiti declaring 'Saddam is an infidel'.

We passed a soccer game between full teams on a grassless pitch on the edge of town, then noticed a large British patrol backed by several armoured vehicles moving slowly down a street. They stopped and took up positions around the high front gate of one house, so we parked and walked up to watch.

A few dozen neighbours had already gathered in excited anticipation. Several told us that the British were raiding the home of 'some bad men'. A soldier confirmed that the commandos were finally trying to track down soldiers and Saddam loyalists suspected of taking part in the stubborn resistance.

This was the first house to be raided. It was the home of the Lazem brothers, a family whose name prompted neighbours to pout and shake their heads slowly, or talk darkly about Ba'ath Party thugs using their political connections to extort money from innocent people.

After fifteen minutes inside the single-storey home, the commandos emerged with an AK-47 assault rifle, spare ammunition magazines and several other pieces of military equipment which pointed to the presence of one of the Iraqi soldiers who had discarded their uniforms and were emerging at night to launch guerrilla attacks on Coalition troops.

A few minutes later, the commandos led the house's owner, 45-year-old port worker Hadi Mared Lazem, and his brother Ali, thirty, a recently married soldier, out of the house in plastic handcuffs.

An armoured personnel carrier had been backed up to the front door but John had positioned himself across the road to try to get a view of whoever emerged from the house. He snapped off one shot showing the brothers' faces as they were bundled into the back of the British vehicle. They were the first men detained in Umm Qasr in such a house search, and the neighbours were delighted.

'They are bad men, Saddam party men,' said one middle-aged man before he was silenced by the appearance of a knot of spectators listening to what he was telling me. Weeding out the Hussein loyalists who were still terrifying the public was an important step towards convincing Iraqis that Saddam would soon be finished and that they should openly support the Coalition. Another Lazem brother, Fadhil, was a particularly loathed Ba'ath Party member, and his brothers were widely accused of aiding his party work and winning kickbacks through his position in the party.

'They have blood on their hands and I am afraid of them,' said one of their nearest neighbours, who claimed that innocent people had gone missing after being informed on by the Lazems.

Two hours after their detention we returned to their home to speak to their relatives about these allegations. They refused to be photographed so John waited outside to keep an eye on the car while Stewart and I were taken inside and seated on rugs on the floor of a tiled lounge room with rough walls. Seven male relatives, led by the brothers' uncle, Abdul Nabi Saber Hatim, joined us to complain about the treatment of the brothers and see if we could do anything to have them released.

Most wore dishdashas, or full-length smocks. Two boys also listened to the discussion but as with most Iraqi homes we were to visit, the women stayed out of sight in a back room. Hospitality is a deeply entrenched Arabic custom, and guests are always offered cold water and cups of sweet black tea. Hatim apologised that the tea we were drinking had been made partially with sea-water because of the town's shortage of fresh water.

The uncle denied that the Lazems had anything to do with the Ba'ath Party or with the armed resistance to the British and US troops. Hadi was a mere port worker and a family man with seven daughters, he said. Yes, he conceded, Ali, who was caught with the gun, had been a soldier but he had deserted from the army just before the invasion and had been visiting from Basra on holidays. I pointed out that everybody in town knew who the leading Ba'ath Party members were, and that several neighbours had pointed to the brothers as Saddam loyalists. Stewart translated my comments as diplomatically as he could, then their uncle smiled and shrugged unconvincingly.

'There is a lot of finger-pointing going on,' he said. 'Lots of people have old grudges and everybody is accusing everybody right now.' The family did not even support Saddam, he insisted, before arguing at great length that the US had no right to overthrow Saddam's Government and should be resisted by all Iraqis.

'This is an invasion, not a liberation,' he said. 'On whose authority have they come here? How would you like it if there was a war in your country?'

The fact that they opposed the Coalition proved little about the family's attitude to Saddam, as many of his fiercest critics were against the war on nationalist grounds. But the Lazems' relatives were particularly blunt in their denunciations of the Coalition. British soldiers had shot dead a fifteen-year-old boy the night before, Hatim insisted. When I asked for details three men spoke up simultaneously with strikingly different versions of the alleged killing.

The boy's tribe had demanded revenge and that was why there might be attacks on the British in the coming days, the uncle said. Traditional tribes, which can have tens of thousands of members, are an important source of loyalty and support across Iraq, as in the rest of the Arab world. Hatim was evasive when I asked for the name of the dead boy or how we might contact his family, and the other men who claimed to know so much about the incident also fell mute when asked for such details.

'The British are also degrading our people by throwing bottles of water and chocolates onto the ground and making people scramble for them,' Hatim said, changing the topic. 'These soldiers are imperialists.'

When I asked how many brothers there were in the Lazem family, Hatim said there were only three – the two detained men and a younger brother, Hussein. He tapped his own temple and said Hussein had 'problems in the head'. Only after I flicked back through my notebook and mentioned the name of Fadhil, the alleged Ba'ath Party member, did Hatim and the other relatives concede that he was another brother.

Deciding there was no value for the family in talking further, the uncle asked us to find out who they should contact for details of the brothers' fate. My legs were already hurting from sitting cross-legged on the floor, so I didn't mind too much as they stood to show it was time for us to go.

We were led back to our car, where John was sweating in the heat. While we were being farewelled one of the younger men in the family, who did not speak English, laughed and used his finger to write 'Down with the USA' in English in the dust on the Pajero's bonnet. We had seen the same slogan on several walls of government buildings and the Ba'ath Party office.

We drove back to the British HQ a few blocks away to keep our promise by asking how the family could find out what had happened to the brothers. A commando who had been involved in the raid on their home said the relatives should present themselves at the gates of the British HQ, then they would be told what was happening to the brothers. The commando said 'off the record' that they had no proof that the brothers had been involved in any attacks but Ali would be grilled closely because he was obviously a soldier.

Now that the British had started scouring the town, the commando said, it was relatively easy to pick out the soldiers pretending to be civilians. 'It's not so much a physical thing. They sort of have a sly look – they look at you differently.'

As we spoke I noticed a tall Iraqi in white plastic-framed glasses, who seemed to be the only person in town wearing a suit. He was surrounded by a small circle of locals and British troops outside the headquarters. This was Najim Abd Mahdi, one of the very first locals to approach the British and offer his assistance. He was busy liaising between the locals and the British military's civil affairs officers and giving the British his own advice on the town's priorities.

A 52-year-old English teacher at the local high school, Mahdi smiled readily and spoke English in a reasonably correct but slightly stilted way. When I approached him he did not want to give his name for publication, explaining that Saddam was still alive.

'It is simple – if he lives, anyone who speaks up now will be dead,' he said, drawing a finger across his own throat.

But everyone in town knew who Mahdi was, so it had been an act of real courage for him to offer to work with the British. Unlike many of Umm Qasr's other opponents of Saddam, Mahdi insisted that he was confident the Coalition would not abandon Iraq and that the old regime was finished.

'I told the British that we do not need food because the Iraqi Government has distributed four to five months' food,' he said. 'We need electricity and water but two things are even more important – freedom and democracy. Only then will we be able to regain our dignity, which was destroyed by Saddam Hussein.

'You don't know our suffering here. People here have been killed, hanged, gone missing forever for challenging Saddam or his sons. We have been cannibalised.

'We don't have a prison in Umm Qasr, we have a graveyard under every foot,' he said passionately. During a 1997 round of repression against religious leaders in the south, forty-five people in Umm Qasr were arrested, he said. Adults in their families were detained for ten months, and some of the forty-five were still missing.

Mahdi's offer of assistance had been seized on by the British, who had many pressing tasks in town. An electrical engineer, Warrant Officer Darren Larmour, stood in a loose queue of people waiting to get Mahdi's attention. He was hoping that Mahdi would help him to find somebody who understood the switching system of the local power station so he could reconnect the electricity supply.

'A couple of people have come forward to help us, including the thief who stole the batteries from the main generators,' Larmour said. 'The batteries went during some looting earlier this week but we have been promised through intermediaries that he will return them.'

If they could get the power back on they could get the water pumps going and the grain silos working, so aid ships could dock. Larmour finally got Mahdi's attention and drove him off to the power station.

We had little choice but to spend a second night at our camping spot, where we found three other media cars preparing to spend the night. One of the other news crews said they had just been north to Basra and that it was less than an hour's drive to the last British checkpoint south of the city. There had been reasonably heavy exchanges of fire from artillery and small arms so it was dangerous to spend too much time at the last checkpoint, where refugees were leaving the city.

We decided we wanted to go there and interview refugees about living conditions in Basra, and John arranged with a Swedish photographer, Jens Munch, that we should travel together for safety.

I was concerned that Jens was on assignment with Olga Craig of Britain's *Sunday Telegraph*, whose copy was distributed to our Fairfax rivals in Australia. That meant the Fairfax papers might get a similar coverage to whatever we saw or photographed alongside the British crew. But John was convinced that we should travel together if we were heading closer to the fighting, so I agreed.

I used my laptop for the first time to write a story about the raid on the Lazem brothers, and was relieved when my mobile successfully 'spoke to' the laptop to transmit the story.

The rumble of artillery was coming from the north as I tapped away at the keyboard, and it kept up for much of the night.

As I was trying to get to sleep Stewart took his boots off, with unpleasant consequences. I insisted he put them outside. To stop stray dogs stealing them in the middle of the night he dropped them into the tent, where John was sound asleep.

3

SOUTHERN IRAQ

We were woken by John's bellowing.

'Jesus Christ, what's with these fucking boots? I'm dying in here. I'm going to be sick!'

He was stomping around bad-temperedly during breakfast when a utility truck pulled up next to us, carrying three young men and a middle-aged mother. The woman climbed down and squatted beside the Pajero, close to tears as her relatives asked for help. Her eight-year-old son, Sattar Jabbar Qate'e, had been injured in a car crash on the first day of the Coalition strike and had been taken away in a helicopter by Coalition forces. Now his family did not know how to find him and she was distraught, fearing that he may have been too seriously injured even to identify himself to the Americans.

Thousands of families had been separated like this all over Iraq and did not know where to go for help. The mother and her relatives had been turned away from the gates of the prison camp across the road and hoped that as Westerners we might be able to help – was there anyone we could call with our satellite phones, anything we could do?

Stewart was keen to do whatever we could but I warned him not to get their hopes up. We had already hardened ourselves to the constant requests for water, as we simply could not hand out bottles to everybody we met.

The tough-minded thing is to apologise and concentrate on your job but this was a direct appeal for us to intervene when we had the power to make a big difference to somebody's life. This difficult balance between concentrating on your journalism and getting involved in people's problems is one of the most unsettling aspects of reporting in any war zone or part of the Third World.

I had been confronted by this basic urge to help while I was covering a Commonwealth meeting in Zimbabwe in 1991. I was in a group of reporters stuck at a small, dusty school in the bush for a couple of hours waiting for the Australian prime minister to arrive in a helicopter. The school's teacher told me the school had no water and I found out that to dig a well would cost only a thousand or so dollars.

Over the next few days a few of us organised a whip-around among the travelling reporters to raise the money. We were all pretty pleased with ourselves and in that case it did not distract us from our work as reporters. There was nothing unique about that experience. Neil Davis, the Australian cameraman who made his name in the wars of South-East Asia, spent quite a bit of time and money helping some children in trouble. But ultimately journalists have to keep their focus on their 'day jobs' – they do not go into crisis situations as aid workers.

Stewart had the most direct contact with Arabic speakers, many of whom were traumatised, terrified or hostile. To some extent he was a filter shielding me from these draining interactions. The best I could suggest was that John and I would pack up the tent and gear so Stewart could drive over to the prison camp and ask the guards what the family should do. He drove off, leaving the mother wailing softly beside the road and her brothers or sons standing about uncomfortably – grateful but also resenting the fact that they had to ask for such help in the first place.

Stewart came back with some advice on which military unit they should approach for information. The boy would be fine, he insisted, and even if he could not identify himself the Coalition authorities would have kept detailed records on where and when he came into their care.

The journalists in the other 4WDs had decided to join us and the *Sunday Telegraph* to form a convoy heading to Basra. When we were packed I called Sydney and found that a comment piece I had written the previous night about the need for the Coalition to do a better job in winning local support had not been published overnight, as *The Australian* had opted for a piece from a US analyst that covered the same territory.

In my piece I had argued that we had always known that the Coalition tanks had the firepower to race up the country towards Baghdad but 'what we did not know ... was how the Iraqi people would react, and the indications so far have been far from encouraging'.

'Journalists travelling with the troops and the "reality TV" approach of the television coverage emphasised the daily progress of the Americans but clouded the fact that Iraqi people have shown little active support for the war,' I wrote. 'This has been especially worrying in the south, where US strategists had hoped for a popular uprising.'

The situation in Umm Qasr had raised worrying longer-term questions, I suggested.

'What happens in the long run when the Americans try to run the country and hand it over to a new regime? Any occupation will be painful and unsettled unless the Iraqis feel more enthusiasm for change than they have shown so far.'

I wanted to freshen up this piece and re-send it but our efforts to help the distressed family had slowed down our packing up and now we had to set off straight away if we were going with the other cars. As we drove north I tapped away at the laptop updating my opinion piece. I hooked it up to the mobile after a few minutes but we had already moved away from Kuwait and I lost the signal before I could send the story.

As we headed north the skyline became heavier with black smoke from Basra, and we were passing burned-out Iraqi tanks, army trucks and artillery pieces. We had decided to wear our flak jackets for drives of any length, certainly when we were heading towards something like the siege of Basra.

After about half an hour we stopped at a British Army checkpoint at a small intersection. Several tanks were controlling the checkpoint, and soldiers were searching vehicles before allowing them to pass. Our little convoy stopped to sound out the soldiers and people fleeing from Basra to help plan our next moves.

John wanted to get some photos here of people leaving Basra. I told Stewart to stay with him and get any details needed for John's captions, while I would drive back a few kilometres to get a mobile phone signal and send that story. I roared back towards the south, the steering wheel in one hand, my mobile in the other and eyes darting between the road and the little bars on the phone indicating whether it had picked up a decent signal.

After about five kilometres the signal was strong enough to transmit. It was dangerous to stop beside an open road because of the threat of drive-by shootings and kidnappings but I pulled over in an isolated spot where I could see anyone approaching for a kilometre in each direction. The laptop was on the seat next to me, and I took about a minute to connect it to the mobile and e-mail the story. I made a frantic phone call to Sydney to make sure they had received it, then went racing back to the checkpoint.

John and Stewart were waiting impatiently beside the road because the rest of our convoy was just leaving. I had broken our rule that we must stay together in uncertain situations. Their expressions showed they were not happy with me but at least I had got back in time. My relief did not last long. Before I had even pulled up some Iraqi youths beside the road were pointing to the rear passenger tyre. It was dead flat, pierced by a flattened bullet casing which must have been lying on the road just a few hundred metres before I made it back. Now John was really pissed off. If we did go on towards Basra we would be driving with no spare tyre and without the comfort of the other media cars. Stewart was less openly angry but later pointed out that if the bullet had flattened the tyre two kilometres earlier I would have been stranded alone.

No sweat, I said, we would just throw on the spare tyre and catch the other cars.

That little operation became a debacle. A crowd gathered as we pulled our food and other gear out of the back to get at the jack, trying desperately to keep an eye on all of our equipment. The jack turned out to be feeble, a little toy-like device which raised a few smirks among the Iraqi men jostling around us. Then we somehow managed to put it under the car's spring so that when the jack was wound out the spring recoiled and the car did not lift fully off the ground.

The only person who seemed to realise this was an Iraqi aged about thirty who had literally lost his tongue. Hundreds of Iraqis had suffered this punishment for crimes like criticising Saddam or his family, and one of his friends told Stewart the man's tongue had been mutilated.

With John and Stewart getting more frustrated and the crowd growing louder in its Arabic offerings of advice, the one guy who knew what was going on was lying on the ground next to the car pointing to the problem and making indecipherable grunts and hand signals.

One of the unwanted volunteers insisted on removing the tyre anyway, just before our puny jack collapsed, dropping the axel onto the road to the loud amusement of the crowd. John, struggling to contain his anger, stalked off through the heat and dust to borrow a sturdy jack from a British armoured vehicle about fifty metres away, then the mute guy climbed under the car and got things sorted out.

As the others packed up I slipped some money to the mute man, a delicate operation because fifteen others decided they had helped and deserved a reward too. We had to struggle to close the doors behind us, then we drove on about ten kilometres and caught the other media cars at the final British checkpoint a few hundred metres this side of the main bridge. John and Stewart were not impressed by my insistence that no damage had been done now that we were back with the other cars.

'Mate, we are now driving with no fucking spare,' John said. 'And I told you I don't like being in places like that on our own.'

He rarely stayed in a bad mood for long, and as usual there was plenty to distract us from any arguments. We parked and walked towards the bridge, a simple concrete structure curving over the river. Beyond it the sky was ominously active with brown smoke from burning buildings and darker, hotter smoke rising more quickly from trenches of oil set alight by the city's defenders in the hope of thwarting laser-guided weapons. The sporadic crack of small-arms fire and occasionally louder artillery explosions kept the soldiers and civilians around the checkpoint looking anxiously towards the city.

Between us and the bridge there was a steady stream of people coming out of the city, many of them distressed and all carrying everything they could of their possessions. Stalled at the checkpoint was another line of traffic trying to go in – mainly men with loads of tomatoes and other food which they said was for their families.

A unit of the Desert Rats, the 7th Armoured Brigade of the Irish Guards, was searching people going both ways but their main focus was on stopping anyone carrying weapons into the city. The whole scene was hot, loud and disorganised, with anger and fear straining nerves everywhere. In the words of one exasperated British soldier: 'This is just a complete cluster-fuck.'

Asked what was going on, he said, 'You know as much as me. We were stopping men of military age and only allowing women and children through until a few hours ago then we got orders saying let everyone in. Now they are saying let nobody in.'

He warned that the bridge and the road on the other side were exposed to occasional sniper fire, and that every couple of hours mortars fired by Iraqis from the back of utility trucks landed close to the road.

The British had decided to avoid any major confrontation in Basra, a city of 1.5 million, but with about sixty per cent of its people lacking clean drinking water they were now considering going into the city.

We took photos and interviewed people leaving Basra. Some said there were dead and injured in the streets but others insisted the local authorities were holding out well. An unemployed villager named Karim Salih said he and his family had been trapped in the city for eight days while visiting on holidays from their home in Zubayr, a town between Basra and Umm Qasr. They had had to walk for two hours to get out. Conditions in Basra were tough, he said, as people were scared of the shooting and bombing. There was not yet an air of total crisis but many had been reduced to drinking salt water while others were even boiling sewage water.

'There are explosions and bombs all the time and people are shooting from nowhere. There is no medicine and no health services. If you have a problem you are stuck with it.'

His one-year-old son Abbas had fallen ill and was having trouble breathing because of the heavy smoke.

Mohammed Mohsin walked towards us with his Bedouin wife, two little girls and son Mohsin. One hundred metres before he reached us the father hoisted his tired son onto his shoulders so the family could hasten their pace, forcing his daughters to trot to keep up. Framed by the smoke behind them the family made a striking portrait for John as they hurried out of the city. When they reached us the father stopped to answer our questions for about a minute.

There was a lot of shooting inside the city, he said, and people were drinking from a river polluted with sewage but they were marshalling their food carefully.

Two of his children, who were barefoot, had just walked six kilometres. Before he hurried on, Mohsin said he had never seen anything like the situation on the city's streets. 'People are scared and there are many wounded,' he said. 'We thought we might be killed trying to leave but I was more afraid of staying. We got a taxi as far as it would take us but a bomb landed near the road and the driver refused to go any further.'

The siege of Basra had become a stand-off between the British forces, who had sealed all main roads into the city, and Iraqi troops who had retreated into the city and were now discarding their uniforms in preparation for urban combat.

Hundreds of thousands of Iranian soldiers failed to take Basra during the Iran–Iraq War in the 1980s and the city had seen centuries of invading armies, from the Persians and Turks through to the British after World War I. It now loomed as a disaster in its own right and a taste of what could lie ahead for Baghdad.

The crews from the other cars in our convoy were also moving about interviewing people but we noticed the *Sunday Telegraph*'s 4WD take off quickly from where it was parked with the other cars, throwing up a cloud of dust, to race into a large compound just off the highway and about a kilometre from the bridge. A soldier told me it was being used as a base by some of the British troops, and I guessed that Olga had got permission from a military contact to go into the compound. She confirmed after the war that she had been invited in to interview refugees who had been shot by Iraqi militia while fleeing the city.

A line of young Iraqi soldiers who had been taken prisoner were then led towards the compound by British soldiers. The prisoners seemed morose but more relieved than resentful, and the British allowed them to talk to a few of us. Stewart stood out as one of the surprisingly few translators working with the smaller one-vehicle media crews. The prisoners told him they had deserted after being ordered to shed their uniforms and bunk down with their weapons in the homes of ordinary citizens.

'We took off our uniforms but did not want to take part in that sort of brutal fighting in our home city,' said one young man of about twenty. 'Our families are still there but now that we have surrendered we can't go back because they (the government) will hang us.'

They were technically deserters rather than combatants, as they had been caught trying to flee Basra. A British soldier said few prisoners were resisting arrest.

'They know they will get a feed and they won't get killed. They know by now that they will get looked after properly.'

As we headed back towards our car we noticed British medics leaning over a heavy European man who lay quivering with pain on a stretcher on the road. 'M1320' had been written in felt pen on his forehead, meaning he had been given morphine at 1.20 p.m. A despondent French reporter standing nearby said the injured man was Alain Dubat, a cameraman from France's Channel Two, who had been hurt after being separated from his reporter. During a mortar attack he had apparently jumped off the road into a trench. He had managed to save his camera but seemed to have shattered his kneecap. The morphine was easing Dubat's shaking and slowing his breathing but his Channel Two colleague, Sabine Albertelli, was clearly distressed. She was gesticulating and speaking animatedly with him in French. I was trying to comfort her when I realised she was mainly worried not about her colleague but about the prospect of being pulled out of Iraq by her editors now that she had no cameraman. She was horrified by the thought.

'What am I going to do without a cameraman? They will try to get me back to France. I don't want to go – I won't go!'

She said they had been waiting with several other carloads of journalists at the checkpoint when the road had suddenly been opened to traffic.

'I got to my car and thought he had jumped into another press car in our convoy so I took off without him,' she said. 'Before I really knew it I was over the bridge and into the city. But I had to come back to find my crew, and there was Alain like this.'

Less than thrilled that she had left him behind, Dubat was walking with another journalist when a mortar was fired from the back of a utility truck. Their passionate words, Albertelli explained matter-of-factly, had actually been a fight about her having driven off leaving him by the road.

After my own drive a little while earlier I felt no need to share this tale with John and Stewart. Newly determined to stick with them, I suggested that we move closer to the bridge. In fact, we walked right to its peak, getting a good view of the city beyond. Smoke rose from five places around the city's low skyline. Few buildings were above two storeys or the height of occasional palm trees.

There were about two kilometres of dried mudflats between the bridge and the outer suburbs, but to the left of the road sat what looked like a large factory complex but was actually a technical college. The British soldiers had told us that there had been sniper fire coming from that complex. The Iraqis were using the small utility trucks as firing platforms for their mortars so that they could drive off into surrounding streets before the British could return fire.

John decided to go further over the bridge to get a better angle. I waited at the top but felt exposed so I moved over to shelter behind a pile of wooden boxes stacked on the left side of the bridge. Only when I had crouched down behind them did I read the English script on the side, which began 'To: Ministry of Defence, Baghdad, Iraq.' I was sheltering behind twenty-three boxes of Semtex plastic explosives which had apparently been positioned to blow up the bridge.

Looking for somebody with whom to share this wonderful news, I trotted a little further down towards Basra to a jeep which was the only vehicle parked on the bridge. Two Western men stood next to it in plain clothes but they were looking at maps and studying the city through binoculars in a way that suggested they had not been civilians all their lives.

They were friendly enough to confirm my suspicions about the plastic explosives. 'They obviously lost control of the bridge before they could set up the detonators,' said one of the men. He had an Australian accent and said his name was Glen but did not want to give away a lot of personal details. They were private security experts working for CNN, and were scouting out the situation for a group of reporters and producers who were waiting a few safe kilometres behind us. This was obviously one of the joys of working with a CNN-style budget – getting ex-SAS men to do their scouting while I was hiding behind boxes of Semtex.

Later in the war another of CNN's 'security advisers' returned fire on some attacking Iraqis with a gun that he just happened to have with him inside their press vehicle. Other journalists were furious at the news. Combatants in Iraq and elsewhere already need little excuse to fire on the press, and the discovery that we might be armed can only put all reporters at further risk.

By now it was 2.45 p.m. and we headed back from the bridge. When we reached the second-last checkpoint a few journalists said a group of Italian reporters had driven into Basra and not returned. Several groups of Iraqis leaving the city had told me earlier that some Western reporters had been arrested.

As we drove south Stewart stopped by a shattered piece of artillery and asked John to take his photo in front of it. John agreed but was not thrilled by the distraction.

Olga and Jens and most of the other news crews who had camped at our spot by the road had decided it was safer to move on rather than returning to the same spot but we figured that having the British troops nearby made our patch of gravel a comparatively safe haven.

Around dusk a US military convoy pulled up near our camping spot for a break and we got chatting to the drivers, who all seemed barely eighteen or nineteen.

They knew little of what had been happening in the war – they were surprised when we told them some news that had been on television before we left Kuwait: that a group of US army mechanics from another convoy had been ambushed in Nasiriyah four days earlier and then paraded by the Iraqis before television cameras, seven of them dead and five as prisoners.

The young drivers were friendly and they told us about their rules of engagement, which required them to adopt a more aggressive posture than that chosen by the British. While the Brits were already wearing soft hats and trying to talk to locals, the Americans were under orders to wear helmets and point their weapons at anybody who approached them.

'Just the way you walked up to me before to say hello, I was allowed to shoot you dead if I wanted to,' one said.

'I don't know you and you just came right up to me. I could tell you weren't Iraqis and you were smiling and no threat but hell, I didn't know if you were faking it.

'We've heard about all sorts of shit happening. Iraqi soldiers are walking up wearing American uniforms, or pretending to surrender and then shooting. Guys like us are not going to take any chances over here, surrounded by these Gooks, we're just going to shoot, and that's what we are ordered to do.'

I corrected him as gently as I could. 'Umm . . . they're not Gooks. That's an expression used during the Vietnam War for Asians – these are Arabs,' I said.

He had clearly seen too many Vietnam War movies. American troops eventually adopted the term 'Hadji' as their slang term for Iraqis. To a Muslim it is a sign of respect, meaning somebody who has made the pilgrimage to Mecca but the soldiers' use of the term had a different source. It came from Hadji Singh, the turbaned side-kick of 1960s Hanna-Barbera cartoon character Johnny Quest. As his name suggests, Hadji Singh was actually Indian but the soldiers applied it to anybody from the Middle East and southern Asia.

For all their teenage bravado the young drivers did not mind admitting they were nervous, even scared. 'Remember, if you hear distant thunder, it ain't thunder,' one half-joked in a little farewell salute.

I wrote a story in longhand for the Sunday papers about what we had seen at the bridge, then tried for the first time to sleep in the tent, a pretty uncomfortable experience as we had no mattress. It did not help that I was trying to keep my flak jacket and gas mask right next to me.

*

I was woken by John and Stewart yelling that we had to hit the road straight away. A Marine from the dug-out across the road had told them that a detachment of British military police was coming to get us. They had heard on their radio that the MPs or military police were going to kick us out of Iraq, and they would be here in about forty minutes.

'Thanks for the warning but why are you telling us?' John had asked.

'Because we're Marines and we have our own MPs – these guys are army MPs so bugger 'em.'

We drove straight to the port in Umm Qasr, more determined than ever to get inside. I had called Patrick Walters, the head of our Canberra bureau, the previous day and asked him to try to find a contact number for the Australian divers, and I called him again as we drove. He had come up with an Australian mobile number which might work. I had not been able to get through by the time we reached the gate with the Saddam mosaic, so we settled down to wait there in the hope that some of the Australian divers would pass through the gates, or that the mobile number would answer.

Several hundred metres away from the port about a dozen Iraqis milled around watching the gates, having already been ordered back by the Marine guards and told not to come any closer.

We were at least allowed to wait near the gates, and as we did a cleanly dressed Iraqi man walked towards us yelling 'Water. Bebi. Water.' The two sentries pointed their weapons at him, yelling for him to stop. He did not seem to understand and kept walking forward with his hands up. Nervous, the Americans screamed more loudly, put their guns to their shoulders and took a firing stance. People all over Iraq were dying in situations just like this and would keep doing so for months. Stewart intervened, warning the Iraqi in Arabic to back off. He yelled something back to Stewart, who explained to the soldiers that he was after water or milk for a new baby. The Marines did not know what to say. I told Stewart that the Marines could not help him because if they did they would have an endless stream of Iraqis coming to the gates for help, which would only make a tense situation worse.

Stewart told the new father that there was no water for him. He turned and walked away. Feeling guilty at my own intervention, I knew that if I had a thirsty baby at home I too would be taking risks and defying the rules of the adult world to find a drink. I considered driving after the guy to give him some of our own water but couldn't work out how to do that without encouraging the attentive audience to make similar approaches to these twitchy American guards. We sat in the heat watching the father walk away.

As we drove back into town to ask locals about car tyre repairs, we were surprised to find a small shack behind the petrol station where several men sat around rusty old tyres and a generator-driven air pump waiting for customers. Almost every other business in town was closed but they said we could pick up the tyre fully repaired the next day for a charge of about US$3. Our heavy use of the inverter had begun to blow fuses in the Pajero but we knew that finding an auto electrician was out of the question. The cigarette lighter was now out of action but there was another connection in the rear compartment where we could plug in the inverter. If that connection went we would have to resort to powering it straight off the battery terminals.

The mobile number I had been calling for the Australian divers finally got through. I explained our situation and the second-ranking officer in the diving unit, a Perth-based lieutenant commander, came to let us in just before lunchtime. He and the rest of the Australian divers were much more welcoming and relaxed about the media than their counterparts in Doha. Extremely proud of their skills and what they were doing in the port, they were keen to lift their unit's profile, something which could bring extra status, funding and opportunities for promotion.

The port area was an expanse of concrete more than a kilometre long, scattered with large warehouses, empty sea containers and ageing port equipment. The concrete ended in a sheer drop of perhaps twenty metres to water deep enough for deep-hulled ships to pull up right alongside the cranes on the dock. Several wheat silos sat a few hundred metres from the dock, linked to it by grain conveyor belts.

Crews from channels Nine and Seven were already inside. They had been allowed to cross the border in Umm Qasr and had driven straight into the port and stayed there. Nine's reporter Michael Usher and his crew even had their own editing equipment. By putting together material sent from elsewhere and doing their own 'stand-ups' to camera on the dock they allowed Nine to add its own Iraq dateline to its material. This practice is perfectly legitimate and is the television equivalent of what we newspaper reporters often do, like sitting in Baghdad pulling stories together from the news wires, websites and other sources so our papers can run the precious dateline 'by Our Reporter, in Baghdad'.

We parked on the tarmac next to Seven's Geoff Parry and Robin Brown, who had often worked together in crisis zones for the network. Kate Geraghty, the Fairfax photographer, and John Hunter Farrell, a freelance defence reporter who had been doing some work for the *Herald*, had also reached the port after being taken aboard an Australian Navy ship. None had ventured far beyond the front gate. The only non-Australian news teams on the docks were two armoured personnel carriers full of Reuters people.

The 32-member Australian diving team was sharing a long, low warehouse with twenty-six British divers and about ninety-five Americans. There were light partitions separating each national group but it quickly became obvious that the Australians and Brits got on much better with each other than with the Americans. According to their neighbours the Americans were less considerate when it came to making noise around the clock, a complaint I had first heard from Australians in Qatar. I also heard off-the-record mutterings that the first wave of US Marines to capture the port had been unnecessarily violent and had later vandalised the docks.

We spent the afternoon talking to the divers and doing some overdue chores – sorting through our kit, hand-washing clothes and draping them over the car to dry. We also had our first 'shower' for three days. The divers had shower stalls rigged up but we did not want to stretch the friendship so we took turns walking off behind a nearby shed with a cake of soap, a towel and two plastic bottles of water.

Apart from a small number of SAS troops in eastern Iraq, these divers, known as Clearance Diving Team 3, were the only members of the Australian military with their boots, or flippers, on the ground in Iraq. While the headline number of Australians involved in the war was 2000 the great majority of those were working on ships in the Gulf, at airbases in surrounding countries or back at headquarters in Doha.

I had lunch on a camp chair on the tarmac, chatting with off-duty divers. Every now and then a pair of divers would head off to the quay in wetsuits for a shift in the water. They and their officers were likable, casual guys who reminded me of friends in Australia who work as firemen – hardworking, well trained and with the camaraderie of a football team.

Based in Perth and Sydney, they had spent a few days in the desert of northern Kuwait before driving here in their unit's own Land Rovers. They had already cleared the port's grain terminal of any landmines and were now clearing the terminals of underwater mines. The immediate aim was to allow a British ship carrying aid, the *Sir Gallahad*, to dock, which was an important public relations goal for the Coalition. The divers were particularly unhappy that they were supposed to leave Iraq in a week to ten days.

'We're here, we're ready and we're keen,' said Jock, a chief petty officer from Perth. 'It's hard for us to understand why they would pull us out when there is so much to be done and we are so well placed to help. It's like training for a game of footy and they leave you on the bench. There are obviously jobs here for us up north and we want to stay and do them. If they will leave us here for a while we can help stop little kiddies stepping on mines.'

The Australians said they had already been asked by British commandos controlling the town to help dispose of land-based bombs and mines but they had been ordered to restrict themselves to their port duties. I told them I was pretty sure that the Australian Government would quickly pull them out. There had been no Australian casualties in the war so far but their work was dangerous and with public opinion against Australia's involvement the government would be desperately keen to get its people out intact.

Their other gripe was about the positive publicity given to the mine-detecting dolphins used by their US counterparts. The dolphins had received enormous attention but the Australians who worked alongside them were less than impressed. The dolphins were trained to find suspicious objects and place markers on them to guide human divers to the targets. They had the valuable ability to search for mines buried under silt but according to the Australians they were less reliable than human divers or mechanical searches with sonar equipment.

'It's all political – the Americans have spent tens of millions of dollars training Flipper so they have to pretend he's a success,' said one diver. 'The dolphins have had all this amazing publicity, but as soon as they put one in the water it shot through. There's a war going on and Flipper goes AWOL!

'He turned up a couple of days later, but in the meantime they had to bring in another one (by helicopter from a US Navy ship) and that meant some of our gear got bumped off the flight.'

I thought this was hilarious and told the divers I wanted to write about it. Such a story would not help relations with their neighbours but the divers were undaunted.

'If you put one to work in Sydney Harbour it would mark a million things because it can't tell the difference between a washing machine and a mine,' one diver said. 'The bottom line, mate, is it's a fish. It's also a very smart fish, so how do you know it hasn't just gone off for a feed instead of working and then thought 'hang on, I'd better mark a few things or they won't give me any fish to eat when I get back'? We're talking about mines here, so that's a pretty big risk to take based on Flipper's say-so.'

The five dolphins from the mine-clearing 'M-7 series' were housed in a warehouse a few hundred metres away. I found their chief handler, Lieutenant Robert Greene, who agreed to let John and I see the dolphins. Three males and two female Atlantic bottlenose dolphins, they were sitting in chest-high tanks, which could be wheeled outside so that cranes could place the dolphins in the water. Lt Greene suspected that we were onto the story about one of his dolphins disappearing and he confirmed that a male named Tacoma had vanished when he was first sent to work.

'Two days later we found him in the same spot where we put him in the water,' he said.

Tacoma was resting in his holding pool with the Navy's oldest dolphin, 33-year-old Makay. Makay's back carried scars from his own AWOL adventure off Florida some years before, when he granted himself a holiday and was attacked by a shark.

Lt Greene, whose team was under considerable pressure because of the US military's large investment in its sea mammal program since 1969, insisted the dolphins had been a great success in Iraq, their first mine-clearing deployment in a war zone.

That night while John slept – somehow – in the tent on concrete and without a mattress, I quite enjoyed knocking out a story for Monday's paper about the Australian divers' reservations, quoting the divers without naming them.

These were the first two pars:

'THE US Navy's mine-clearing dolphins have been the surprise media stars of the Iraq War, but they have not exactly won over Australian divers working alongside them.

The polite way to express their scepticism about the mine-clearing skills of the dolphins is to question their reliability and cost efficiency, but there is another way to put it.

'Flipper's f. . . ed, mate,' was how one diver saw things yes-terday [. . .]'

I knew the Americans would not be happy when they heard about the report and that the Australian commanders would be less than thrilled by anything that might offend their allies. That could all rebound uncomfortably on us while we were relying on the mili-tary's hospitality but I wasn't too fussed. I knew it was what the divers believed and I had asked their permission to report their com-ments.

*

The next morning I called *The Australian* and each of our papers in Melbourne, Sydney, Brisbane and Adelaide to make sure they knew that there were several stories coming for Monday's papers – one report with John's striking photos of refugees fleeing Basra, a story and photo on the Australian divers' low opinion of their dolphin allies, a report on the divers wanting to stay, and another photo story that would come a few hours later about the Australian divers helping to distribute aid in Umm Qasr. A woman I spoke to in the *Herald-Sun*'s newsroom joked that it was going to be the 'memorial Peter Wilson edition', then got tongue-tied as she apologised that she didn't mean to say 'memorial' as I was obviously not going to die. I was amused. She was mortified.

Phil Pyke, a Tasmanian policeman and captain in the Army Reserve, was serving as a media officer for the diving unit and was the most helpful person we had come across in such a role. That day he was to lead a group of the divers into town to distribute aid, which would be the first occasion in the whole war on which Australian troops would meet ordinary Iraqis, apart from any local contact that the small contingent of SAS troops might have had out in the desert.

Armed with M4 carbines, Pyke's team were nervous about going into town. Our convoy of two navy jeeps, the Channel Nine and Seven cars and our Pajero was held up at an intersection on the edge of town as the soldiers tried to locate a water distribution site. As we waited in the heat a couple of the divers obliged the cameras by handing out parcels of food to children beside the road. The usual crowd gathered but it quickly became unruly and then bad-tempered. A middle-aged man in a black shirt yelled at children not to accept the food.

'You are embarrassing all Iraqis, having your photos taken like zoo animals leaping for food at feeding time,' he chastised them.

He had a point. All that the cameramen wanted was a dignified shot of the divers handing out food but the children kept running in together and snatching at the food, then fighting among themselves for it. Stewart was our only hope of communicating with the children but he was reluctant to get involved because he basically agreed with the bearded man that the whole event was in poor taste.

He and I had sharp words. I too found a free-for-all demeaning but that was precisely why I wanted him to calm the children down. I was tired of the whole set-up myself and tempers were fraying.

We always spoke to as many people as possible when we were on the streets and I noticed a group of seven young men who were better dressed and more neatly groomed than most people in Umm Qasr, who tended to be scruffy, with poor skin and lean features. This lot were middle-class out-of-towners, and seemed to be increasingly afraid of the fact that they stood out.

The leader of the little band mustered up the courage to approach us. Ali Hassan, twenty-seven, explained – first in halting English and then quickly in Arabic when he realised Stewart could speak it – that they were all university graduates of military age who had left Basra to try to get out of Iraq. When he learned he had approached a journalist rather than the sort of foreigner who might be able to get him out of the country, Ali hesitated nervously but continued talking for a while to explain himself.

'Our families are all still in Basra but they told us to go so we would not be taken by the army,' he said. 'They make you fight and if you won't, they just kill you. There is already shooting and looting in the streets and shortages of water and food but things are getting much worse for young men because they have started to round us up.'

When a good friend was seized in his home they decided to take their chances. A 6 p.m. curfew stopped them leaving at night so they left Basra at dawn that day, sneaking out through friends' homes to avoid road blocks.

'If the soldiers see young men leaving they accuse you of being traitors and abandoning your city,' he said. 'It is very dangerous.' Once out of the city they paid for a lift for the sixty kilometres to the border.

A physical education graduate who had only ever been able to find work as a labourer, Ali said he wanted to go to Kuwait or 'any other safe country' that would accept them because he had the same aspirations as educated young men anywhere in the world.

'I want to work and study more and be able to live freely, and travel to many countries. I would like to have a holiday in Paris one day. I have had enough of Iraq – I have no future here. Here there is nothing for us.'

Ali stopped talking whenever prying ears came within range, and at one point I stopped the conversation to tell an eavesdropper to go away. Asked whether he would stay and help rebuild Iraq if the US-led Coalition managed to overthrow Saddam and install a democratic regime, Ali said yes but he was highly sceptical that it would ever be worth staying.

'Of course we would rather stay – why would we want to go away from our families? But I just don't believe that things are going to change. In 1991 [when the US encouraged an uprising against Saddam then offered no support] we were all young but even we saw people being executed on the streets.

'They took them out of their homes, dragged them away from their mothers and killed them. Things might improve but they might not and it could take a very long time. And I only have one life to live.'

I wanted to write a story about him, to show that the terrified exodus from Basra was not all exhausted old women and photo-genic family groups carrying their possessions over their shoulders. Ali agreed to a photo and story on the condition that I did not use his full name because his family was still in Basra. I asked John to take his photograph as he spoke.

They were travelling with no luggage at all so as not to look like refugees. Locals were starting to pay more attention to Ali and his conversation with us, and he knew by now that there was nothing we could do for them. He offered disappointed farewells, then led his friends off, walking quickly and quietly around the nearest corner.

Eventually our convoy took off again and found its way to a vacant block of land where a tanker truck was to distribute water. Family groups lined up with plastic containers and amid much shoving the water started flowing into barrels and buckets.

Once again it was poorly organised and many of the locals found it frustrating and humiliating. Even the navy divers, who were happy to finally get out of the port and meet some Iraqis but did not have an interpreter, could pick up on the ambivalence of the locals, and they too were uncomfortable that families were having to fight for water and scramble for food.

Chief Petty Officer Richard Hocking – at thirty-nine one of Australia's most senior military divers – said it was frustrating to see the town without water and people becoming increasingly angry at the Coalition over their worsening living conditions.

'I know that sometimes these things take time but it really would be nice to get the water to the people more quickly,' said Hocking.

Some British reporters had also been invited to see the water distribution and one, from the *Independent*, asked me if I would 'lend' him Stewart to do some translating.

I said no as Stewart was starting to get overtaxed by such requests and we had to leave before the rest of the convoy for an appointment to watch some divers at work back at the port. As we walked off, a middle-aged man who could see that Stewart was the only interpreter among the foreigners started to yell at me that the way the water was being distributed was an affront to their dignity.

'We are not animals. This is treating us like animals. George Bush just wants our oil. I will never forgive him for treating us like this,' he fumed. 'They promised us we would be taken care of – it's been ten days, so where is our water? There are twenty-five million Saddams in Iraq, we will hit you all.' This threat that every Iraqi was 'a Saddam' was one I would hear several times in the next few days.

I understood his anger but the longer and louder he yelled at me the less patient I became. I told Stewart to ask the man whether he realised that the shortage of water had been exacerbated by looting by Iraqis, including the theft of the four large batteries from the town's main electricity generators a week earlier. This was not one of my diplomatic triumphs.

The man, a portly figure of about fifty, literally shook with rage and waved his fists, turning his abuse from George Bush to me. The looting was the fault of the Coalition for allowing it to happen, he screamed.

I asked again whether he thought the Iraqi thieves shared any responsibility at all. In the face of his rage I became calmer and quieter, which just angered him more. It was an uneven confrontation – I had the option of walking away and getting into our air-conditioned 4WD, with its stock of water bottles, leaving him standing in the field with an empty water bucket and a thirsty family.

His rudeness had turned me into an offended victim in the eyes of his neighbours, even though his anger was totally understandable and I was a fair enough target as the only foreigner he had met with an interpreter.

As we reached our car two other men ran after us, out of the hearing of their furious friend, to apologise for his behaviour. He had gone over the top, they said, and everyone realised I was not responsible for their problems. They warned, though, that while the locals had always opposed Saddam, their frustration at the lack of the promised aid could dangerously sour attitudes to the Coalition.

We did a quick tour of the town, then watched the divers at work in the port. Somebody had brought along a clothes line so with that strung up beside the car we had a quiet evening doing more chores and sorting out the back of the Pajero.

I had been asked to write a news story and a feature article for *The Australian*'s weekly Media section on how John went about transmitting photos from Iraq, and how it compared to his work in East Timor.

Before writing I checked the Internet, where I read that US forces had ordered another round of bombing in and around Baghdad. This news was presented as a piece of strategy, an almost clinical explanation of the latest logistics exercise, which could never convey the flesh and blood consequences of such decisions.

One person who was about to feel those consequences was Ismail Abbas, a fifty-year-old driver and part-time farm worker from the village of Zafaraniya, on the southern edge of Baghdad. As we had been unpacking the Pajero, Abbas was unpacking his own car about 450 kilometres to the north of us.

I had never heard of Abbas, of course, but I would learn later that he and his family arrived home at 6 p.m. after spending a week with relatives further south in the ancient capital Babylon. They had gone to Babylon to try to avoid Coalition bombing but a series of fatal Coalition attacks there convinced Abbas that his family would be better off back in Baghdad.

While he and his two wives, Layla abd Hamza and Azhar Ali, unloaded their bedding and clothes, the children ran to tell their friends about their trip. Nestled among a dozen palm trees on the edge of a broad stretch of cornfields, their small home was in a hamlet of nine other cement-block houses which were mostly owned by cousins and more distant relatives. The extended family had been living in the area for several generations, and Abbas had spent twenty years in his house, which measured just nine metres square and had two rooms plus a tiny kitchen and a bathroom.

The younger children were excited to be back with their play-mates but at dusk they were ordered inside for dinner. By 9 p.m. everyone was in bed. Abbas slept in one room with his second wife, Azhar, who was seven months pregnant, and their two sons, Ali, twelve, and Abbas, ten. He had married Azhar, twenty-two years his junior, after his first wife had delivered four daughters – Lamya'a, who was now 21, Asma'a, 18, Hana'a, 15 and Shahla'a, 14.

The enlarged family stayed under the one roof, as is the local custom. Azhar promptly gave birth to Ali, finally providing a male to lead the younger generation. The first wife, Layla, had her own son Hamza a year later and then two more daughters – Hadeel, who turned eight while the family was in Babylon, and three-year-old Maha.

Layla slept in the larger second room with six of her children – Asma'a, the second oldest was already married and living with her husband's family. It was a cold night so the family were tucked under heavy acrylic blankets.

Just before midnight an American missile ploughed into their little hamlet, its blinding explosion destroying eight houses and leaving Ismail Abbas's home a burning pile of rubble on top of the family. A gas bottle exploded in the kitchen as the smaller room caught fire, its bedding and blankets bursting into flames on top of Ismail and his wife and two sons.

The other room did not burn. Fifteen-year-old Hana'a told me later that she woke up trapped under cement blocks and wooden beams, screaming with her sisters for help as flames up to three metres high engulfed what was left of the other room.

The girls' uncle, Mohammed abd Hamzah al Sultany, heard the explosion from his home about a kilometre away and ran to help. Thirty-seven-year-old Mohammed, who is Layla's brother as well as Ismail's distant cousin, says he arrived panting to help neighbours pull the girls out.

One of those neighbours, burly farmer Karim Jassim Ahmed, heard young Ali calling 'I'm here, I'm here' from amid the flames. Ahmed, a father of eight whose own home was just ten metres away, found the twelve year old trapped under rubble and his still-smouldering blanket.

The boy's parents and brother were already dead, their corpses terribly burned. Ali had also been horribly scorched and was screaming in pain. The only part of his body that seemed not to have been burned was his face, which had not been covered by the blanket. Ahmed told me later that as he dragged Ali clear he saw the boy's left hand fall off 'right in front of my face'.

Electric wires were snapping and sparking in the burning wreckage, and water from burst pipes was creating dangerous puddles. Ahmed was burned on the lower left leg by a flying electric cable, then when he tried to lift up Ismail's body he was knocked off his feet by an electric jolt.

No ambulances or emergency services had arrived, and neighbours scrambled from house to house trying to help survivors. A roof beam had kept most of the ceiling about forty-five centimetres off the floor of the second room, saving the girls' lives. Their uncle Mohammed and two others eventually prised it up to drag Layla and her terrified children free.

Ahmed, a strong bear of a man, carried Ali up to a raised road which runs by the hamlet and loaded him into the back of a neighbour's Toyota Corona which raced him off to one of Baghdad's biggest hospitals, Al-Kindi. Several of Ali's sisters were sent to that and another hospital but none was seriously injured.

Apart from Ali's parents and brother, thirteen neighbours, all relatives, died in the hamlet.

By the time they were being pulled from the rubble I had finished my stories and was wrestling with my mobile and laptop in the front seat of the Pajero to send off my e-mail. I checked the Internet again, and saw some news of more direct interest to me than the earlier report about Baghdad being bombed.

Terry Lloyd's two ITV colleagues were still missing near Basra; another British reporter, Gaby Rado of Channel Four, had died in northern Iraq in what may have been a suicide, and a Newsday reporter and photographer had gone missing from their hotel in Baghdad, apparently detained by Iraqi officials.

The BBC's director of news, Richard Sambrook, was reported saying that the corporation had decided it was now too dangerous to have correspondents working 'unilaterally' in southern Iraq.

'Other than in Baghdad and in northern Iraq, it's extremely difficult for us to work independently on safety grounds – as the death of an ITN team showed – so we are inhibited from independent journalism in a way that we weren't during the first Gulf war,' he told the *Independent*.

The BBC felt it was safest for its reporters to be embedded. 'But that in itself is not enough – you need to have other ways of finding out what is going on,' he said, without suggesting what those other ways might be.

The only good news on the 'journalists in distress' front was that a group of Italian reporters who had entered Basra two days earlier and been arrested by Iraqi officials had somehow turned up safely in Baghdad.

I called *The Australian* to make sure it had received my e-mail despatches and mentioned the surprising fate of the Italian journalists in a brief chat with the news editor, Matthew Stevens. 'That could be the way to get to Baghdad,' he joked.

'Yeah – a free trip! I should try it,' I said, and we both laughed.

By now it was after 3 a.m. The three-hour time difference to London meant it was about midnight there when I called Pilita to let her know I was OK. She said the *Sunday Telegraph* had carried a front-page report by Olga Craig which was billed as the first by a Western journalist from inside Basra. It told how she and the photographer Jens Munch had driven around the city's streets for a few kilometres, getting a surprised and occasionally surly response from any locals they passed or tried to engage – they did not have a translator so real conversations were out of the question.

Olga wrote that four armed Iraqi soldiers sitting in a doorway had looked at her in disbelief but had not prevented her from reversing and driving away. It was not clear from the report exactly where they had entered the city, where they had gone, and whether they had been alone, given that I had seen them driving into the British military base on the edge of the city.

Olga told me months later that the day after our trip together to the bridge, while John and Stewart and I were in the port at Umm Qasr interviewing the divers, she and Jens had gone back to the bridge and told the Desert Rats that they were contemplating driving into the city.

The soldiers advised against it but they decided to take their chances anyway.

'It was 3.30 on Saturday afternoon and we're a Sunday paper – we figured that a week later Basra would have fallen, so if we were going to do it, it had to be then,' she said. 'So we just drove across the bridge.'

They drove around for about forty minutes before leaving safely to be questioned by the British soldiers, who were as keen as we were for any information about the living conditions in the city.

4

ARREST

On Monday morning we made a decision we would regret for weeks. It was nearly 8.30 a.m. when I woke in the front passenger seat after about five hours' sleep.

John had already been up for an hour after another uncomfortable night on the tarmac. Stewart was also up, having slept soundly through my swearing at his snoring.

As I scratched around looking for a clean bowl for the Fruit Loops we had brought from Kuwait, John was upbeat.

'We've already got our first yarn of the day lined up – it's too easy,' he said. After a week of promising to restore the water supply to Umm Qasr, the British were finally due to open a water pipeline from Kuwait, and they planned to turn it into a media event.

'Instead of getting a boring shot of a crowd standing around the pipe,' he suggested, 'let's find a family who'll take us back to their home so I can get them washing their kids or doing something else with the water.'

To do that we would need enough space in the car for extra passengers. And that is when we made our brilliant decision – we would take a lot of gear out of the Pajero so we could travel lightly for the day. Until now we had travelled with everything – the camping equipment, food and water, clothes, the lot – so we could change plans at any time and camp wherever we wanted.

But today we would travel light. We left the tent standing on the tarmac about twenty metres from the navy divers' warehouse, along with our sleeping gear and most of our supplies, taking only enough food and water for the day.

Stewart was so confident about the security at the port, which was surrounded by a high wall and guarded by US Marines, that he even left his passport and credit cards in the tent. John's suitcase stayed on the Pajero's roof-rack simply because it was heavy and easier to leave there but Stewart and I threw our bags into the tent, so the two of us had only the clothes we were wearing.

We left the port in the same small media convoy as the previous day, guided by two Australian Navy jeeps. The water pipe was supposed to be opened in a former UN compound a couple of kilometres away, near the Kuwaiti border. Typically, even this little event was delayed, leaving exasperated families queuing in the midday heat outside the compound's barbed wire fences. The delay meant we would probably just miss our next set of deadlines for Tuesday morning's papers in Australia.

Our daily scheduling decisions and even sleeping times had been shaped by the eight-hour time difference to Australia, which meant we needed to file by about 10.30 a.m. for anything other than big news to comfortably make the next day's first editions. Most of Australia had moved off daylight saving on the weekend, reducing our time 'handicap' to seven hours, and Iraq would go onto daylight saving later that night, taking it down to six hours. Gaining that extra couple of hours would make a huge difference to what we could achieve in a morning.

Waiting for the pipe ceremony we used the time, as usual, to talk to locals. Stewart, with his perfect Arabic, was a fantastic asset. It was only the journalists travelling independently who could talk candidly to Iraqis but I was still amazed by how many of the 'unilaterals' we came across had not bothered to hire translators. Apart from the obvious need to find out what people were thinking it was a lot safer when making travel decisions to be able to ask a farmer in a field 'Is that road safe?'

The Basra uprising trumpeted by the Coalition had clearly never happened, and the conversations made possible by Stewart's Arabic had shown that the Coalition was much less popular in southern Iraq than the White House and Pentagon had expected. Many Iraqis saw the invasion as an attack on their nation rather than an attack on Saddam's regime, and even those happy to see Saddam go were intimidated by the Saddam loyalists in their midst and genuinely upset at the way people were being treated by the Coalition.

Standing in front of his mud-brick home on a dusty side-street near the UN compound, a middle-aged father became the umpteenth person to complain that the Coalition had promised in radio broadcasts and propaganda leaflets to maintain services and had immediately broken those promises. As usual a huddle of about twenty people gathered to listen and offer their own complaints.

These open-air sessions were not a lot of fun, as people often ended up berating us for all the failings of the Coalition. They were especially hard work for Stewart, who had to contend with half a dozen people speaking or yelling at once, and me insisting that he ask a certain question or translate the comments of whoever I found interesting.

One forty-year-old man stood out in today's pack. Dressed unusually neatly in cardigan and trousers, he condemned the Coalition calmly and firmly rather than echoing the shrill anger of the crowd.

'We were eating, we were drinking and then they invaded. These people are behaving like invaders not liberators,' he said in Arabic. 'In Basra ordinary families are getting caught in the cross-fire, the invaders don't care and people are blaming the Americans.'

He gave his name as Ahmed To'ma and said he lived in Zubayr, south of Basra, and worked in Basra. That made him even more interesting. People fleeing Basra were giving conflicting messages about the conditions there, which was now one of the most important questions in the battle for control of the south. It would also be a valuable indicator of what lay ahead when the Coalition reached Baghdad, because if the regime could hold Basra this would lift its confidence about defending the capital.

To'ma said it was so easy to get in and out of the city safely that he had driven from there today to get water. In fact, he could take us back and guide us around Basra, he said. That would be a lot more interesting than the opening of a water pipe.

He had his own car and at 1 p.m. we followed To'ma and two friends travelling with him north out of Umm Qasr. Once out on the open road he pulled over so we could talk without the prying crowds. Both his friends wore traditional dishdasha. One was Jaffa abu Zainab, a 34-year-old Iraqi with a narrow face and wiry frame, and the other said he was one of about fifty Sudanese who were stuck in Basra trying to get home to escape the war.

To'ma revealed that he was an Iraqi policeman and a Saddam loyalist. 'Other police would arrest you if they caught you in Basra but I can get you in and out,' he said. Some foreign journalists were already staying at the Sheraton in Basra, he said, although he did not know their nationalities. This was obviously going to cost us a reasonable bribe but a guided tour would be worth it.

Following him further north through flat, sandy farming fields we discussed the risks of going into the city but we were all excited about the prospect of being shown around Basra. We had had a few of these high points in the past few days, when we marvelled at our own brilliance and the fantastic stories and photos we were about to produce.

We also found ourselves hilariously witty. John tried to mask his excitement with a casual observation about the farms flashing by the car windows. He knew that Iraq was where mankind first settled in one place and learned to plant crops.

'These people have been working those fields that way for thousands of years, just eking out a living,' he said.

'Yep,' I agreed, savouring his cliché, 'they're pretty experienced ekers.'

Stewart chipped in. 'That's all they do – eke, eke, eke, all day long.'

'There's nothing like a hard day's eking,' I rabbited on, as John swore at us from the back seat.

We were now almost out of mobile phone range. During another brief stop for To'ma to refuel we made quick calls so that if we ran into trouble people would know where we were. John rang his girlfriend Nadine but the other mobiles did not work. Stewart used my Thuraya to call a friend in Kuwait, then I called *The Australian*'s head office. The editor was not at work but the editor-in-chief, Chris Mitchell, was in so I asked to speak to him. Standing in a heavy sweat by the side of the highway I was put straight on hold because he was in a conversation and a news assistant did not want to disturb him.

John recalls me yelling obscenities into the desert. By the time I could convince somebody to put me through our new guides were starting to drive off and I only had a few seconds to tell Chris what we were planning. He just had time to tell us to be careful before I had to hang up.

To'ma pulled up on the outskirts of Zubayr, an unattractive town where the mood was particularly hostile to Westerners. British troops patrolling the town had often been shot at, and two or three young men had thrown rocks at our car when we drove past a few days earlier.

To'ma told us to wait on the highway about two kilometres away rather than risk an ugly reception inside the town while he quickly saw his family. The wait stretched into an hour or so and it was not a pleasant one. We were in full view of a British checkpoint but a dozen teenagers surrounded the car banging on the windows and aggressively demanding water, using two of their few English words – 'Mister, water!' – and becoming increasingly surly when we refused.

When I pointed to the large bottles of water that two of them were already carrying they changed tack, demanding food, cigarettes and money. The challenge was to discourage them without being rude enough to start trouble.

To'ma's travelling companion, Zainab, eventually walked back to us. To'ma had heard that the British checkpoints were blocking entry to Basra so he wanted to meet us at 10.30 a.m. the next day to try again. Zainab spelled out for the first time that they expected to be paid to lead us in and out of Basra, a deal we were happy to make.

We were already sweaty and anxious, and the excitement in the Pajero swung straight to cranky disappointment. We agreed to push on anyway to see what was happening on the edge of Basra, and drove virtually in silence for the remaining fifteen kilometres. The last British checkpoint had been moved just over the bridge on the city's edge. We drove over the bridge then I put on my flak jacket to walk the last hundred metres to talk to the British officer at the checkpoint, while John and Stewart spoke to some of the refugees trudging out of Basra and a few Western journalists hanging around the checkpoint.

Alex Cosby, a friendly young captain in the Desert Rats, told me the British had made two or three incursions from the south over the past couple of days, finding increasingly half-hearted resistance.

'We push in to see what the enemy is doing and they seem to be less enthusiastic each time about challenging us,' he said. 'It's almost as if they are being paid or forced to fire something at us and they just want to get a shot off and disappear. So they stick an RPG (rocket-propelled grenade) around a corner and fire it without really aiming, or just fire it in our general direction and run off.'

The British were still allowing people to cross the checkpoint, despite what To'ma had heard. I asked Cosby if he thought it would be safe for us to drive into the outer streets and he said it might be. While the risk would obviously be ours he was pretty confident that the mortar fire and snipers had stopped. The technical college to the left of the road had been bombed by the British overnight and there had been no more shooting at the road, he said.

I went back to the car to get John to take a photograph of Cosby but when I told him what Cosby had said about the snipers John surprised me.

'Let's just do it then – let's drive in, get what we want and get out quickly,' he said.

We had been making constant decisions on logistics, directions and stories but this was the biggest decision of the lot.

It was also the sort of decision where group dynamics and the frustrations of the past few hours could sway judgments. The high of finding a cop willing to take us into Basra for a bribe had been replaced by exasperation and John, who was usually quite cautious, had decided not to wait until the next morning. I knew by now that he tended to balance things up carefully but that once committed to action he was hard to sway.

I was happy to go, figuring that if the snipers and mortar were under control the biggest danger was being arrested by Iraqi soldiers or police, and there was no reason to believe they would harm us. Coalition troops had already shot up Terry Lloyd's ITN vehicles and would later kill several more reporters but there had not been a single report of the Iraqis doing so. I knew by now that Olga Craig had driven into Basra without being harassed and that the Italians who had ventured into the city had since surfaced in Baghdad, which was turning out to be the safest place in Iraq for foreign journalists.

That meant two of us were ready to drive on. When we reached the car and told Stewart he winced and shook his head. John had spent a good deal of time amusing all of us over the previous week by joking with Stewart and we were all getting on extremely well. He now climbed into the back seat and told Stewart to stop carping and get on with it by driving through the checkpoint.

I told John to ease up because we could not take a risk like this unless each of us was comfortable with it. To break the tension I got back out of the car and took my flak jacket off to let everyone calm down.

High in my thoughts was the experience of the three-member Channel Seven crew killed by Indonesian troops in East Timor in 1975. I had taken a close interest in their deaths because of my friendship with the family of Tony Stewart, the crew's nineteen-year-old soundman, and had researched the tragedy in the 1980s while writing a thesis on the history of Australian journalists in Indonesia.

The Seven trio were killed after entering the town of Balibo, in the path of Indonesia's invasion force, and witnessing an advance that Indonesia claimed was not happening. An East Timorese witness who had tried to talk them out of driving to Balibo told me later that reporter Greg Shackleton had been the keenest to take the risk. I had often wondered about the dynamics among the three as they made that decision. The cameraman Greg Cunningham was the only one with any war experience, having worked in Vietnam, but he was not as forceful a personality as Shackleton, and the young soundman would have gone along with anything they decided.

Twenty-seven years later, in an invasion on the other side of the world, I was determined there would be no bullying – we would only take this risk if each of us genuinely felt it was a good idea. I did not want that responsibility on my head and would soon be grateful that we took the time to make sure everybody was on side.

John told Stewart that the goal would be to talk to just enough people and take just enough photos to get some real sense of the conditions in the city, then to get out as quickly as possible.

I told him I wanted to go too but if he did not agree that was fine, we could come back tomorrow with our 'hired' Iraqi policeman. After a couple of minutes Stewart decided to give it a go.

His daily rate of US$300 a day was not to be sniffed at but Stewart had always been mainly motivated by his adventurous curiosity. A couple of weeks earlier he had been helping Canadian businessmen do business in Kuwait. Before that he had worked in a marketing and advertising agency and held a string of jobs like selling time-share units, none of which had really excited him.

Now he was showing real talent for media work and having a ball, living and dressing the part of a war correspondent in a photographer's vest and checked Arab scarf. John and I preferred plain white T-shirts, although on this day I was wearing my long-sleeved mountain-climbing shirt for the first time and John was wearing his only dry T-shirt, one he had bought at the Coalition base in Doha.

Stewart got as big a kick as John and I when we came up with good photos and stories, and I loved his enthusiasm, even if it did spill into his insistence that we take his photo in front of wrecked tanks and landmarks. Now, as he donned his helmet and flak jacket and jumped back behind the wheel, Stewart slipped into his full-enthusiasm mode.

Just after 3.30 p.m. we drove past the two British tanks protecting the checkpoint, tagging on to half a dozen private vehicles heading across the flood plains into the city – a collection of old passenger cars and small vans which looked nothing like our 4WD. I prodded Stewart to speed up so we were close to the other cars rather than presenting an isolated target.

After 700 metres we had passed the technical college on our left. There was another 500 metres of open land, or rather dried mudflats, on both sides of the road before we reached the first houses on our right. We passed two burned-out Iraqi tanks beside the road then saw that a third 'dead' tank had been positioned to block the road ahead, about 3 kilometres north of the bridge.

We took the first street to the right and slowed down, motoring at thirty kilometres an hour down a comfortable suburban street, called the Arabic equivalent of Engineer Street, which was lined with one- and two-storey houses and flooded blocks of empty land. Inside the Pajero there was no chit-chat or joking.

After what seemed a kilometre but was actually a few hundred metres we pulled up beside a group of men chatting on the footpath outside a double-storey home. They did not know how to react when we climbed out and introduced ourselves but when we ploughed straight into an interview they were quite happy to answer our questions.

This was the first proper interview conducted by the Western media in Basra during the war, and it was the oddest interview in my twenty-four years of journalism. With their city being attacked by Coalition troops the last thing these men expected was to be approached in the street by an 'enemy' news team and asked how they felt about it all.

We were trying to act relaxed but also to get through the interview and photos as quickly as possible. Sabih Abdullah, a grandfather and the owner of the house, was wearing a cardigan over a checked shirt and business trousers, and sandals over socks. He said the twelve people who lived in the house – he and his wife, their five sons, three of their wives and two grandchildren – were getting ready to leave because of the intermittent bombing in the area. They were going to stay at his brother's home on the other side of Basra.

Conscious that a group of neighbours had gathered to listen, Abdullah, who said he worked in Basra's grain silos, began spouting the party line about the city being comfortable, secure 'but most of all united behind the official party and leadership'.

'Despite the bombardment of the last fourteen days we thank Allah that everything is stable. I doubt that the Americans can do anything to hurt us because there is strong resolve and high morale [in the city]. Everybody is behind Saddam and there is a lot of unity.'

When pushed, he admitted that people were suffering from drinking brackish water from wells – 'It is disgusting to drink and bad for your health' – and that families were starting to panic because of the fighting.

'Everybody has food but the schools are closed.'

'So at least the children are happy!' I said. He and his neighbours laughed with surprise at my attempted joke.

'Some houses are getting hit and a lot of people are being injured, so there is some panic among families and children,' he said.

The eldest of his five sons, Nashwan Abdullah, said his wife had been due to have a caesarean section the day before but it had been postponed because of the siege.

John had just taken his final photograph of Sabih and two of his five sons when we were grabbed.

A thickset man in an olive-green uniform carrying an automatic weapon suddenly walked into the middle of the interview demanding in Arabic to know what was going on. A few seconds later two cars pulled up carrying four men in plain clothes.

Having a translator, unlike the *Sunday Telegraph* crew, had allowed us to stop for a real interview but that had made us a stationary target, a crucial difference. We had stayed still just long enough for word of our presence to be reported and acted on.

We headed for our car, saying we were leaving, but the character in uniform and his colleagues had other ideas. A tall, handsome man in a white dishdasha produced a handgun and pushed us towards one of their cars.

Stewart tried to argue that we would come along in our own car but the issue was not up for debate – they took our car keys and within 20 seconds the three of us were shoved into the back of their small car. As it sped off the man with the handgun twisted around in the front passenger seat to face us, then slid the top of his gun back to cock it and pointed it at our faces.

I learned later that the neighbours who saw us taken away assumed we would quickly have our throats slit, as some of the men who grabbed us, including the tall, slender man with the handgun, were members of the Fedayeen Saddam, a militia run by Saddam's son Uday, who were supposedly willing to die to protect the old regime.

We were jammed in tight, with our bullet-proof vests and John's cameras squeezing us together as Stewart translated our protests that we were just journalists. I was surprised how calm I felt but became seriously worried when the car appeared to be heading towards empty land near the river rather than into town.

'Jesus,' I thought, 'they're not delivering us to the authorities, they are taking us to the side of the river to shoot us on the spot.'

Could this really be it? What would I do if they did pull up in an open stretch of land? Run? Fight? Beg?

I had read that things seem to move in slow motion at times like this, and they did for me, perhaps because my mind was racing along in problem-solving mode, assessing several possibilities and what we should do in each case. I kept talking to the man with the gun and trying to smile and make friendly eye contact. He was clearly nervous and told us several times in Arabic to relax.

The car made a few more quick turns then to our great relief pulled up outside an official-looking building. We did not know it at the time but it was a house that had been converted into a local office of the Ba'ath Party.

John told me later that he had been reassured by how calm I seemed but his scariest moment was when he looked across at one point during that car ride and saw fear in my eyes, no doubt when I thought we were being taken to the riverside.

A dozen men in olive uniforms, several carrying AK-47s, stood outside the station glaring at us. Several had checked headscarves or kaffiyah wrapped around their heads but we did not know what branch or branches of the Iraqi security apparatus we were dealing with. As we were taken out of the small car three men pulled up behind us in our Pajero.

We were rushed into the office of the head of the operation, a man in his mid-fifties who was leaning back in his seat behind a large desk. He had a composed air and a stiff way of smoking a cigarette from between two straight fingers held horizontally to his mouth. The office was coated in fine sand-storm dust, with thin carpets and mostly bricked-in windows.

A large portrait of Saddam Hussein smiled down from behind his desk, while another grinned back at it from the other end of the room and yet another was carved in plaster on a side wall. John and I took off our flak jackets – Stewart had taken his off before the interview in the street, and it was still in the Pajero. John realised with horror that the T-shirt he had bought in Doha had a US military 'Desert Scorpion' emblem on the left breast, so he sat with his left hand rubbing his chin to obscure it. He was the only one in the room who noticed it but it made him even more nervous. The three of us sat on a couch along the only wall that did not have a Saddam portrait. The captain's desk was to our right, and the other two walls had couches. In all there were couches for nine others and they quickly filled with men in olive or light khaki uniforms – every one wearing a Saddam moustache – as we tried to explain ourselves.

Our press passes were taken from us and handed to the captain, who demanded to know what we were doing in Iraq, let alone in Basra. I did most of the talking and Stewart translated, trying to convey my air of being contrite without conceding guilt. The captain said that as far as he could see we were potentially spies accompanying the enemy and at the very least if we really were journalists we had broken the law by entering Iraq without visas. I admitted that we had entered without visas but pointed out that we were not 'accompanying' the enemy as we were travelling independently.

I stressed that British military police had been trying to expel us from Iraq because the Coalition preferred to deal with officially 'embedded' journalists. That was my main message – we were independent. A junior came bustling in to report ominously that our car was from Kuwait – Iraq's worst enemy in the region – waving the piece of black masking tape that had been covering the word 'Kuwait' on the number plates. There was also 'military equipment' in the car, another underling announced, meaning our helmets and gas masks.

The captain made several calls on an old-style black telephone, eventually putting it down and looking up pompously. 'Welcome to the harsh climate of Basra,' he declared in Arabic, 'which is going to stand up to every aggressor and enemy force.' I feigned interest in his rhetoric. I had brought in my backpack to keep my passport and cash with me, and now I pulled out my notebook as if keen to record his fascinating words.

His nine subordinates stared at us with disapproval rather than malice as I explained through Stewart that we had only entered Iraq and then Basra to try to hear the views of ordinary Iraqis. The Australian people were divided on the merits of the war so we had come to let them know the true situation in Iraq.

Without openly conceding that we were not spies the captain soon seemed to accept that we were journalists. After consulting one of the uniformed men, a lean man with combed-back greying hair and a horsy grin, he informed us that we had broken Article 24 of the Iraqi criminal code, dealing with visas, which normally carried a prison sentence of up to seven years.

John, who was nervously licking his lips to cope with a dry mouth, chipped in that he did actually have a visa for Iraq. 'But when we got to the border the Americans had already been through and there were no Iraqi border guards around to stamp my passport,' he said with a smile. Nobody laughed when Stewart translated.

The only person in a laughing mood at all was the lean guy, who described himself in Arabic as a lawyer volunteering to fight the enemy. He was the only one to speak any English and he took some delight in berating the 'invaders' to us in English, finishing most of his comments with an annoying laugh at the futility of the invasion.

'They say they are going to liberate us by bombing us. (laughter) They want to steal oil under the cover of liberating us,' he said. 'They have planes that can bomb us, they have surrounded the city but they cannot enter Basra – if they enter any city they will be killed. Wait until the April heat starts next week, the British will die in the desert heat.' (laughter).

We had been arrested at about 3.45 p.m., and at 4.25 p.m. we were given tea, the traditional Iraqi welcome for guests. Even when they have arrested you and they have limited drinking water for themselves, the Iraqis still offer you tea.

At 4.33 John asked if he could take a photo, a request which was sniffed at. We seemed to be waiting for somebody to arrive, and the tension was increasing. I tried to ease it by joking that if we were spies we were the worst ones in Iraq because our devious strategy consisted of driving straight into town and talking to people in the street. Nobody smiled but two men nodded that it was a fair point.

'Our procedures are very legal and we will follow the laws,' the captain said. It was in ancient Iraq that legal codes were first written down and we often encountered a real attachment among Iraqis to the concept of rule by law, even if that concept had been perverted by Saddam's regime.

The guy with the annoying laugh filled most silences with his own little interventions. 'You want to kill me, my mother, our children ... why? Children are playing in the street and there's bombing. (laughter) What do you people want?'

After another few minutes we were offered water. 'I suppose a beer is out of the question?' said John. Stewart hesitated, then translated the request. At this, most of the Iraqis did laugh for the only time during the encounter.

Ten minutes later a more senior official arrived. Tall and heavy, he wore a black and white kaffiyah and said his name was Mustafa. He sat down and went over much of the same territory as the captain. The captain, who was the head of the local Ba'ath militia, deferred to him, and I learned later that the new arrival was from the Mukhabarat, or secret police. He was more aggressive, demanding to know why Australians had come to Iraq to kill civilians.

'We have no fight with Australia, we wish it was not attacking us,' he stormed. 'In your countries the people do not agree with this war [while] in Iraq the people are with the Government against the war, so the real dictatorship is in your countries, not Iraq.'

The three invading countries, he said, were all controlled by Jewish interests. For half an hour he lectured us and went over our explanation of how we came to be 'behind Iraqi lines'. He got angry with me at one point when I referred to 'the Coalition'.

'Don't call them a Coalition – call them invaders. It's only three countries and they are in an invasion.'

He was right, of course. Other countries like Spain and Italy would later offer token contributions of troops but for the actual war George W. Bush really only won British and Australian support. That hardly merited the grand term '*Coalition*' but the Coalition's insistence on calling itself that had successfully rubbed off on me.

'You throw volcanic lava at women and children and say you have come to help them,' he snorted, berating us in a little performance that was obviously designed to impress his colleagues.

We would be staying at the Sheraton for the night, he announced, then travelling the next day to Baghdad, where our fate would be decided. We were going to get first-hand experience 'that there is the rule of law in Iraq and the Government is in control'.

Mustafa stood and told us to follow him out of the station, leaving us to make an awkward farewell with the captain and his men. We were genuinely relieved to have been well treated but it was not exactly a moment for big smiles and hearty goodbyes.

When John and I climbed into the Pajero with a driver and a uniformed guard carrying an AK-47, we saw straight away that our binoculars and some expensive camera equipment had disappeared but we were hardly going to complain. In fact I was surprised that our gas masks, chemical warfare suits and flak jackets had not been taken by the uniformed men, who would certainly need some protection in the days ahead.

I would learn much later that one of the men who had been sitting opposite us during our hour or so in the office was killed by a British artillery shell a few hours later, and that the handsome young man in the white dishdasha who had pointed the gun at us was the son of a tribal leader from a village to the west. He was killed three days later in a clash with a tank when the British began seizing large parts of the city.

Stewart was made to travel in another car with Mustafa and another armed guard. We were eventually driven along a boulevard on the western bank of the Shatt al-Arab waterway, into which flow both the Tigris and the Euphrates rivers. Once one of the most prosperous cities in the region and known as the Gulf's 'Venice', Basra had taken on a shabby feel after a decade of war with nearby Iran, then another decade of UN trade sanctions.

The boulevard was lined on the left by once-grand two-storey villas and on the river side by palm trees and another reminder of the past hardship, the larger-than-life statues of 150 'martyrs' from the war with Iran, each pointing an accusing finger south-east across the river towards Iran.

Large fishing boats were tied up in front of the Sheraton, a hulking five-storey building on the left of the boulevard. The hotel's driveway had been scarred by an explosion from some sort of missile and the whole place had a deserted feel, with overgrown gardens and algae in the driveway fountain.

Our escorts took the Kuwaiti plates off our car and made us hand over our mobile phones and work equipment. Stewart realised that his pocket knife and mobile phone had also gone missing from the Pajero.

We were allowed to take a box of food and some clothes into the hotel but a search by Mustafa found that John had left a small camera among his clothes. It had genuinely been an accident but Mustafa was furious. Glaring, he told Stewart to translate a simple message: 'Don't make too many more mistakes.'

In the lobby we were marched to a corner and told to sit on large leather couches for more questioning by Mustafa.

'How many British tanks did you see? Have any British ships arrived at Umm Qasr? Do the British troops have water? Are they well supplied? What is their strategy?'

We were happy to answer most of those questions because all that information had been reported on the BBC. Our biggest concern was that he would not let us telephone home to tell our families we were OK. With our empty tent sitting back on the dock in Umm Qasr we knew we would soon be reported missing, and the anxiety this would cause our families and partners began to eat at us.

Mustafa stopped his questioning mid-sentence and pointed accusingly at John's breast, demanding to know what the scorpion emblem meant. I was as taken aback as the Iraqi but John waved it off as a souvenir. Thankfully, Mustafa had accepted by now that we were journalists.

Next to the lobby was an enormous enclosed courtyard, with an open space reaching five storeys high to the roof of the building. On each level the courtyard was ringed by an open corridor lined with long pots of plants and the doors to about 20 rooms. A large piano sat in one corner of the cavernous courtyard.

The hotel had 198 rooms but only one other group of guests – a four-member crew from Al-Jazeera, the Arabic news network on which I had written a news feature two weeks earlier in Qatar.

As we were being hectored in the lobby by Mustafa one of the Al-Jazeera crew stepped out of the lift and came over with a surprised smile to find out who we were. Mustafa angrily sent him away. As he retreated into the lift I ignored Mustafa's glare and blurted out 'We're Australian journalists who have been arrested. Can you please let somebody know we are here?'

Nobody has ever reported getting any such message from Al-Jazeera.

I was led to the reception desk, where clocks giving the time in New York, London, Tokyo and Baghdad seemed just a touch pretentious under the circumstances. The manager said I had to pay US$107 cash for a room for the night! He seemed embarrassed that we were prisoners rather than guests but he was not going to miss the opportunity to get his hands on some hard cash.

He then led the three of us and Mustafa, plus one of the drivers and a young uniformed soldier named Ali to a top-storey suite. Spacious but dirty and run-down, it had a big lounge–dining area, a small kitchen, a bathroom and a bedroom with two single beds. Sliding glass doors and large windows looked out from the living room onto a wide balcony, where four concrete arches framed a broad view of the river.

Mustafa explained that our driver and Ali, who still carried his AK-47, would spend the night with us, and we were not to leave the room. As he left he stopped at the door and turned with a flourish. For the first time he looked at us without menace.

'I will soon be leaving for the frontline and I feel a bond with you because you have also been brave enough to be on the frontline,' he said, pausing for Stewart to translate. 'I want to call on that bond now by asking a very important question which could save my life.'

We agreed to answer, wary of some final trick question. His query was a surprise.

'Will I face chemical weapons and other weapons of mass destruction from the Coalition?'

Relieved, we assured him that the Coalition would not use chemical weapons. He was even more relieved than we were. 'Salaam [Peace],' he said with a happy nod of the head before leaving.

Whenever Coalition troops had found gas masks in Iraqi trenches or bunkers in the previous two weeks the Coalition's spokesmen, and much of the Western media, had reported grimly that this was further evidence that the Iraqis were preparing to use chemical weapons. It had not occurred to me that the Iraqi troops were worried that such weapons would actually be used by the Coalition and that the only reason more gas masks had not been found was that the Iraqis did not have enough to go around.

For the rest of the night we were locked in with the driver Mohammed, a beefy thirty-four year old in a sports shirt and slacks, and Ali, who said he was eighteen. We were worried about the next day's journey because we knew major tank battles were underway between Basra and Baghdad, and we had heard news reports that the road to Baghdad had been cut. Mohammed said it was still open but was regularly bombed by the invaders.

With Stewart interpreting, Mohammed gave us yet another lecture about the evils of the war, which showed a pretty keen knowledge of the internal politics of the Coalition members, including the Australian public's opposition to John Howard over the war.

'Tony Blair will get a shock in Britain's [1 May] municipal elections, and US public opinion will also turn as dead Americans are brought home from Iraq. The Iraqis will defend our cities and a ceasefire will have to be declared,' Mohammed said confidently.

Bush, he noted, had not even won his own election in 2000, so he would have no chance next time around.

'To get what he wants Bush will have to wipe out the whole population of Iraq and the world won't tolerate that. And even if we lose today our children will come back and liberate Iraq.'

I wandered out into the dark of the balcony to escape the lecture. Palm trees and open land could be seen on the far river bank through the evening haze. Lights reflected on the water but the sky was too hazy to see the stars, even though there was little ground light. There were a few lights of moving cars and every now and then the whole grid of street lights across the river blacked out. A pontoon bridge to our left carried the occasional vehicle across the river. Artillery rumbled in the distance and on this side of the river the lights of the hotel and surrounding streets went out occasionally.

In other circumstances the palm trees and river would have made an exotic sight. Further upstream to our left was Sinbad Island, where the legendary sailor supposedly began his journeys. But I was preoccupied – we might not get through the next day's drive in one piece, and there was no way of knowing what awaited us if we did reach Baghdad.

I was dwelling on what Pilita and my family would be going through when the young soldier Ali appeared beside me. He spoke almost no English but I realised that he wasn't checking up on me – there was no escape from the balcony. As I looked up at the moon he put a comforting hand on my shoulder, an unexpected show of sympathy which was all it took to bring tears to my eyes.

We walked back inside, where Mohammed was still spouting his opinions on the war, despite the fact that Stewart was obviously exhausted by the stress of the day. Australia's former UN weapons inspector Richard Butler had become 'a mouthpiece for the Americans', Mohammed said, but his successor Hans Blix was greatly admired by the Iraqis for the fair way he went about his work.

I had been encouraging Stewart to ask personal details about the people we interviewed – hobbies, families, anything that might show them as real people – and we had time now to get anything we wanted about Mohammed.

He was a Sunni Muslim from Baghdad and had two children, Abdullah, six, and Aya, three. He would be driving us to Baghdad, he said, and would take us to meet his wife. He normally worked in the Ministry of Health but had been working with the Fedayeen for the past two months.

Alcohol is legal in Iraq but none was served in the Sheraton. Instead the hotel manager brought tea and cola for us all, which cost me another US$12. I was being forced to buy drinks for our own guards but out of habit I added a US$1 tip anyway. Apologising that we were his involuntary guests, the manager said he had no chef but would cook our dinner himself.

He returned with minced beef omelettes with chips, salad and pita bread, which were eaten with no cutlery and little appetite. He delivered the food with his deputy manager, and they were joshing each other in an attempt to lighten our mood. The deputy referred to his boss as 'the galley hand' for having cooked dinner, and the manager theatrically aimed a kick at his assistant's backside.

Eating with his hands, Mohammed was enjoying the sound of his own voice and bragged about his role in putting down the anti-Saddam uprisings which followed the first Gulf War, uprisings which the regime blamed on Iranian infiltrators.

'I was part of a cleansing mission to Nasariyah and got a medal for being shot in the arm by one of those infiltrators,' he said between mouthfuls. This friendly and garrulous man we were eating with was proudly telling us that he had taken part in the massacres that wiped out tens of thousands of Shi'ite Iraqis.

At 9.10 p.m. we all jumped at an explosion which sounded as if it was barely a hundred metres from the hotel. I guessed, quite correctly, that Coalition missiles would soon hit the hotel. The question was whether it would be tonight, while we were still there. Ten minutes later we were joined by another guard carrying an AK-47, who wore the robes and headscarf of the Fedayeen. John convinced himself that if this new arrival wrapped the headscarf around his face like a mask we were in big trouble. He did, and John quietly excused himself and went to bed.

The bedroom was dusty and shabby, and there was no water in the shower or toilets. But they were the first beds we had seen for days. A spare mattress was brought in and placed on the floor so the three of us could sleep in the one room, and our guards insisted that the door be left open. Stewart volunteered for the mattress. Lying in the dark we discussed the fact that he did not have his passport, and wondered whether that was a good thing or not. Its absence might raise dangerous suspicions in Baghdad but it might have been even worse to have a passport with visas showing that he worked for a Western embassy in Kuwait.

Stewart joked that he was surely entitled to a bonus for the new stress involved in this job and I replied that average wages in Baghdad were apparently quite low. John was in no mood for joking – he was particularly worried about the next day's drive. At least, we agreed, we would be able to personally deliver some cash to Ian McPhedran, who we knew was running low on US dollars. We all smiled at what Ian's face would be like when we knocked on his door to announce 'Cash delivery for Mr McPhedran'.

At 5.45 a.m. we were woken by heavy machine-gun fire close to the hotel as British troops fought their way into the city from the west. I was the last to wake. We had been told to be ready at 8.30 a.m. and I had become so used to war sounds and explosions that when I got my bearings and realised it was 'only' machine gun fire and a ground incursion I dozed off for another two and a half hours.

When I was fully awake I realised that John and Stewart were both anxious now, and with good reason. We knew that a major tank battle was underway north of Basra, and we were about to drive straight into it. I pointed out that it was April Fool's Day but they were not up for black humour. We barely picked at a breakfast of bread, fig jam and tea (US$10). Trying not to dwell on the trip ahead, Stewart and I discussed our strategy for when we reached Baghdad – should we ask the Iraqis for permission to stay there, to come back and report in Basra, or to leave the country so we could re-enter through Kuwait?

In any case it was a good thing that we did not spend the rest of the day at the Basra Sheraton. That night it was hit by four direct hits from Coalition missiles. Al-Jazeera was convinced its journalists had been deliberately targeted, as US warplanes had also bombed the network's bureau in Kabul during the conflict in Afghanistan. The Pentagon offered the implausible claim that it did not realise that Al-Jazeera, the only network broadcasting from Kabul, was in the city. Others saw it as a deliberate attack by the Bush administration, which had long accused Al-Jazeera of being 'Osama bin

Laden's network' for having broadcast the Al-Qaeda leader's taped messages.

Al-Jazeera had actually shown an unprecedented degree of independence since being launched by the Emir of Qatar in 1996, its refusal to toe government lines upsetting virtually every regime in a region where broadcasters had always been closely controlled by unelected governments. Its large audience in the Arab world meant it was always going to be an important player in the reporting of the Iraq war, and I had interviewed one of its executives, Jihad Ballout, during our time in Qatar. Ballout told me that after the Kabul experience the network was making special efforts to avoid a repeat attack by the Coalition.

'We have given them our addresses in Baghdad and Basra, even our map coordinates so they will not do it again,' he said. 'Or if they do, it won't be an accident.'

The Arab network protested furiously after the Basra attack but did not know that it would soon suffer a much harder blow from the Americans.

We were on the road at 8.50 a.m. Stewart was ordered into a late-model taxi with two minders while John and I were put into our 4WD with a new driver and two new guards, one of whom was armed and in uniform. Stewart was nervous at being separated like this as he feared that, in his words, 'They probably figure they can do what they want to some Arabic translator and nobody will care'.

Despite Mohammed's long-winded promises the previous night to take us to his home in Baghdad and introduce us to all his powerful friends in Saddam's Government, we never saw him again. I was told later, by one of the Ba'ath Party members who had been present when we were first taken to the party office in Basra, that the young soldier Ali survived the war.

I sat in the front seat and the guards did not object when I put my notebook on my knees so I could take notes during this next leg of our Iraqi road trip. Driving through Basra we saw plenty of men carrying guns but not a single uniform. Deserters had already told us a few days earlier that soldiers in the city had been ordered to shed their uniforms and melt into the population. Quite a few buildings were bombed out, and we could see people pumping drinking water out of filthy canals and filling sandbags for defensive positions at major intersections.

The driver, a middle-aged man who was also named Ali, spoke some English and opened a brief conversation by saying he was pleased by what he called 'the huge demonstrations' in Australia against the war. Almost every Iraqi official we came across drew a similar distinction between the attitudes of Australia's government and its public.

The traffic was surprisingly heavy and we queued for some time at a petrol station. The going rate was about one US cent a litre. It was mid-morning when we passed the city's final Saddam statue and headed out past Basra University on the double-lane highway to the north.

The first military uniform we saw was five minutes out of the city, at a sandbagged checkpoint. There was a reasonable amount of civilian traffic on the highway, ranging from commercial trucks to families on donkey-drawn carts. We passed one burned Iraqi tank being carried on the back of a truck towards Basra, then three other tanks heading into the city under their own steam.

Power pylons in the open fields a few hundred metres west of our two-lane highway were doubled over after US attacks. Two-storey mud-brick homes soon gave way to mud houses of the simple, boxy style that had been built here, amid the first-ever cultivated flood plains and fields between the Tigris and Euphrates rivers, for thousands of years. Young men walked with guns, and military vehicles appeared regularly but there were also knots of children playing soccer and other games by the road. Here we saw the first of the very few Republican Guard soldiers we would see in the whole trip. Most of the elite guards, in their distinctive red berets, were apparently being mustered in Baghdad to defend the capital. Three minutes later we were in the middle of the battle that we had feared we would run into.

We had just passed through the town of Qurna, where the Tigris and Euphrates meet, and traditionally reputed to be the site of the Garden of Eden, when the highway gently curved to pass through an open stretch of flood plains, into which large holes and earth fortifications had been carved to protect tanks. Four or five Iraqi tanks were spread around the field to the left of us and another couple could be seen to the right, the closest perhaps fifty metres from the road. There was little other traffic on this stretch of road but our driver, Ali, was not particularly worried – we had already passed half a dozen tanks since leaving Basra.

After a few seconds, though, we realised that these tanks were actually firing and being fired on by missiles or unseen warplanes. Explosions were going off around them, sending up fountains of dirt and smoke. They were heavily armoured but we suddenly felt as vulnerable as if the Pajero was made of cardboard.

As we accelerated, I asked the driver if they were Iraqi tanks and he nodded tensely. A shell or missile then hit a tank about two hundred metres from us, slightly in front and to our left. Ali put his foot to the floor. By the time a ball of flame had rolled up from the tank, reaching twenty metres into the air, we were past it, so the force of the blast thumped into the left of the car from behind. John, sitting in the back left seat behind the driver, felt it hit the door like a solid impact. In the front passenger seat my left eardrum 'popped' with the pressure.

Ali was now hunched over the wheel pushing the Pajero to its limits and the two Iraqi guards in the back urged him on in Arabic once or twice. Nobody else spoke and the car filled with the built-in chime letting the driver know he was exceeding the speed limit of 120 kilometres per hour.

Further up the road several burned-out civilian trucks made it clear that the highway itself was a Coalition target. The large steel power pylons running alongside the road were obviously another target. In one stretch six out of seven had been twisted and bent in half, dragged down by a direct hit on one pylon.

The cigarette smoking in the back seat was now furious. John had given up before coming to Iraq but today he was almost chain-smoking, and the guards sitting next to him were quickly sucking on their own smokes. The traffic around us was also showing signs of stress. A bus sped along with the door of its luggage compartment flapping open, while a semi-trailer rigged up for carrying cars raced on with its loading ramps bouncing behind on the road in a shower of sparks.

We were passing through the marshlands, home of the Marsh Arabs who had been heavily oppressed by Saddam in retaliation for rising against him in 1991. More and more of the homes by the road were flying black flags to mark a festival of the Shi'ite Muslims, another group to suffer heavily under Saddam, a member of the Sunni minority. The Shia made up sixty per cent of Iraq's population but a much heavier proportion in southern Iraq.

Three young soldiers overtook us on motorbikes with automatic rifles strapped across their backs. They seemed remarkably exposed and vulnerable as they leaned forward into the wind just a metre outside my window and it occurred to me that at least one of them would probably be dead by the end of the month.

At 11.01 a.m. – I had time and plenty of nervous energy on my hands so I was taking meticulous notes – we passed four Iraqi tanks in another battlefield setting on the right of the road. Beyond them I could see explosions throwing up plumes of dirt and smoke which looked like distant trees. These and other military vehicles we saw were usually surrounded by high piles of dirt to protect them from anything but a direct hit.

The sandy soil slowly took on richer hues. More children played soccer by the road and markets were open in small towns. After long years of war with Iran and then Kuwait, and another decade of US and British warplanes flying overhead to impose no-fly zones, Iraqis were responding more calmly than would most nations to the idea of foreign armies being on their territory.

Just before noon we stopped at a roadside café for a ten-minute toilet break and to wash the sand off our faces, then we took on petrol. Half an hour later we came upon a traffic pile-up at a bridge that had been all but destroyed. A direct hit had completely buckled one lane, and the other was tilting at a dangerous angle. Our guards jumped the queue by explaining their human cargo to the soldiers managing the bridge and our cars crawled across ahead of the waiting buses, beaten-up passenger cars and two trucks laden with tomatoes.

At the edges of several towns we were stopped by checkpoints which Saddam's regime had long used to monitor civilian travel. The rationale was to stop criminals and detect foreigners moving illicitly around the country but the system also strengthened the government's grip on the ordinary population. Four hours into the journey we found ourselves overtaking more and more army trucks, a nervous venture as they were obviously Coalition targets.

By two in the afternoon the soil around us had changed from the yellow–orange of the south to a rich brown. The light traffic also took on a different hue because there were more city taxis – small white sedans with their corner panels painted orange. Then the sky ahead of us quickly darkened with smoke from oil-filled trenches. This was Baghdad. A heavy dark cloud grew across most of the horizon ahead and the air in our car soon reeked of oil. We passed close to one of the trenches. It was about fifty metres long, with flames leaping two metres to mingle with the charcoal-grey smoke meant to block the Coalition's laser-guided missiles.

The truth was that the Coalition's technology had largely moved on to satellite-guided weaponry; the most the smoke clouds could do was to reassure the capital's population that at least some effort was being made to defend their city.

Five hours after leaving Basra we were in the southern suburbs of Baghdad and fifteen minutes later we were in the centre of the city, near the Al-Rashid Hotel which had been the long-time home of foreign journalists, businessmen and diplomats. But for the next three hours we were driven around the city's streets while our guards waited to be told where to take us. There was no mobile phone network in Baghdad so we were constantly stopping to use land lines.

Baghdad sits on a flat plain and is a low-rise city, so even an elevated motorway offers a long view over a sprawling, dusty metropolis of more than five million. The whole urban vista, even its palm trees, seemed painted in a monochrome of orange–brown sand, crying out for a good cleansing rain. Minarets, mosques and monuments pointed to a sky busy with a dozen huge plumes of black smoke and occasional bursts of anti-aircraft fire.

Most shops were closed, some even barricaded, and the traffic lights were not working, leaving intersections in the hands of a 'Dad's Army' of retirees directing traffic in business suits topped with green battle helmets. At one point we spent about half an hour idling on a street corner, within sight of the 'Mother of All Battles' mosque, a Saddam extravagance which has minarets in the shape of Scud missiles and gun barrels. Inside, Saddam had had Koran verses written on the walls in an ink mixed with his own blood.

While our escorts waited for orders on what to do with us we watched a US jet leave a vapour trail high in a pale-blue sky, anti-aircraft cannons firing off token resistance. At 5.12 p.m., eight hours after we had left Basra, we arrived at the Palestine Meridien Hotel on the banks of the Tigris. It was right next to the Baghdad Sheraton, the only other hotel where journalists were now allowed to stay, and both were directly across the river from the presidential compound that we and the rest of the world had seen on television as the 'ground zero' of Coalition bombing. The Al-Rashid, which we could see further beyond the presidential compound, and these two hotels were the highest and most prominent buildings on Baghdad's skyline.

A couple of minders came out of the hotel to accept responsibility for us, and our escorts from Basra wasted no time heading off. I apologised to the driver, Ali, saying I was sorry they had been forced to make such a risky drive and wishing him a safe return south. We were told to bring along clothes and other basics from the car, as we were now under house arrest in the Palestine Hotel.

5

INSIDE THE PALESTINE HOTEL

The lobby of the Palestine Hotel was dimly lit – the power supply was almost exhausted – and thick with preoccupied people. About thirty foreign reporters walked about as if they were looking for somebody in the crowd, while middle-aged Iraqi men in business shirts or jackets stood alone or in small knots with worried looks on their faces.

Two days earlier the bombing of the Information Ministry had led the Iraqi bureaucrats responsible for 'minding' the foreign press to move into the Palestine alongside their charges. Apart from anything else they thought they were less likely to be bombed again if they were under the same roof as the foreign press.

At the far end of the lobby were a bank of elevators and the entrance to the hotel dining room, the Orient Express restaurant. The reception desk was along the right wall, and a row of shopfronts along the left. The first space was a closed Internet café, then came a shop selling Iraqi art and craft, an Iraqi Airways office, a store selling clothes and watches and a tiny office of the state-owned Rafidain Bank. In the middle of those stores two flights of granite steps led up to a café under a sign 'Aladin Rest'. We were directed up to the café and pointed to seats at the far end, away from other journalists who were breaking off conversations to watch us curiously. The café ceiling was curved to give the impression of an oriental palace but the furnishings were more 1960s, with low-set brown leather couches and chairs grouped around knee-high coffee tables. The floor was tiled in blue and the walls bore twenty-year-old drawings of old Baghdad street scenes.

The effect was a mixture of movie sets – a hint of Rick's Café from Casablanca with ominous minders lurking among correspondents, combined with a Colditz film in which prisoners surreptitiously swapped notes and whispered in half a dozen languages. Occasionally a 'human shield', or foreign peace activist, would pass through, bringing a straggly, often eccentric touch. Some were dressed as 'ferals', with loose T-shirts and wild hair styles, while others wore old-fashioned shirts or floral skirts straight from a 1960s hippy movie. As we headed to our seats one reporter, a Somali-born Briton, walked over cautiously.

'Are you guys OK?'

'We don't know. We're supposedly under arrest,' I said. 'We really need to call home but they've taken our phones.'

'Don't worry, we'll let you use a phone,' he said before getting details of who we were and where we had been arrested.

He was Rageh Omaar, the BBC's 36-year-old former South Africa correspondent who was already becoming the most famous reporter in Baghdad. His good looks and calm manner had made him a cult figure in Britain, where people had for weeks been wearing T-shirts bearing his face and his new nickname – 'Scud Stud'.

As we waited nervously in our corner a French television journalist sidled over furtively. He was wearing a khaki photographer's jacket with a black and white kaffiyah around his neck, the standard uniform for anyone trying to look like a correspondent in an exotic Arabic setting. He gave a conspiratorial whisper out of the side of his mouth.

'Write down a number and I'll make a call for you.'

I scribbled down our names and the number of The Australian's news desk in Sydney and slipped it to him.

Fifteen minutes later, as we were being lectured and questioned by three 'minders', he strolled past and gave a thumbs-up. I realised now that it was the middle of the night in Sydney and I should have given him somebody's home number but he had at least been able to leave a recorded message saying that we had turned up in Baghdad.

John showed one of the minders a photo of Ian McPhedran that he happened to be carrying in his money belt, and the man nodded that Ian was staying in this hotel. Ian would be more than just a friendly face for us – he would be our direct link to home and work, with his own phone and computer. Losing patience with yet another round of the same questions and warnings, John stomped over to the front desk and asked for Ian's room number. The receptionist gave him the number but then called him back with a bizarre update – Mr McPhedran had just checked out.

Ian had been expelled from Baghdad earlier that day – while we were being driven here he was on the road to Jordan. The previous day he and a reporter from the *Sunday Times* in South Africa had left the Palestine Hotel without their official minders to inspect bomb damage to the Information Ministry's old offices and to pick up some equipment they had left there. They were unlucky enough to run into the bully who ran the minders, Uday al-Tai, the director-general of the Information Ministry, who was furious that they had broken the rules by leaving the hotel without a minder. He snatched their passes and ordered his minions to expel them immediately.

For another hour we were questioned by several minders who refused to let us use a phone and seemed unclear about which of them was to be responsible for us. Before long we realised that even among the minders there was distrust and power games, with the Information Ministry employees not even sure which part of the security apparatus employed some of their colleagues. They were a mixed bunch. Ali, a tall man with a gentle manner and reassuring air, was the most sympathetic, while some of his colleagues were openly aggressive. They calmly informed us that we would be permanently losing the Pajero and the Thuraya satellite phone. I was unhappy, as I had just bought the phone in London for £750 but John went pale at the thought of the $30,000 imprint on his card.

We told them this amounted to theft, which brought an angry response – we were lucky not to be getting a seven-year jail sentence for entering Iraq without visas, one minder said. Our other phones, cameras and computers would all be locked away and returned to us when we were eventually allowed to leave the hotel. We were to stay inside the hotel until a decision was made on whether to expel us or give us press visas. In the meantime any journalism was out of the question and would be harshly punished.

'You are in a very serious situation. Leaving the hotel is forbidden and if you work without a visa you will be put in prison,' said the surliest of them, a slightly built younger man with a moustache and permanent scowl.

A three-man French television crew arrested south of Basra had already been waiting more than a week for such a decision, the minders said, and seven Italian reporters seized in Basra were also in limbo. The Italians worked for seven different newspapers but had entered Basra in a single convoy the day before Olga Craig – three days before us – and been held at a road block.

The French and most of the Italians had told the minders they wanted to go home, and they had the French Government and the Vatican – which had kept its Baghdad embassy open – lobbying for their release. We said we wanted to stay and do our work rather than be deported. When they finally let us talk to other reporters in the café for a few minutes we discovered that the Frenchman who had made the call for us was one of the arrested French television crew.

We were taken to the eleventh floor of the hotel. Each of the seventeen floors had a similar layout, with one long corridor down the centre. There were twenty-nine rooms on each floor, including a suite at either end which connected rooms in each corner to provide the expanded suite with two balconies and sweeping views of the city. The four passenger lifts were in the core of the hotel, stairwells were tucked away towards each end and there was one service lift, which I often used because of overcrowding in the main lifts. The hotel was twenty years old and the carpet, blue with black stripes, had obviously never been replaced.

Our room, 1104, had dirty walls, worn-through carpet and two tired single beds. Once again an extra mattress was to be put on the floor because no other rooms were available. With staff from the Information Ministry shifting into the hotel it would be a struggle to find a second room, let alone the two more rooms we wanted. The situation was not helped by the fact that some journalists in the Sheraton were maintaining empty 'backup' rooms in the Palestine, but the minders said that if any of those reporters would help us out we could apply for permission to sleep in such a room.

We were told that more senior officials would soon be coming to search our gear and in the meantime Abu Tayef, who had a slow smile and shifty, hooded eyes, stayed to watch us. 'Abu' means 'father of' and is often used with the name of a man's eldest son, so that Abu Tayef was the father of Tayef. While we waited for our visitors I remembered that tucked away in my bag was the young woman's Ba'ath Party membership file I had taken from the party office in Umm Qasr. That might not go down too well when it turned up in the search, I realised. I asked Stewart and John to keep Abu Tayef talking, then I took the file out to the balcony and threw it into the night. It blew straight back towards me and drifted onto the balcony of the room below.

Two other minders finally arrived, including the director- general al-Tai and a snarling thick-set character in a cheap black jacket and black shirt. Al-Tai went through our bags, confiscating virtually all of our equipment. My shortwave radio was the only thing he left beyond our clothes, some toiletries and a cardboard box of food from the Pajero. John still had his full suitcase but Stewart and I had little more than what we were wearing, in my case my light green mountain-climbing shirt and tan jeans.

When John protested about his cameras being taken al-Tai flashed a quiet anger – we were lucky we were not in jail so we shouldn't push our luck, he fumed. As they went out the door with our most precious equipment crammed into a cardboard box I realised they had also taken my notebook. I ran out into the corridor and snatched it back from the top of the box. The man in black, who had been carrying the box, started to yell but I clutched it to my chest and protested that I wanted to read it, not to write in it or use it to do any reporting. Abu Tayef stepped between us, shrugged and said something on my behalf in Arabic, then al-Tai let me keep it, to my enormous relief.

Al-Tai said that a guard would eventually be posted outside our door but in the meantime we could go down to the restaurant and try to find some food. Guarding our door seemed pointless if we were allowed to move around the hotel but we could hardly argue. Our real priority was to get on a phone. We went to the restaurant, where we paid for a hot buffet of grilled chicken, rice and chops, followed by an orange for dessert, and ate quickly. I went back for thirds. It was not great cuisine but I have always believed in the concept of 'comfort food'.

We knew that Ian had been working closely with some British journalists, and when he heard English accents from two men sitting near us John began eavesdropping. He walked over and introduced himself to photographer Stuart Clarke, who was eating with the

Sunday Times's Jon Swain, a correspondent since the Vietnam War. When John explained our situation Stuart, who was a friend of Ian's, showed immediate generosity. He proposed that John should accompany him straight upstairs to use his mobile phone and that Jon would let me use his. I had met Swain once before at a dinner with mutual friends in London, and we chatted while he finished his meal before going up to his room.

I called Pilita, who was finishing a late day in her office at the *Financial Times*.

'God, where are you?' was her frantic response when she heard my voice. News Ltd had done a poor job of alerting our relatives to our situation. In fact the first she had heard was when a friend in *The Australian*'s Canberra bureau sent her an e-mail asking whether she had heard from me. Word had got around the paper that I had not called in for thirty-six hours and that we were overdue. Pilita e-mailed back to her friend: 'What do you mean, overdue?'

The news that we were missing had started to feature on Australian radio reports and television news bulletins, which was how most of our friends and family heard. Nobody had contacted John's mother to tell her we were missing. The first she knew of any trouble was when John rang her. John's girlfriend Nadine's grandmother became physically ill at her bowls club when she heard a radio report that he was missing.

I gave Pilita a quick summary of what had happened and asked her to call my parents and try to get somebody at Channel Seven or in the army to get Stewart's passport from the dock in Umm Qasr.

John and I met back in the hotel room before returning to the café to begin the uncomfortable exercise of imposing on fellow journalists to use their phones.

The first reporter I approached had his own troubles. A Lithuanian radio journalist, he was almost in tears because the Iraqis had just told him to leave Baghdad. He had not been attending their daily press conferences so they wanted him out. His satellite phone was flat, he said, but the place to go for help was the Reuters room on the fifteenth floor.

'Ask for two boys named Goran and Taras – they are great guys and will help you out.'

The Reuters suite was busy, with several people filing stories and news footage but they were indeed welcoming when we walked in and began explaining ourselves. Taras Protsyuk, a cameraman with clean, handsome features and a ready smile, was Ukrainian-born but lived in Poland, and was going through the process of becoming a Polish citizen. Goran Tomasevic was a Croatian photographer, tired and unshaven with a world-weary manner.

Taras Protsyuk, the Reuters TV cameraman in an undated file photo.

Taras had been hunched over some editing equipment when we arrived but he listened to our pleas for a few seconds then said 'Of course – use the phone'. Goran turned and walked away, but only to pick something up. When he returned he had the biggest bottle of Grants whisky I had ever seen – about eighty centimetres high. 'You need to *drink*!' he said, issuing a firm diagnosis and prescription rather than a suggestion.

While I was following Goran's orders, John called the News Ltd switchboard and was put through to Michael Stutchbury at home. It was barely dawn in Sydney but he was already being pressured at home by radio stations seeking interviews about his missing news team. Few people realise the stress on editors who send reporters to dangerous places. Michael literally laughed with relief to hear from us.

We made a few more calls, then settled in to talk to Goran and Taras over whisky and Turkish Efes beer.

The Reuters crew were in a great position in more ways than one. Their suite at the end of the building allowed their cameras to scan Baghdad's skyline. Iraqi officials insisted it was against the rules to film from the balconies but Reuters had tripod-mounted cameras rolling 24 hours a day to capture explosions or any other action on the skyline. Television stations around the world were subscribing to the live Baghdad backdrop for their own reports.

Reuters was also in a great position competitively. CNN and

Fox had been kicked out of Baghdad for allegedly being too pro-American, and the other US networks and Associated Press's television operation had all closed their bureaux or withdrawn their foreign staff. Reuters had eighteen people here and was the only news agency offering a full television service out of Baghdad.

Taras and Goran were the perfect people for us to talk to – they had been through plenty of tight moments as war cameramen and they were happy to listen, drink and talk. Taras, who was wearing a baseball cap and a constant smile, read our thoughts by saying the worst part was being worried about what your loved ones were hearing. He recalled that while working in Chechnya he had once been knocked unconscious by a Russian bomb. His leg was broken and he had to be stretchered out but the worst thing, he said, was that a radio station in Poland reported that he was dead. His wife Lidia, who had just had their first son, Denis, (now eight) heard that report.

Taras did not play up his war stories from conflicts like Bosnia, Kosovo, Pakistan and Afghanistan. It was only later that I learned he had been arrested for three days for entering Serbia without a visa during the Kosovo War, and beaten by plainclothes policemen while filming demonstrations in Pristina in 1998.

After high school he had studied aeronautical engineering at the Leningrad Military Academy in the hope of becoming a cosmonaut but was asked to leave after joining a hunger strike in support of Ukrainian independence. The collapse of the Soviet Union killed off any last chance of a space career, so he began working as a media translator with his six languages, which included Arabic. He then taught himself camera work, editing and reporting before joining Reuters in 1993 and moved from Kiev to Reuters' Warsaw bureau six years later. Now thirty-five, he was considered brave but not reckless and was popular among his colleagues because of the self-effacing charm we were now enjoying.

Our Reuters friends were surprised to hear that the highway we came up was still open, and told us that a 4WD carrying *The Times* of London's reporter Daniel McGrory had just been shot up in an ambush after entering Iraq. McGrory had agreed before the war that I could travel with him, plans I had dropped when I learned that John was coming with me. McGrory was not injured in the ambush.

Taras and Goran filled us in about the war. Only 5000

Republican Guard soldiers had been in action so far, so they were presumably being saved to defend Baghdad. The question was whether the conquering of Baghdad was going to be a painless drive into the city like the fall of Paris in 1944, or something like the siege of Stalingrad, or perhaps even the anarchy of Mogadishu. Taras remarked that the war had not turned out as expected. Everybody had thought the journalists in Baghdad might be bombed by the Americans or killed by the Iraqis but the capital had turned out to be the safest place in the country for foreign reporters.

'It is guys like you who went out [in the field] who have been getting killed. Look at us – we have water, food, even beer,' he said as he raised his glass. 'And no one is going to shoot at this hotel.'

We all laughed and kept drinking and swapping rumours and tips. I would remember that exchange only when John reminded me of it, some time after Taras had been proved terribly wrong.

I went down and got Stewart so he could come up and use a Reuters phone, while I took a turn waiting in the room to mind our remaining gear and in case our minders came back with more instructions. This was the start of a tedious process of having to share the one room key between us, which meant we had to keep track of each other's movements or risk being locked out.

Stewart said that while I had been out Paul McGeough had visited from the adjoining Sheraton. He had left a business card and when I called him well after midnight I declared that no visitors would be accepted unless they arrived bearing alcohol. He said he could not come over tonight because he had to finish a story for a deadline but he would visit the next morning. We had become a bit of a news item in Australia – he had already been asked about us by a radio station – and he asked what had happened to us.

After I had hung up I realised it was only morning in Australia and couldn't figure out why he had to file at this hour. In fact he had become a one-man multimedia industry, with almost every radio and television station in Australia relying on him for news from Baghdad. When Stewart and John came down from the Reuters suite Stewart was edgy and unhappy about how we were handling our predicament. For the previous two days he had been remarkably calm but now that John and I were relaxing he was testy and worried, and thought it was dangerous for us to drink. He felt we were still 'on a knife edge' and could even be killed by the Iraqis. He had heard our Iraqi drivers speaking threateningly about us in Arabic, he said, and it had rattled him. We argued about how cautious we should be, while Stewart paced around the room and I sat on the balcony watching the flashes and flares of the nightly Coalition bombardment of Baghdad.

I thought we were a lot safer now that we were in the hotel with other journalists, and that he was being alarmist. In fact, I wanted to file a story about what had happened to us and what we had seen on the drive from Basra. There was every chance, I argued, that the Information Ministry would not be closely monitoring the Australian press. Most Baghdad phone lines were down, the Iraqi Embassy had been kicked out of Canberra and the Iraqi Government had quite a bit on its plate. If we kept the story off our newspapers' websites we just might get away with it. If they did pick up that we had broken the rules we could apologise and promise not to do it again. There was some risk involved but I thought we should at least consider it.

Stewart was dead against the idea. I said I would not file a story unless he agreed, as doing so would impose a risk on all of us. John, on the other hand, had found a badly needed release in a few drinks and was more relaxed than he had been for days. Or so I thought.

At 4 a.m. I was sitting alone on the balcony still watching the amazing spectacle of Baghdad being bombed around us when the bedroom behind me was filled with a muffled scream. A loud nightmare was an understandable release of tension for John, and a reminder that I would need to be aware of how we were each dealing with the pressure.

*

We were woken by a Muslim call to prayer being broadcast through tinny loudspeakers about a hundred metres away. In the morning light we could see that our balcony looked out on the busiest landscape I had ever seen. There was so much going on out there that we could – and did – watch it and listen to it for hours.

For one thing, Saddam Hussein was right outside the window. Sitting in the middle of a traffic roundabout directly in front of the balcony was a large statue of Saddam with one arm raised, a statue which would later become world famous. The roundabout, called Firdos or Paradise Square, was busy with buses, donkey-drawn carts and occasional Iraqi military vehicles. On the far side of the roundabout was the source of the call to prayer that belted out each morning and occasionally during heavy bombing raids – the Shahid Mosque, with its elegant minaret and a large dome covered in tiles of spectacular greens and blues.

Beyond the mosque was a wide view of the city under a hectic sky. American helicopter gunships looped in tight circles then buzzed away, and fighter-bomber jets occasionally flashed confidently across the sky, knowing that the Iraqi air defences had been pounded into impotence. Six oil trenches were on fire, with their heavy black smoke rising rapidly because of the great heat generated by oil fires. More conventional fires, caused by Coalition attacks, burned in several places, sending up lighter, slower-moving smoke.

To the right we could see the Tigris River and part of the large presidential compound beyond it. That was the riverside area that the world had seen being bombed over the past two weeks, and a smoky haze still hung over it. The hotel balconies were shielded by a waist-high wall and concrete lattice-work which partly hid the view but might also give the room some protection from the heat and hopefully even shrapnel. Directly below our balcony were the lawns and driveway of the hotel. We could see our Pajero parked amid the hustle of the scene, like an old friend looking out of place in a foreign environment.

Television networks had set up dozens of tents and broadcast points on the roof of a lower wing of the hotel, which formed a viewing platform on which reporters could speak to their own cameras with the city skyline behind them. The presence of TV crews from time zones around the world made that lower roof the world's main eye on Baghdad and meant that at almost any time of the night or day we could look down and see at least one TV reporter, if not a dozen, doing their 'stand-ups' or reports to camera. The reporters often wore their bullet-proof vests for those broadcasts but from our vantage point we were amused to see that the off-camera producers, sound technicians and cameramen rarely wore their jackets, suggesting they were an on-camera prop to heighten the drama.

Our first breakfast in Baghdad came from our remaining MREs

– cold cappuccino from a drink powder mixed with water, a sweet pastry and cheese and crackers.

Paul McGeough visited later in the morning. He was a welcoming face but did not hide his disappointment that our arrival meant he had not even had a full day as the only Australian reporter in town. The *Herald* had been planning to promote his exclusive status on their front page after the expulsion of McPhedran.

Access to a phone was our biggest headache and Paul said he would be happy for us to use his phone. The problem was getting to it as we were not allowed to leave our hotel. He said it would be difficult for him to bring his phone across to our hotel but he would see what he could do. I learned after the war that he had had a spare room in our hotel throughout the war but it would obviously have been dangerous for him to set up his phone there for us to use. Staying in Baghdad had to be his main priority and being caught with rule-breakers like us in his spare room would not have helped – as one British journalist put it, we were the officially designated bad boys of the foreign press, confined to our rooms, or at least our hotel, for being naughty. In any case there were plenty of other phones in the Palestine we could borrow.

Paul left, promising to e-mail Pilita telling her how we were. We did not see him again but he kept tabs on our welfare through other reporters and kept Pilita informed through e-mails and phone calls to his wife Pam Williams. The hotel phones were only good for calling the front desk or other rooms but we soon received a call from an English reporter, Stephen Martin of the *Sunday Mirror*. He had met Ian McPhedran in Baghdad and they had invested together in a generator and a few other pieces of equipment, so in Ian's absence half that generator was ours. More importantly, we were welcome to use his phone at any time, he said, which was the best news we had had since we arrived. I went straight up to his room, 1327, but he had already raced out on a job.

The accredited foreign reporters did have the occasional event to attend. The Iraqis were holding press conferences in the lower wing of the hotel and taking busloads of reporters to news events which might serve the Iraqi Government's purposes, like visiting a civilian bombing site. This was when we started to realise just how restricted were the two hundred or so reporters in Baghdad.

The Information Ministry decided who they could speak to and its minders sat in on all interviews with Iraqis. Even with their minders in tow they needed permission to go anywhere, and that had become almost impossible to obtain. Since the start of the bombing they were generally allowed out of the press hotels only on ministry bus tours, forcing them to look desperately from their bus windows for any hint of how the Iraqi people and military were faring.

They had nothing like the freedom we had enjoyed in the south and, ironically enough, they had little more freedom of independent movement than we now had during our house arrest. What they did have were two valuable things. One was locally hired drivers and fixers. While some were untrustworthy or ineffective, others were excellent. They could run shopping errands and chase information for the correspondents, becoming particularly important as the journalists' movements became more tightly restricted. Their other big asset was satellite telephones and Internet access in their rooms. The Iraqis had originally forced the journalists to keep their sat phones at the Information Ministry but had now allowed them to use their equipment in their rooms. That meant a reporter could file stories from his or her room and just as importantly they could receive all the news being collated by news editors around the world.

Thousands of those editors were sifting through the masses of material from official sources and embedded reporters, each of whom had one small fragment of the big picture. The original information might have come from a *Jerusalem Post* reporter embedded with British Marines or a *New York Times* report out of Washington but it could all be pulled together in a Baghdad hotel room, enhanced with a dash of local colour and the reporter's own analysis, then filed with that famous Baghdad dateline. Few readers knew that the person whose name appeared at the top of the story might have actually interviewed nobody that day and seen only what could be spied from their balcony window. The same thing had happened, of course, in stories around the world.

This evolution of foreign corresponding, and the technological revolution that produced it, has happened within the career span of current journalists. Forty-two when I went to Iraq, I was hardly a wrinkly old veteran but even I began my career in a big-city newsroom powered by typewriters. My first 'correspondent' job was in the Sydney bureau of Melbourne's *Sun-News Pictorial* in 1983, when the bureau needed two full-time telex operators to convert our typed pages into a series of holes in rolls of paper tape which could be fed through a telex machine.

When I went on my first foreign posting, to Tokyo in 1985, I was given a manual from the company's 'Melbourne Herald Cable Service', which still included a chapter advising reporters how to keep down their word counts, as cables once had to be paid for by the word. It was that pricing system that produced a bizarre form of truncated 'cable-ese' and some famous, perhaps apocryphal, exchanges between correspondents and their editors.

'Why unnews?' one editor is said to have cabled an unproductive correspondent.

'Unnews is good news,' came the answer.

'Unnews is unjob,' was the response.

My favourite was the three-word cable in which a disgruntled correspondent halved what would usually be a six-word message to his editor: 'Upstick job arsewards.'

Instead of delivering typed pages to a cable office, correspondents can now sit in a hotel room – or on a beach for that matter – comfortably cruising the databanks and websites of the world on their laptops. But all these developments depend on access to a telephone, so that even if I was simply to dictate a story to somebody in Sydney we would first have to beg for precious sat phone time from people who were preoccupied with their own deadlines and concerns.

It was even tougher for Stewart. When he approached strangers in the hotel asking to use their phones he ran into a professional caste system, with many reporters and photographers less likely to help out a translator–fixer. Whenever I did get my hands on a phone I would try to wrangle Stewart a few minutes on it as well.

I went down to the lower roof on this first morning to cruise the broadcast tents in search of a phone I might borrow. In the BBC tent I met cameraman Duncan Stone, a tall Englishman who was extremely helpful. He said his fellow BBC cameraman was an Australian, Andrew 'Killer' Kilrain. I did not know Killer personally but recognised that distinctive name – he had worked in the Canberra press gallery when I did a decade or so earlier. The BBC team were as surprised as the Reuter guys by the news that the Iraqis were still using the main highway from Basra. The advice from Duncan and BBC reporter Paul Wood was that after that drive we were lucky to be alive and we should not push our luck by trying to file.

Four other journalists – two working for the US newspaper *Newsday*, and freelance photographers from Denmark and the US – had been taken from the Palestine just over a week earlier and locked in the terrifying Abu Ghraib prison for working as reporters on tourist or peace activist visas. Within the next day or so news would come through that they had been released to Jordan after heavy lobbying by groups ranging from the Vatican to Yasser Arafat but it was not an encouraging precedent for anyone considering working with no visa at all.

I found the detained French television crew in the café and we discussed life under house arrest. The Iraqis had warned them not even to allow any publicity in France about their plight.

'They told us the best thing is to just stay quiet, so we have – but now we have been here eleven days and we're going crazy,' one said.

It turned out that there was something almost as frustrating as sitting in Kuwait trying to get over the border: sitting in the middle of the world's biggest story being unable to file. I had lunch with a new minder who had been assigned to us – a short, overweight fifty year old named Abu Mohammed who said that before the war he had worked as an interpreter. Softly spoken and not at all aggressive, he said he thought our status would be determined in a day or two. He also announced that we had to move up two floors to room 1316. It was in much worse shape than our first room and felt more like a prison cell than a hotel room. It was grimier, with a filthy bathroom that received almost no natural light. During the frequent power blackouts the bathroom and toilet were virtually pitch black, so we had to rely on candles even to go to the toilet.

When we complained, our minder warned that some of his colleagues still wanted to get us out of the hotel altogether. A chair was placed at our door and a guard sat in it for that afternoon but must then have been assigned to more useful duties. Our minder offered to get some shopping done for us so I asked for beer, biscuits and two white T-shirts and gave him US$70, knowing that most of that would go into his own pocket. It was an easy way to slip him a first, small bribe.

Steve Martin

We eventually found Stephen Martin in his room. He was a short thirty-two year old with the latest wire-framed glasses and a quick sense of fun. More used to reporting for the *Sunday Mirror* on crime and what he called 'celebrity shagging', he had grabbed every chance for more heavyweight assignments and this was his first real war. His conversation was full of light-hearted London patois – 'old chap', 'lovely jubbly,' and 'Baggers' (for Baghdad) and he was full of comic double entendres but there was nothing old world about him. He had a sharp fashion sense, which stood out amid the Vietnam-era 'correspondent look' and khaki vests around us. His CD player also stood out: other rooms were filled with news radio or perhaps classical music but Steve's equipment was more likely to be playing music by Paul Weller. Steve said he had taken to Ian because he seemed 'a lot less up his own arse than some of the people here'.

Also visiting him when we dropped into his room were two Fleet Street veterans. Ross Benson of the *Daily Mail* was permanently dapper. When others were down to dirty jeans and T-shirts Ross would somehow be working in a pressed blazer, looking ready for a cocktail party. Anton Antonowicz, of the *Daily Mirror*, seemed to be at war with his own photographer Mike Moore. The pressures of the war had brought out some simmering work dispute and by the time we arrived they were barely speaking, let alone working well together.

Life in Baghdad had so far been safe and comfortable for the foreign press but it had also been hugely stressful. Personal conflicts were just one of the ways people responded – some were drinking close to a bottle of whisky a night, and others simply became painful to deal with.

One reporter–photographer team who seemed to be getting on well were Stuart Clarke and reporter Bob Graham, who were among the few other teams we met who were sharing a room in the Palestine. They were among the very few freelance teams in Baghdad.

The deep pockets of a large employer were usually needed to fund the bribes and other overheads needed to get an Iraqi visa and pay the extortionate daily fees charged by the Information Ministry for the right to operate in Baghdad but Bob and Stuart were a wily pair who had set themselves up nicely.

Deciding in 2002 that war was inevitable, they had asked several British exporters how they organised Iraqi visas for their sales reps. They eventually found their way to Fawaz Zureikat, a Jordanian businessman with strong Iraqi connections, who agreed to get their passports stamped by the Iraqi Ministry of Trade. After two preparatory trips they entered Baghdad ten days before the war carrying three months' supplies, including banned communications equipment hidden in sealed boxes of cereal and bags of rice. They also carried hundreds of tea bags, as their operation seemed to be fuelled by endless cups of the stuff.

They went in with the backing of the Mail group, including the *Daily Mail*, the *Mail on Sunday* and the *Evening Standard*, but by the time we arrived they seemed to be working for half the world's newspaper readership. As other papers pulled out their reporters or missed out on visas, Bob and Stuart's empire expanded to include *Expressen* in Sweden, the *New York Post*, London's *Sun*, *News of the World*, *Sunday Mirror* and *Sunday Express*, and the *Sun-Herald* in Sydney.

Stuart, forty-eight, was lean, blond and laid-back, a gentle-natured foil to the more mercurial and gregarious Bob. A top sportsman in his day, Bob was beefy enough at fifty-four to have discovered in Baghdad that he could not actually fit into his chemical and biological weapons suit, despite it being a Large. While Stuart would join us for meals in the hotel buffet, Bob was determined to avoid any risk of illness, so he sustained himself with chocolate bars, tea and tinned food cooked in his own

Stuart Clarke

Bob Graham

room. Bob ran his operation with the efficiency of a small business, and had had 150 stories published in their various outlets in three weeks.

I was surprised to see how closely many of the British reporters and newspapers cooperated. If two events were on at once they would often share photographs and perhaps even split the workload, meeting up afterwards to swap quotes and details, which they called 'giving a fill' to each other. That is rare in Australia, where there are only two major newspaper groups so reporters tend to be in more direct competition. We would never expect McGeough to help us file stories, for instance, as that would undermine his own papers' advantage over their only competitors – us.

But the British industry is so crowded, with about a dozen daily papers available in London, that they tend to serve distinct markets – the *Mirror* and *Mail* are both tabloids but the *Mirror* is pitched at a Labour-voting audience while the *Mail* chases more conservative readers. The result is that they tend to operate as if they have separate audiences, reducing the head-to-head competition. The occasional bit of cooperation made more sense than ever in hazardous circumstances like Iraq.

Every reporter had stocked his or her room (there were few women reporters in Baghdad) with dozens of plastic bottles of water but I noticed that Steve's was also equipped with several two-dozen slabs of Efes beer cans. My shopping deal with our minder, Abu Mohammed, eventually produced one slab of a Jordanian beer called Rubicon which was not to our taste, so we borrowed an Efes slab from Steve. The minder had also produced two T-shirts and a large box of industrial-strength biscuits (eating them was like chewing on wheat-flavoured concrete).

While we were spending much of the afternoon worrying about our shopping, 150 kilometres to our north a three-man BBC team was grappling with a deadly dilemma that had nagged at me for two months. At Kifri, a small town on the frontline between Kurdish forces and Saddam's military, experienced BBC reporter Jim Muir decided that afternoon to do a live broadcast by video phone from a recently abandoned Iraqi military dug-out. A Kurdish military commander warned Muir, his 31-year-old producer Stuart Hughes and Kaveh Ibrahim Golestan, a Pulitzer Prize-winning Iranian freelance cameraman, that the Iraqis had occasionally been shelling their abandoned positions, and he gave them a young local guide.

They had been forced to shelter from mortars several times in the previous few weeks and as they drove to the dug-out, a series of trenches on top of a hill, the guide directed Muir to park on low ground to its left to shield them from Iraqi view. The moment they stepped out of the car an explosion hit Hughes. The next two or three seconds were chaos. The badly injured Hughes crawled behind a car wheel for cover while Muir ran behind the car and dived to the ground to shelter from further shells. The Kurdish guide ran off up the hill shouting the Kurdish word for 'Mortar' and Golestan ran for cover on lower ground to the left. Then there were two more explosions and Golestan, a 52-year-old with an adult son and mentor to dozens of young Iranian photographers, lay dead.

Hughes had not been hit by a mortar at all. His first step out of the car had planted his right foot straight onto a landmine. All of them thought it was a mortar and Golestan's instinctive reaction had simply taken him deeper into the minefield. Even when he realised that it was a minefield, Muir did what he was not supposed to do, by running to Golestan, dragging his body back and lifting him into the car.

During the Hostile Environment course we had been told that if a mortar exploded nearby you should throw yourself to the ground because the shrapnel flies up and out from the point of impact. But if the explosion was caused by a landmine then throwing yourself to the ground was the last thing you wanted to do – in a minefield you should not take another step, let alone stretch out on the ground. So how do you tell the difference?

The answer, according to our instructor, was to remember what you had heard before the explosion, as mortar shells usually whistle through the air. The problem is that a trained firer can attach weights to the tail fins to stabilise their flight, reducing or even stopping the whistle – soldiers call them 'silent killers' for a reason.

'There might not be a whistle,' our instructor conceded, 'but the shell is still falling through the air so you should still hear something.'

Months later, when Stuart Hughes was back at work after having his leg amputated below the knee, I called him to try to clarify the landmine/mortar dilemma. He said he had done a similar 'hostile environment' course before the war but even now he was still not sure how he was supposed to have told the difference between a mortar and a landmine.

'When you feel a bang you just get out of the way. I certainly didn't have the presence of mind to think "Now let's see, did I hear the whistle of an incoming mortar?" The only thing in my head was "I have been hit, I'm badly hurt and the next one is going to take me out".'

Paul Rees, the former British Marines trainer who founded Centurion Risk Assessments, the firm that ran my training course, says the correct response to a first explosion is to crouch as low as possible without taking another step.

'Freeze, kneel down and wait for another explosion. If there isn't one then it was a mine, so you don't go to the ground. If there is another bang it's mortars, then you do get to the ground.'

Which is all very well, of course, unless you have just had half your foot removed and your eardrums assaulted, like Hughes, and are not exactly thinking clearly.

Back in Baghdad, I found myself sharing an elevator after dinner with Peter Arnett, the New Zealand-born American television reporter who had become a star reporting from Baghdad for CNN during the first Gulf War. I said hello and he latched onto my accent.

'You're the Aussie guys who've been arrested! I've been searching everywhere for you guys,' he said with his loud American twang.

He had come to Baghdad to make a documentary for National Geographic but when the NBC network pulled out its own crew it asked him to stand in as its man on the spot. He also had a few other 'strings', including the Australian radio stations 3AW and 2UE, which had asked him to track us down. Those broadcasters were all lucky to have him on hand – Arnett was in Baghdad because of his love of a big story rather than what they were paying him. Short, bald and with a bent nose from his amateur boxing days, he had won a Pulitzer Prize as far back as 1966 for his Vietnam War reporting and as a self-employed sixty-eight year old did not need to be in Baghdad. He took me back to his room, where he recorded a radio interview about our experiences. Loud and friendly, he let me call Pilita and my parents and handed me a bottle of whisky as I left.

I dropped in on Taras and Goran to check on the progress of the US advance, before triumphantly delivering Arnett's whisky to our room. John was excited to hear who I had been with, as he had recently read Arnett's autobiography and wanted to meet him. I called my new mate and he came straight up for a beer. John was thrilled but too embarrassed to tell Arnett he had just read his book, so naturally I did.

Arnett said the Americans had made a breakthrough and were only twenty kilometres 'from Baghdad's environs', meaning they were just fifty kilometres from where we sat. He then told us about his own controversy. He had been sacked by NBC two days earlier for giving an interview to Iraq's state-controlled television channel in which he said the US advance had slowed down because the Pentagon had underestimated Iraqi resistance, a comment which Republican Congressmen described as boosting enemy morale.

'I was just telling the truth, and a damn obvious truth too,' he said. He had expressed the same views to television stations from several other countries but he conceded it had been poor judgment to say it on Iraqi TV.

'I'm in shock and awe!' he joked. 'I've been fired and I don't even work for the bastards.'

Britain's *Daily Mirror*, which had been running a vigorous anti-war campaign, had hired him immediately, trumpeting that Arnett had been 'Fired by America for telling the truth. Hired by the *Daily Mirror* to carry on telling it.' A petition had gone up in the lobby of the Palestine on which dozens of reporters protested at NBC's actions.

When he left we tackled his bottle of whisky. Stewart's fears had eased and he agreed that we should try to file a report and pictures if John could borrow a camera. We would try to get some material to Sydney and decide later whether to run it.

The next morning, Thursday 3 April, I went back up to the fifteenth floor to hear from Taras that there had been heavy bombing throughout the previous night. As the US advance got closer today's explosions grew louder and more frequent, with real thumps ringing out all day. Taras said the road from Jordan, the safest way in and out of Baghdad, had been cut. I was not sure whether to be worried or happy about this news, as it might make it easier for us to resist being expelled.

The detained French crew definitely wanted out but when I spoke to the Italians they were divided – three wanted to stay, four wanted to go. I called my parents from Steve Martin's room at 12.30 p.m.

My youngest sister Jenine had taken leave from her job as a country schoolteacher and driven to Melbourne to be with my parents, Tom and Mary. Another sister, Marlene, lives two doors from my parents and between them they were putting in long hours monitoring the media.

They had contacted Foreign Minister Alexander Downer's office and asked him to do whatever he could but his staff pointed out that it had no representation in Baghdad and had expelled Iraqi diplomats from Canberra. The phone was passed around at my parents' home in Thornbury so I could have a few words with everybody. They were all obviously worried but Dad, typically, was joking.

'No need to hurry back, mate. I've never had so many people at the bowls club buy me drinks to steady my nerves – the sympathy factor's fantastic!'

I called Michael Stutchbury to update him, telling him that if we did get expelled we wanted to head straight back to Kuwait and retrace our steps into Iraq. There was silence on the phone, then a laugh of disbelief.

'Not for this paper, you won't be,' he said.

The view in Sydney was that we should stay in Baghdad if we judged that to be safe, otherwise get out by any safe route – and then quit while we were ahead. Editors are in an extremely awkward situation in these conversations: he obviously wanted us to stay and file stories but he was careful not to pressure us.

In any case our chances of staying were being reduced by over-crowding in the hotel. To ease the shortage of rooms the Iraqis had posted a list of fifty-one people who had to leave Baghdad, suppos-edly so that other reporters waiting in Jordan could replace them. Stephen Martin was on the list. His strategy was to stall as long as possible and hope that the regime fell apart before it could act on the expulsion. He mused that an intelligent person might accept the expulsion order rather than trying to stay, and he was keen to get home to witness his family's latest breakthrough – eighteen-month-old Rosie endlessly proclaiming her first word – 'Pooh!'

But Steve also joked that a harsh fate awaited him at home – his partner Caroline was planning a caravan holiday at Scarborough. The choice as he saw it was 'a caravan holiday with the family and mother-in-law or having my goolies hacked off by Saddam's secret police – yes, the secret police every time!'

Steve's driver, Salah al Musawi, agreed to do a shopping run for me, and I gave him money for beer, socks, underpants, T-shirts and a business shirt for Stewart. I liked Salah instantly. He was an ele-gant fifty-five year old who had eschewed the popular Iraqi grooming style of dyeing his hair and moustache black like Saddam, instead allowing his hair to go almost white. While some drivers and fixers were oily or clearly dishonest, Salah had a quiet, dignified air that made me trust him, a first impression that was backed up by the experiences of several British reporters who had employed him in recent years.

His excellent English came from his time as a chief steward for Iraqi Airlines, a prestigious position which allowed him to travel the world before Saddam isolated his country. When he was working for the airline Salah had often visited his sister-in-law Fawzia in London, where she was mar-ried to an English doctor, and even took his wife and four children on hol-idays to places like Rio de Janeiro. 'My children loved his visits,' Fawzia told me later in London. 'If we were out walking he would send them into a

Salah al Musawi

shop with a handful of money and stand in the doorway to keep me out while they bought all the sweets and things I wouldn't let them have.'

But when the airline sacked its staff, driving for foreigners was one of the few ways a middle-class Iraqi not connected to the regime could earn a good US-dollar salary. Salah and his 45-year-old wife Zubaydah were supporting daughters Nawar, 25, and Abeer, 21, and two sons at school – Ali, 16, and Hasaneen, 12.

A good driver could make all the difference to a reporter's safety and state of mind, as well as lifting the quality of their journalism, and Salah was trusted and held in an unusual amount of affection by his press employers.

But these were dangerous relationships, and the stakes were much higher for the Iraqi member of the partnership. Any suspicions among Iraqi officials that he was not loyal to the regime would have had brutal consequences. Salah was no supporter of the Saddam regime and had long trodden the tightrope of privately sympathising with the foreign reporters for whom he worked.

At 5.30 p.m. John and I visited Bob and Stuart in their room, 826, to tell them that we wanted to defy the ban on us working by writing about the interview in Basra, our arrest and the trip to Baghdad. They instantly offered to help, even though being caught would have seen them expelled at the very least, and they had a lot to lose. As freelancers they had invested a lot of their own time and money in setting themselves up here in Baghdad, and the risk was now paying off, as the flight of hundreds of reporters had left newspapers around the world hungry for 'a feed' from Baghdad.

Stuart lent John a camera and led him off so John could take some shots of the skyline from our room. Bob dug out a spare laptop for me. He had brought it along as a backup, given the lack of any 'help desk' if his main laptop broke down. He put it on the bottom of a cardboard box then filled the box with fruit and bottles of water so I could carry it back to our room without being detected. We still

Inside the Palestine. Stuart Clarke took this shot of John and me in the room he shared with Bob Graham, which was much nicer than our room. Stuart then lent John a camera to capture the view through the lattice work outside our window. The statue in Firdos Square would become an icon of Saddam's fall.

did not have a sat phone but I could write my story in our room, then bring it back for Bob to transmit. I checked my e-mail account on his laptop and looked at a few Internet news sites. The Americans were only six kilometres from Baghdad and claiming they could take over the airport whenever they wanted.

By 6 p.m. the sky was darkening early as the Iraqis churned out more smoke than ever from their oil trenches. Back in our room with my new box of 'fruit', I could see that one oil trench was raging out of control, with flames leaping much higher than usual. As I watched it from the balcony I could hear Ross Benson, who was also on the expulsion list, negotiating in the next room with a furtive-looking Iraqi for a ride to Jordan or Damascus for US$300 a seat.

Half an hour later there was a major blackout. Our room was left without power, and the hotel's noisy generators provided light only to the hotel lobby, making for long, dark walks up the stairs. Reporters groped their way along our corridor asking each other for torches or candles, and somebody swore furiously in Spanish a few rooms away. A blackout on deadline was no fun, especially if you lost hours of work on a computer or some television editing equipment. Tempers were being lost all over the building, and the mood was one of growing crisis.

We went back to Bob and Stuart's room so Stuart could take a photo of us to go with my report. Still worried about his lack of a passport and how the Iraqis might react to his Kuwaiti connections, Stewart decided it was too dangerous for him to take part in the photo. Stuart Clarke photographed John and me sitting on the bed, then standing on the balcony with the skyline behind us. We did not exactly feel like smiling and the resulting photos looked like something from a prison camp.

The hotel was full of stories about reporters having their empty rooms searched by government minders or robbed by hotel staff. Stuart carried most of his cash in his shoes – he could fit US$8000 in each shoe although it added about two centimetres to his height – but Bob had had $4000 stolen from his room. I told John and Stewart that now that the laptop was hidden in our bedside drawer we must never leave the room unattended. They solemnly agreed and I went off to Steve's room to make a phone call. John and Stewart promptly got bored and left the room to go up to the Reuters suite.

Stewart at least turned up on time for an appointment we had in the restaurant to have dinner with our minder, Abu Mohammed. John came into the restaurant later, after a few drinks with the Reuters guys and then with Stuart Clarke. He rolled his eyes at the sight of the minder as if dinner with him would be too boring for words, and took his grilled chicken and rice off to eat with some of the British reporters.

Three unusually loud and close explosions sent a murmur through the dining room. Our Iraqi dinner companion shrugged his shoulders with resignation. He was giving nothing away as Stewart and I campaigned for the right to do some work, and the truth was that any decisions would be made well over his head. In an odd way he was as much a prisoner as we were – if all went well we might be home in a few weeks but it was hard to see a comfortable life ahead for the regime's servants, not all of whom were evil killers.

John joined us for a cup of tea after dinner, joking as he sat down that I was a slacker. I should be back in the room writing my story, he declared.

'This guy procrastinates! Just finish the thing – bang it out and file it,' he chided me.

I stared daggers at him but the minder did not pick up on this little disclosure. Ten minutes later John referred again to the fact that I had a story to write. Stewart suspected that our minder was now deliberately missing the point but we could not be sure. I had not done any writing that afternoon, and not just because I was avoiding my homework. I was more nervous than ever about being caught because Bob and Stuart had reminded us that several people had been jailed for working without proper visas.

We returned to our room to find that the crumbling power system meant no water was being pumped into the toilets at all. To flush we had to pour water into the bowl from plastic bottles, making our candle-lit bathroom visits even more unpleasant. Still avoiding my story, I sat on the balcony late into the night tuning into the BBC for news and watching the skyline lit up by explosions.

Below our balcony the hotel's generator and the massed back-up generators of the TV networks were droning out more loudly than ever, producing a din that would continue for the rest of our time in Baghdad.

After that night's pathetic efforts at security I felt it was safer to take Bob's laptop back to his room and handwrite my story. I could type it into the laptop later, minimising the time the computer was in our room. I finally got my head down on Friday morning, going through my notes to begin constructing an account of what we had seen.

Salah delivered the fruits of his shopping expedition. With the city braced for attack it was not easy to shop out there and some of his purchases were shockers. The most disappointing was four dozen cans of the worst beer any of us had ever tasted, a Turkish drop called Bavarian. With a stagger-inducing 12.3 per cent alcohol content it tasted like a mixture of whisky and beer. Salah had also found three pairs of white boxer shorts big enough to stretch from the belly button to the knees. They were so bad that they were funny and with no air conditioning we took to sleeping in them and wearing them around our room like a team uniform.

His better finds were a bottle of Teacher's whisky, a long-sleeved shirt for Stewart and some toilet paper purchased on his own initiative. By now I had had two or three conversations with Salah and I was pleased when he said that if Steve's expulsion was enforced he would like to work for me. We agreed that he would, leaving the details to work out when Steve's fate was decided.

The power was still out and the toilet was becoming a real problem, as hand-flushing did not do a thorough job. I went to Bob and Stuart's room to check my e-mail and Bob announced that the Americans had taken the airport. I then went to Peter Arnett's room and called Sydney to say Stuart had sent our five photos to the *Sun* in London, which would send them on to Australia.

Ross Benson had received good news. Despite being on the expulsion list he had now been told that he could stay, so Steve Martin was determined to ignore the edict as well. The hotel's rickety generators were powering away to try to cope with the growing blackouts but the hotel infrastructure seemed to be coming apart. Water was pouring from the roof in one corner of the lobby. More alarming was the cascade of water down the walls of the electric fuse box just across the corridor from our room. The carpet next to it was waterlogged and I wondered whether anyone had ever been electrocuted by stepping on damp carpet. Our room had not been cleaned for days and sightings of hotel workers were rare. Our minder arrived with another shopping order of food, water and detergent so we could wash some clothes.

Boredom was our new problem. When the electricity had been working Iraqi television had been quite amusing in small doses. It consisted of endless singalongs for Saddam, with small variations on the one theme. Twenty-odd workers and soldiers would stand uncomfortably singing in praise of Saddam, with the most enthusiastic cheerleader tending to be a chap waving a gun to mark the beat.

'Saddam has confused his enemy,' began one snappy little number, 'Saddam is ours and we will stay with him until we die, he is our Saddam and we will defend him unto death.'

John and Stewart had started to read novels donated by Bob and Stuart. Between prowling the corridors for information, tuning into the BBC and lying awake listening to explosions, I had been getting only four hours sleep a night but this afternoon for the first time I managed a decent nap.

Stewart had cleverly found out which room our equipment was being held in – room 511. He had invented some urgent reason why he needed to get something from the gear and hectored the minders until they agreed to let him into the room. He could see that all our equipment, and that of the French and Italians, was still there.

I went downstairs to eat early so I could write in the evening. On the way back, I visited Killer in the BBC office. He said the minders were starting to disappear and the whole system could break down in a couple of days.

While I was out John had found my notebook in our room and enriched my notes with references to my healthy appetite and personal hygiene. At least I suspect it was him. I had left my draft story at the point of us being arrested, and the following paragraph had been added in a handwriting other than my own.

'Feder then fought both men to the ground and physically took us all to safety.'

Most reporters in the Palestine thought the regime would now fall quickly, which might mean a dangerous collapse of order. The restaurant was full of guesswork about how we would be treated by departing remnants of the regime. When they returned from dinner John and Stewart said the minders in the lobby had thinned out. We decided to try to get our gas masks and vests out of the car and into our room first thing in the morning.

I sat up for a few hours writing by candlelight. The explosions overnight were closer and louder than anything before, so John and Stewart also got little sleep. Several large buildings were set alight by the bombing and we could now clearly hear machine gun fire. The early light of Saturday morning revealed far fewer cars outside the hotel but the Pajero was still there. Worried that some Iraqi official would escape in it, we had been talking about letting down a couple of tyres to prevent anyone making a fast escape.

The wind had changed direction so that oil clouds were now coming straight at us along the river, and the skyline was a blur. At noon two truckloads of young Iraqi soldiers towing a large artillery piece drove by the hotel, with the soldiers cheering for the sake of the foreign press.

'It's pretty weird – there they are now but you just know that most of them will be dead really soon,' John said.

Sirens sounded throughout the morning. The regime was on its last legs. The only question was when the Americans would arrive.

While I typed my story into Bob's laptop, Stewart, John and the French television crew hassled every minder they could find until one let them get our gas masks and flak jackets out of our cars.

John and Stewart used the opportunity to turn on the car radio and leave the interior light on in the hope of running the battery flat. Stewart also jammed a small piece of wood into a tyre valve but could not get the air to keep escaping.

Sitting on the balcony watching the attacks come closer and listening to the BBC's commentary on the short-wave radio was like being front-row spectators at a deadly sporting spectacle, except there was always a chance we would find ourselves part of the game.

When the BBC reported that US troops were already in Baghdad, John began pacing and getting more anxious than ever. I had at least been able to keep myself distracted by writing, and Stewart had been busily working on the minders but John was going out of his head without his cameras.

The Americans had cut the road north from Baghdad to Saddam's home city, Tikrit, and had moved into the south of the capital. The Iraqi Information Minister, Comical Ali, declared that the city and airport remained in Iraqi hands following a supposedly successful counter-attack by the Republican Guard to seize back the airport.

'The operation is moving in our interest and I think we are going to finalise it soon,' he said in a press conference below us in the hotel, claiming the ministry could not take reporters to the airport for another few hours because there was still some shooting going on.

In Qatar, US spokesman Frank Thorpe responded that the Americans already had members of the media with their own troops, who happened to be on the tarmac of the airport. 'Substantial numbers' of US troops had entered the capital, he said, and had come within three or four kilometres of the press hotels.

'We saw an opportunity last night to go forward and confront the Republican Guard so we took the opportunity to challenge them and go forward up the main thoroughfare to destroy more enemy forces that may be in the area.' It had not been an attempt to occupy or 'slice off' part of the city, he said, but US forces were now 'in the heart of the city'.

The US statement was challenged by BBC radio correspondent Andrew Gilligan. Gilligan would later become famous for a sceptical and inaccurate report about the Blair Government's rationale for war, which sparked a row between the BBC and Downing Street during which his initial confidential source, government weapons scientist Dr David Kelly, committed suicide.

Gilligan, who was reporting from the BBC tent beneath us, said there were no US troops in the heart of the city. In some southern suburbs there were burned-out armoured vehicles and other evidence that the Americans had been there but they had moved on and the Iraqis remained in control, he said. Gilligan was right – the Americans had indeed rampaged their way into the sprawling city but they had not yet reached that ill-defined place, 'the heart of the city'.

Saddam was being given reason to regret having built such an elaborate system of wide highways in and around Baghdad. The Americans were sending armoured columns on 'thunder runs', blasting their way down the wide, straight roads without being pinned down in the sort of guerrilla street fighting they had been dreading.

Two M1 Abrams tanks seemed to lead each column, filling the road and firing on any vehicle that looked suspicious, followed by Bradley fighting vehicles and humvees. Their superior firepower allowed them to stand off and destroy any Iraqi units from a distance but anxious young tank gunners were also 'taking out' family cars and taxis as well as military vehicles. And yet there were still some signs of normal life in the city. Civilian traffic had not completely disappeared and a petrol station visible from our balcony was still doing business.

At 4.30 p.m. American spokesmen said they were moving more troops into the airport to secure it for use as an air base and as the Americans' main operating centre near the capital. More than just the loss of an important asset, the fall of the airport was a fatal blow to any credibility the Iraqi regime's spokesmen had left, as people living near the airport could see that it was indeed controlled by the Americans.

I decided to file my story first thing in the morning. By now the hotel's generators were struggling. Paraffin lamps were being used on the reception desk in the lobby and the lifts were totally dark. Somehow the restaurant kept serving hot buffets for lunch and dinner but the standard had become atrocious, with even the rice tasting burnt. That night we spent some more time with the Reuters guys, discussing the fact that the battle was on our doorstep and would hopefully soon be over. I felt like we had been in this hotel for a year, not just a few days, and that I had known these people for half my life.

When I went to Bob's room early on the morning of Sunday 6 April to send my story I got a nasty surprise – the laptop on which I had written several thousand words had no software to transmit the story. It also lacked a drive to copy the story onto a floppy disk.

I went to the BBC tent for technical advice and the cameraman Duncan Stone managed to get my story out of the computer by copying it to a card normally used for storing photos. After an anxious morning the story was sent on BBC equipment. It ran at some length with John's photographs in the next day's newspapers.

By now the stress of the past few weeks had brought a cold sore up on my lip. Embarrassingly, John developed one too, as Steve Martin delighted in pointing out that morning.

Steve and Salah left the hotel for lunch at one of the few restaurants still open, which offered a restricted menu of kebabs and mezze plates. Even to go there they had to take Steve's minder, a nasty alcoholic named Mohammed, who generally made a special effort to be extremely rude to Salah, no doubt suspecting where Salah's political sympathies lay.

Steve had no trips planned for the afternoon so on the drive back from lunch he told Salah to go home early. Salah thought he knew a laundrette that was still open so he took some of Steve's shirts and other washing. He also took Steve's new Iraqi press card because he thought that enough businesses were open for him to get it laminated somewhere. When Steve waved goodbye to Salah in his white sedan outside the hotel it was the last time he would ever see him.

That afternoon we saw quite a few children in the hotel for the first time, and Iraqi families pushing large trolleys of food to hotel rooms. Well-placed Iraqis were obviously moving their families here for protection. The power was mostly gone and water was flowing only briefly in the morning and evening, making it pretty important that we grabbed the chance to flush the toilet. Even the phone in our room was now cut off, so we could no longer call other rooms.

We had dinner with the newest arrival at the Palestine, a French reporter from *Raids* magazine – France's version of *Soldier of Fortune* – who had also been arrested and brought to Baghdad. To call Yves Debay 'gung ho' would be an understatement. He was a thick-set former soldier who fought as a mercenary for the white Rhodesians and now apparently went from war zone to war zone relishing the conflicts rather than the causes. The US special forces would come to the hotel soon, he declared, so when we heard close shooting we should all stay in our rooms.

That night we went for a drink in the BBC crew's rooms, which formed a suite like the Reuters rooms. Nobody was stupid enough to swap our horrible Bavarian beer for anything else, and even we were struggling to drink it warm. Our fridge had no power but the BBC had a generator, so some borrowed fridge space came in handy. Like most reporters cooped up in Baghdad the British were interested in our stories about the mood in the south and the drive to Baghdad. The cameramen amused themselves by teasing Rageh Omaar about his new fame. Rageh admitted to becoming increasingly jittery – he had been in Baghdad for a long stint and had had a dream in which he was hurt in the very last moments of the war. Those moments were about to arrive.

6

BAGHDAD FALLS

The next day at dawn, Monday 7 April, the heavy explosions of recent nights came closer than ever, then they were joined by bursts of machine gun fire just outside our window. Although we didn't know it then, this was the last full day of Saddam Hussein's 24-year-old regime.

By eight the light had improved enough for us to see the source of the commotion. About a kilometre away, directly across the river on the exposed western bank of the Tigris, US and Iraqi troops were having a firefight inside the presidential compound.

About twenty American soldiers could be seen running crouched along the river bank from our left. They came under fire from machine guns and grenades and dived to the ground. We could see Iraqis, some half-dressed, running away along the river bank to our right, a few pulling off their uniforms as they ran. This humiliating retreat of Saddam's 'elite' Republican Guard was being beamed live around the world from the cameras journalists were training from their hotel balconies around us.

Heavy-calibre machine-gun bullets were punching into the river, sending up spouts of water, so we put on our flak jackets and crouched below our balcony wall to watch, hardly believing that the first land assault on Saddam's palaces was playing out right in front us.

Ross Benson was watching from the window of the adjoining room, and we began yelling questions and comments back and forward.

'Can you see those vehicles – what are they, tanks?' Ross yelled. Two US Bradley fighting vehicles had come into sight and were moving about on a road about a hundred metres above the river bank.

'I don't know, not tanks. Are those planes actually firing on the compound?' I called back, as two US jets circled overhead.

Just after 8.30 the Iraqi defenders set fire to an oil-filled trench to generate smoke cover. Five minutes later, both the fighting vehicles fired their cannons. We saw people lying on the river banks, either dead or taking cover. Incredibly, back on this side of the river, light traffic, including public buses, was flowing through Firdos Square and we could make out a queue of cars sitting patiently at the nearby petrol station.

I scribbled out an account of what we had seen and at about 10 a.m. I ran down to Steve Martin's room to borrow his satellite phone. I called Sydney and told them that now that I had already broken the Iraqi rules by filing the previous day's feature I would keep doing so until the Iraqis stopped me.

I asked a copytaker to call me back, to reduce the cost on Steve's phone, then dictated a sixteen-paragraph description of the palace fighting, which went onto the bottom of *The Australian*'s front page. Even when McPhedran had been allowed to operate from Baghdad, the News Ltd papers had tended to use his material for colour and first-person descriptions, relying on reporters in New York or Washington to pull together the 'splash' from official statements and the flood of other news reports. Rory Callinan had long given up on Doha, where the Coalition was releasing little useful information.

Dozens of television cameras in our hotel were capturing the fighting and I knew the footage would scare our families so when I had sent the story, I called Pilita to tell her we were OK. I left a message on my parents' answering machine, then quickly called Glad Peterson, a very close aunt who I knew would be anxiously watching the TV coverage.

Back in our room, the short-wave radio was quoting an embedded journalist from Sky TV saying the Americans had entered the presidential compound to test its defences but had then decided to stay and were now holding three buildings. One US soldier was apparently swimming in Saddam's pool, and there was TV footage of celebrating soldiers throwing their helmets into the air. It was all moving much faster than we had expected.

Just as Baghdad's elaborate highway system and broad boulevards were helping the Americans, so was its sprawling size. The scale of the five-million-population capital had been expected to make it hard to capture but instead made it difficult to defend in the face of such a fast-moving foe, which could pick its own places to stand and fight.

One place they chose was near a major intersection on Al Zaitoun Street in the Mansour district, which Steve's driver Salah approached just after 9 a.m.

Salah had decided that the arrival of the US tanks on the streets made it too dangerous to keep working. Because there were no functioning telephones, he told his wife Zubaydah over breakfast that he wanted to tell Steve in person that he would not be in for a few days. He had not been able to find a laundry open so he had washed and dried Steve's clothes himself, and wanted to return them.

Witnesses later told his family that he waited at the intersection for a green light then drove on towards a short tunnel, not knowing that at least one American tank was in the tunnel. The tank fired into a small car in front of him, killing its three occupants – a man, a woman and a child. Trapped, Salah tried to do a U-turn but had only just started to mount the traffic island when heavy-calibre bullets smashed into the front of his car. He was shot in the head through the windscreen and died sitting at the wheel. The next vehicle, carrying a large family, was also hit. A tank later pushed Salah's car around to block the road, his body still in the driver's seat. A small contingent of Marines found Steve's press pass in Salah's pocket and thought he was Steve, something Steve learned a week later when he bumped into one of the same Marines. Not only did they fail to contact Steve's paper, the *Sunday Mirror*; the Americans, in blocking off the road, prevented anybody else getting to the bodies of Salah or the people in the other passenger cars around him.

All Steve and the rest of us knew at the time was that Salah did not turn up for work, but that was not too extraordinary as many other drivers and fixers were staying home.

Before noon the Iraqi Information Minister, Mohammed Saeed al-Sahhaf, held a press conference on the lower roof below our balcony to announce that the Americans had been fought back and driven out of the presidential compound.

'There are no American infidels in Baghdad, never!' he vowed.

A small group had tried to enter the city but most had had their throats cut. 'Those rascals are now committing suicide on the gates of Baghdad.'

As we looked down at Al-Sahhaf and the reporters around him, following his press conference on the BBC, a turn of the head showed the Bradley fighting vehicles still sitting brazenly in full view on the open river bank, and from time to time machine guns and tank fire still rang out. The Americans were daring the Iraqis to respond, knowing that any move to bring out Iraqi tanks would be met with US air power.

The sights, sounds and smells of the war had bombarded our senses since we arrived in Baghdad. Now, with the heavy smoke in the air, you could even feel the oil, grit and sweat on your face.

The hotel was in full war mode. Armed Iraqi troops guarded the front door, while arguments between reporters and minders erupted

Above and overleaf:
The US Marines arrive in central Baghdad. Having just 'liberated' his cameras from our fleeing Iraqi minders, John went out onto the streets with a British TV crew to record the history of the Americans approaching Firdos Square.

in the crowded lobby. Late in the afternoon I saw the Information Ministry's Uday al-Tai scream at a German television reporter that he was going to be expelled from Iraq for some sort of breach of the rules. The reporter was almost in tears as he pleaded for a reprieve but Uday was being a bully while he still could. The reporter was not just worried about missing the climax of the war – this was not exactly a good time to try to drive to Jordan.

What everybody in the Palestine Hotel wanted to know was when the Americans would arrive to 'liberate' the press, and how the Iraqis would handle such a takeover. The presence of Iraqi families in the hotel was an encouraging sign that the regime did not intend to attack the Palestine.

That evening was a decisive one for the journalists under 'house arrest' in the Palestine. Abu Tayef announced during dinner that we would get a decision on our future within an hour. We were spread around several tables in the restaurant and some of the French and Italians began moving from table to table in excitement. Most had been keen for days to get out but the dangers of travelling had swung the debate back in favour of staying. I argued that the road to Jordan was not safe, which was true, and that we should be united in refusing to go – we should declare that if they tried to force us onto the road we would protest to the Red Cross.

As we were debating the best way forward, Yves Debay, from *Raids*, cleared his throat and offered the benefits of his vast war experience. The other French reporters were already wary of this burly former paratrooper and he had little in common with the Italians, who seemed more like cerebral opinion writers and columnists than the average war correspondent.

The answer was simple, Yves declared. If they tried to expel us we should literally go berserk and become violent. During one period of detention in some war or another, he explained, he had forced his captors to return some confiscated equipment simply by going off his head and tearing his room apart. Sixty seconds earlier there had been six people talking at once but Yves's suggestion brought silence. One of the Italians sat with a spoonful of food suspended halfway to his open mouth, staring at the man from *Raids*, who clearly was not joking. After a few seconds heads turned and conversation slowly resumed, leaving Yves to shrug in disappointment. One of the less war-like Frenchmen eventually warned Abu Tayef on our behalf that we would not accept expulsion. He went away to pass this message to his superiors.

On the way back to our room I went into the BBC suite to pick up some of our horrible beer from their fridge. Their bureau chief Paul Danahar was working on a report and Rageh was looking out the window at the scene across the river. I said 'Hi', grabbed our Bavarian from the fridge and was heading straight back out the door when Rageh called me over to look through the zoom of a camera fitted with a night vision lens at the amazing scene in the compound – American troops were lounging around, confident enough to have their helmets off. Danahar apparently wanted Rageh to get on with his work and turned his temper on me, abruptly asking me to get out so Rageh could do some work. Rageh was embarrassed and I was less than thrilled to be caught in the middle of their domestic.

Abu Tayef eventually came to each of our rooms with the verdict – a decision had been deferred. This was a win as the regime seemed unlikely to last long enough to take any more decisions.

As the three of us lay in our parallel beds that night, John mentioned that he had been having dreams which incorporated the sounds of war, only to wake each morning to find that the war was real. This night I had my own discomforting dream, which was probably triggered by a story of Stewart's about some adventure wind-surfing among big waves. I dreamt I was trying to navigate a small boat through huge, dark seas, and was constantly being lifted up by one enormous wave after another only to drop helplessly into space off the back of the waves, trying desperately to keep the boat balanced as it plunged into the dark.

We had gone to sleep expecting the Iraqis to launch a counter-attack on the presidential compound overnight. At 4.50 a.m. we were woken by whistles in the compound, followed by machine gun fire and sharp explosions. We guessed that the whistles were being used to signal an infantry attack or by sentries to alert defenders of an attack. The sound of close-quarters fighting continued for almost two hours. And yet dawn showed that the American vehicles were still sitting there in full view, a major victory in the propaganda war.

The Americans were trying to force the regime to implode but what was the Iraqi strategy for victory? They could only be banking on outrage overseas, especially in the rest of the Arab world, forcing the Americans to stop their assault. That was simply not happening – the supposed fury of 'the Arab Street' was not erupting in support for Saddam.

We did not know it at the time but just before 7 a.m. that morning, Tuesday 8 April, a US jet fighter made two passes over the Al-Jazeera network's building just over a kilometre along the river from our hotel and then hit it with two air-to-surface missiles. The precaution of giving the Pentagon the coordinates of all its offices had not prevented an attack on their team in the Basra Sheraton, and now the Baghdad bureau had been targeted.

Al-Jazeera's office was a well-known two-storey villa which stood out on the river bank and had a large sign reading 'TV' mounted on its facade. Reporter Tareq Ayyoub, a 35-year-old Jordanian with a one-year-old daughter, was killed on the roof just as he was about to go on air. The survivors were evacuated to the nearby office of the Abu Dhabi television network, the only other base of the foreign press in Baghdad apart from our hotels. Soon after they arrived, US shells ploughed into the Abu Dhabi building, flattening part of the building. Staff from the two networks were trapped in the wreckage but there were no more deaths.

Al-Jazeera had been angrily accused of bias by both Washington and the Iraqis. The Pentagon was furious that it had aired graphic footage of Iraqi civilian casualties and American soldiers who had been killed or captured, while the Iraqi Information Minister, Comical Ali, was indignant that the Qatari network was reporting the fact that US troops were inside the palace compound, instead of accepting his own ludicrous version of events.

Just after 9 a.m. the American vehicles in the palace compound moved out of sight. From Steve Martin's balcony on the other side of the hotel we could see that several US tanks had driven onto the two major bridges further to the right along the river. They were firing virtually straight across the bridges at Iraqi defenders sheltering in buildings on our side of the river. Helicopter gunships backed up the tanks, buzzing here and there to launch their own rockets.

I filed another story about what I had watched that morning, noting that more Iraqi families had started to move into the hotel in the belief that they would be safe here from US attack. John went to

the Reuters suite to ask Goran if he could borrow a camera but Goran could not spare one. The agency's whole team had been working frantically since dawn.

Paul Pasquale, a stocky thirty-six year old who had left the British Army at twenty-two to become a cameraman, was filming US A-10 tankbuster aircraft from the lower roof and sending live footage to London, while Taras was on the balcony of his own bedroom, room 1503, filming the tank offensive. The only time Taras left his camera was to rush in and out of the adjoining room, 1502, where the television editing was being done, to hand over tapes and quickly explain his shots to producer Ahmed Seif.

Samia Nakhoul, the Lebanese-born chief of Reuters' Gulf bureau, went once to Taras's balcony and looked at the action through his camera. They hardly had time to speak before she went back to the balcony of 1502 to watch the US attacks on the Rashid military camp further to the east, dashing back to the phone occasionally to update her reports.

At about 11 a.m. Stuart Clarke took John up to the room of Mike Moore, the *Daily Mail*'s photographer, so John could take a few shots with Stuart's backup camera. Moore's room was on the seventeenth floor at the river end of the hotel, above the BBC suite and at the opposite end to the Reuters room, so its balcony gave them excellent views of the US tanks on the Jumhuriyah Bridge, 1.7 kilometres away. They wondered aloud among themselves why one of the tanks kept swinging its turret around and pointing it at our hotel.

John was back in our room when I returned from filing some time after 11.30, and we watched the presidential compound together for a while. In the other direction, behind the mosque, we could see two helicopters circling at speed and firing their cannons at a target about two kilometres from us.

I stepped in from the balcony to tell John that a Japanese photographer I had met might be able to lend him a camera but before

The grisly scenes on the Sinak Bridge over the Tigris River on 10 April, the first day after Saddam's fall. Iraqis had launched suicidal attacks on US tanks parked on the edge of the bridge. An American journalist pretended to interview the burned corpse. Note the Iraqis who could see the whole scene. John Feder

he could say anything there was an enormous bang over our heads. The impact shook the room, sending us both diving to the floor. Something had hit the hotel.

We scrambled into our flak jackets and ran into the corridor to see a dozen stunned journalists coming out of other rooms. We raced up a flight to the fourteenth floor. There was yelling and smoke in the corridor, with a few reporters running towards the smoke coming out of the end suite.

People were screaming for a doctor and saying that somebody was hurt in that suite. It was right under 1503, the Reuters room, so I ran up another flight. It was a similar scene, except this time I could see Iraqi men crying and others rushing in tears out of the Reuters suite.

I bolted back down to our room to grab the home-made first aid kit I had put together a few weeks earlier, then ran back up to the fifteenth floor, sweating in my heavy vest. I pushed my way into 1503, past several men who were standing around the two single beds yelling that there was no doctor.

The frame of the sliding door onto the balcony was still intact but most of its glass had been blown back into the room. Taras was lying on his back on the carpet with his feet still out on the balcony. Shattered glass was all around him and his video camera and tripod lay next to him, where he had been blown in from the balcony.

Two Arab men who I assumed were Iraqis working for Reuters were grabbing their own hair and wailing. Taras was splattered with blood and not moving. The only person who was trying to help him was a 42-year-old French photographer from Associated Press, Jerome Delay, who was kneeling beside him. By the time he got there – just before me – the less serious casualties had been rushed out but Taras was still unattended.

'The people who were first on the scene looked after those who were conscious first because they were screaming,' Delay told me later. 'I suppose that is natural because they were not professional emergency people but it meant Taras was left lying there, not breathing.'

Jerome had done the same sort of emergency first aid training as me, so when we started working on Taras our priority was to make sure he could breathe, before stopping any major bleeds and then getting him to hospital.

I threw some furniture out of the way so I could kneel on the other side of Taras, then we forced open his jaws, and he took a deep gasp of air. His eyes were half-open but rolled around out of control whenever we moved his head, and he did not respond when we spoke to him.

I yelled at the two crying men to get out as they were not helping. Behind them I could see that a TV crew had squeezed into the room to try to record the scene.

We tilted Taras's head back to open his air passage, and Jerome and I took turns supporting his head to make sure he kept breathing while we checked for major wounds.

I looked for the source of the bleeding under his shirt and found an ugly answer. His intestines and some organs were spilling out of his abdomen. Behind me I could hear somebody yelling 'Oh my God, look at him! He's dead, my God ... look at his guts!' We had been told on the course at Heckfield Place that people who are not fully conscious can often hear what is going on around them, so I yelled 'Shut up' over my shoulder and did my best to reassure him.

'You're alright mate, you'll be fine ... This isn't serious, it's not too bad.'

Amid all the confusion, I had mistaken Taras for his colleague, Goran Tomasevic, and I called him 'Goran' at least twice as I tried to see if he was conscious.

Two Arab men in the room had been yelling Goran's name when I entered and at first I was bending over Taras from above and looking at his face upside-down. Both men had dark hair and the normally clean-shaven Taras had not had time to shave for a couple of days, so for the first time all week he had stubble like Goran's. Once I had decided it was Goran I did not take time to step back and look at his face the right way up, because checking his identity was the last thing on my mind.

There was a large pool of blood under his left leg so I asked Jerome to cut open the pants on that leg so we could check for heavy bleeding before trying to move him. He used scissors from my kit. The leg was unmarked.

Rather than trying to shove anything back into his ruptured belly we draped a large bandage around his midriff, more to keep the contents in place than to staunch any bleeding. Several men cleared a space behind me and laid out a blanket as a stretcher. Four or five of us lifted him onto it, then he was raced out of the room. I stayed on my knees, dazed, until Rageh Omaar yelled at me to follow him out in case of a second attack.

I met John in the adjoining Reuters room and we had a confusing conversation. He asked how I was coping and said he had seen me helping Taras but I said no, I had been working on Goran.

The lobby downstairs was chaotic. Children were crying, and confused reporters and scared hotel workers were pushing through the crowd as the last of the wounded were being bundled into cars at the front doors.

Jose Couso, a 37-year-old cameraman with Spanish network Telecinco, was carried out with a belt tied as a tourniquet trying to stop the blood spurting from one leg. He had been standing on the balcony under Reuters and was hit by shrapnel in the leg, chest and jaw.

Steve Martin watched two of the wounded being loaded into the back of a people carrier, their blood trailing down the hotel steps, then quietly went upstairs to vomit in his toilet.

Nobody was optimistic about any serious casualty who arrived right now at a Baghdad hospital. They had been swamped for days by civilian casualties, and children were already dying on trolleys in crowded hospital corridors.

One of the injured being taken to hospital at that moment was Paul Pasquale from Reuters. He had taken a break from his work on the lower roof and gone up for a chat with Taras. Paul told me months later that he went out onto the balcony and sat on a metal stool to the right of Taras and his tripod. They had worked together in Bosnia, Kosovo and Afghanistan and were close enough friends that Paul lit up a smoke for Taras without asking if he wanted it. Taras had stopped filming but was still scanning the city through his camera.

'He was starting to relax and just sort of saying "Phew that was amazing",' said Paul, who was reaching up to hand the lit cigarette to Taras when there was an explosion on the exterior wall of the hotel just to their left.

Shrapnel sliced into them, and they were thrown back through the glass door, with Taras landing on top of Paul. The tendons in

Paul's left hand and foot were severed, his right arm, face and belly were gouged by metal and large chunks of muscle were blown from his right hip and thigh, so Paul initially assumed he was more badly injured than his friend.

'I asked him to get off me but he didn't move or say anything. My hands weren't working so I had to use my elbows to move and get him off. As I got out from under him I could see the injuries on his front and I knew he wasn't going to make it.

'I thought whoever hit us is going to do it again so I crawled on my back away from the balcony. I only made it to the bed then I leaned myself against it and started calling for help. I could see the blood pissing out of my leg but my hands weren't working so I couldn't do anything about it. I was watching myself bleed to death.

'The first person who came in was an Asian woman but she just looked at me and started screaming, sort of collapsing to her knees. Then some Iraqi guys came in and one tried to lift me by my foot, which was already half hanging off. That's when I really screamed.'

Trained in first aid in the army, Paul told them to use a blanket as a stretcher, and he was carried out of the room.

Samia Nakhoul had been on the balcony of room 1502 with Iraqi photographer Faleh Kheiber.

'He said "Samia, look!",' Samia recalled later. 'There was an orange glow in the sky and we looked left for a second (at the blast). I felt a lid of fire hit my head and we were all on the floor screaming and shouting in pain.'

Shrapnel lodged in her brain, and Kheiber's nose was smashed, his blood spurting over the long white zoom lens of his camera.

I made my way downstairs and through the bewildered crowd in the lobby to the hotel's front doors, then went through them for the first time since we had been placed under house arrest. None of the minders was going to notice me in the chaos and I was determined to look at the damage from the outside to try to work out where the blast had come from and how it could have injured people on both the fourteenth and fifteenth floors.

The consensus among the journalists was that there was no way the Americans would have fired on the Palestine – everybody in Iraq, indeed millions of people around the world, knew that it was full of Western reporters. One reporter confronted the Information

Ministry's Uday al-Tai in the lobby and openly accused the Iraqis of firing on the hotel. But it was hard to imagine why the Iraqis would attack a hotel where well-connected families had begun to take refuge.

Looking up from the lawn at the front of the hotel I could see a crater about thirty centimetres wide in the outside wall beside 1503's balcony, and several smaller holes there and on the ceiling of the balcony. The explosion had clearly blasted up into the roof of the balcony. The damage was at the end of the hotel furthest from the Tigris, meaning it faced away from the scene of that morning's fighting, ruling out a stray shot from the presidential compound, where the main US force was.

Standing next to me on the lawn looking at the same thing was Giovanni Porzio, a journalist from the Italian magazine *Panorama*. He said he had been standing on the balcony directly above the Reuters office when the blast knocked him off his feet.

'I was in a Spanish TV reporter's room and I went out on the balcony so I could get a nice view of the city as I was talking to my son on the sat phone,' he said. 'I heard this amazing noise and then saw small pieces of shrapnel and smoke flying up past the balcony about forty centimetres in front of my nose. I fell to the ground and could not hear anything for ten seconds.'

Looking at the impact crater I was convinced that the shot had been fired towards the river, meaning it had come from behind us in the part of the city held by the Iraqis, so it must have been fired by Iraqis. The Reuters cameramen had told us that they had been ordered several times by the Iraqis to stay inside off the balcony, so perhaps this was some sort of punishment, or a warning to all the press to follow those rules.

By now it was about 12.45 p.m., or 6.45 p.m. in Sydney. Deadline was approaching and I decided that the best way to capture the brutality and panic of the previous forty-five minutes was simply to recount what I had witnessed as plainly as I could.

I headed back to our room and scribbled out a report, then took my notebook to Bob Graham's room so I could dictate the story on his phone. He needed to use the phone so I typed the story out on his laptop to send it as a quick e-mail, rather than tying up his phone.

Towards the end I looked down from the screen and saw that

my hands and forearms were covered in blood, and my fingers were shaking as they hovered over the keyboard. They did not look like my hands. I still thought it was Goran who had been injured. John, Ross Benson and Bob and Stuart were in an animated conversation behind me, swapping whatever they knew and trying to work out what the attack meant for our safety. John said later that my forehead was glistening with beads of sweat as I typed, even though nobody else in the room was particularly hot.

Many reporters had agreed to distinctive door knocks to avoid being surprised by an official 'visit' or room search. Right now that was the last thing on anybody's mind, and a loud banging on the door saw it quickly opened.

In walked two angry-looking Iraqi minders. I was hunched over Bob's laptop with my back to the door, breaking the rules by writing a story. That was enough to get Bob and Stuart, as well as me, into serious trouble but it was not the only reason everyone stiffened. Sitting on the desk in full view were two pieces of illegal equipment: a B-Gan data transfer device which Bob had brought into the country sealed in a box of corn flakes and a Thuraya satellite phone which had entered in a bag of rice. Both were fitted with GPS which the Iraqis considered spying equipment warranting heavy punishment.

The minders walked straight towards me at the far end of the room, then right past and out onto the balcony. Coming back inside they snarled that we would be punished if we hung white bed sheets of surrender from the balcony, as some reporters had done, then they stalked out of the room.

As everyone else exhaled I finished the last few lines and sent the story at 2.06 Baghdad time. That was 8.06 p.m. in Sydney, early enough to be dropped into the first editions but late enough to mean there would be little time for handling the copy.

With the story gone I was then interviewed by a few of the other reporters for their own stories about what had happened in Room 1503. A little while later Bob and Stuart were handing around cups of tea when Anton Antonowicz came in to say that grim news had come back from the hospital.

Jose Couso, the Spanish cameraman who had kept talking about his two sons as he was driven to hospital, had had his leg amputated. Then he had died.

Taras had not even lasted that long. We did not know the details then but the hotel lift taking him down had stopped at all fifteen floors. Then a local driver who was told to rush to the nearest hospital wasted precious time by taking him to a small clinic that was close by but could never handle a case like his. Two nurses there cried when they saw his injuries and told the people carrying him to take him straight on to a proper hospital.

According to the French cameraman Jerome Delay, who travelled with him in the back of a utility truck, Taras was groaning until just before they reached the Olympic Hospital. Jerome saw him stop breathing and applied mouth-to-mouth resuscitation but when they got him onto an emergency table at the hospital a few minutes later the doctors said it was too late.

The news was a blow but not really a surprise.

'But you mean Goran, not Taras,' I corrected Anton. No, he said, the Reuters people had confirmed that it was definitely Taras. I felt like I had been slapped in the face. I could not believe that I had not even noticed whose life I had been trying to save. I said out loud that I was a fucking idiot but Ross and Bob scoffed at me for being distressed.

'He was dying, for God's sake. Checking his bloody ID was the last thing you needed to think about,' Ross said.

I called Michael Stutchbury in Sydney and told him what had happened. He was also totally supportive, saying he was amazed that I had been able to file at all. He pointed out that mine was the first eyewitness account published in any newspaper in the world, and said there was plenty of time to correct the story, as it was running on page one, and to pass the correction around the other News Ltd newspapers. He put me through to a copytaker and I recited some additional paragraphs which corrected Taras's identity, updated his condition by saying he had died, and explained to readers that I had mistaken him for Goran. It did not make me look brilliant but it was what happened.

Because of the late hour in Sydney I had to file these extra paragraphs 'off the top' of my head, meaning I was composing the story as I spoke. If newspaper journalism is the first draft of history then this sort of work, which goes straight from the spoken word into print, is the hastily scribbled notes of history.

I finally got a chance to go back to our room to wash my hands and forearms. As I tried to open the door my hands were shaking and I fumbled and dropped the key, then had to concentrate on getting it into the hole. I realised that this was probably normal in the circumstances but Stewart was waiting behind me to get into the room and I was embarrassed by how long it took me.

There was still no power in the bathroom so I lit another candle. Flickering in the dark and the silence it turned the bathroom into an oddly calm spot, and as I washed the blood from my hands I let myself cry.

I cupped water to my face for a while and was drying myself when Stewart called me out onto the balcony to listen to some extraordinary news on the radio. I had reported that the Iraqis must have fired on the hotel but the American military was now admitting that it had been one of their tanks.

I raced back to Bob's room and called Sydney again.

'I can't believe it but it was the Americans, not the Iraqis,' I told Stutchbury.

He already knew. The wire services were carrying the US admission and the editors had corrected my mistake.

I was gob-smacked by the US confession. I couldn't work out how their tanks could possibly have hit that side of the hotel, let alone why they would fire on the press hotel. The US explanation was that one of the tanks on the Jumhuriyah Bridge had come under fire from the hotel, so its crew had fired in self-defence.

That was simply nonsense. With reporters on the roof, in most rooms and on dozens of balconies it was hard to imagine how any sort of weapon could have been fired undetected from the hotel. Television footage from the roof showed the tank slowly turning its turret towards the hotel, lifting its cannon, then pausing for quite a while before firing straight at the camera. The soundtrack picked up no trace of any shooting from the hotel before the tank fired.

As for the angle of the shot, the tank must have struck a glancing blow on the end of the hotel. It must also have been using a shell intended to damage people rather than buildings, otherwise the crater would have been much larger.

Several hours after the Americans had admitted firing on the hotel the BBC's Andrew Gilligan gave a live radio interview saying he had made his own inspection of the damage and still thought it virtually impossible for the US tank to have fired on the Reuters room.

'I have to say I rather doubt it and, having been underneath it and looking up now just before it got dark at the hole again in the side of the hotel, I still doubt it,' he said.

'For a start the damage to the hotel is superficial, it's only the masonry that's been torn off in a very small area. A tank shell would have done more damage, I feel. Secondly the angle that the tank would have to have reached to hit that roof, it would more or less have had to have shot just round the corner and I don't think even the Americans have got those kinds of weapons.'

Gilligan's rather implausible theory was that there may have been simultaneous strikes on the hotel – that while the US tank had obviously fired on the hotel the deaths of the newsmen 'might have been the responsibility of someone else, maybe some Saddam Fedayeen with a rocket-propelled grenade, who did not like the fact the Reuters guy was shooting footage from his balcony at the time of the attack'.

I do not believe there was a second attack, but Gilligan's report shows the confusion swirling around the whole incident.

At about 3.30 p.m. I was with a group of reporters in the lobby trying to make sense of the US admission when Bob introduced me to Stephen Farrell of *The Times*, one of several reporters who had managed to get into Baghdad from Jordan over the past day or so. Like most reporters staying next door in the Sheraton he had not known about the attack at the time and was now interviewing witnesses for details. I told him what I had seen, then Farrell said he had been looking for me anyway. His foreign news editor, Martin Fletcher, had told him to keep an eye out for me. Martin was a good friend with whom I had shared an office when we were both Washington correspondents.

The Information Ministry's rules seemed more trivial by the hour so I went with Farrell across to his room in the Sheraton. The Sheraton rooms were luxurious compared to our dingy little cells in the Palestine, with lots of space, clean bathrooms, a reasonable electricity supply, plenty of light and sweeping river views.

Farrell called Martin and mentioned that I had given him firsthand details of the attack on the Palestine. Martin had been chasing me to check on my welfare but now he also wanted me to write a piece for *The Times* about the attack. From Bob's room I e-mailed *The Times* a reworked version of *The Australian*'s story.

John and I then found Goran in his room. Taras's friend blinked back tears as we tried to express our sympathy.

Samia underwent successful brain surgery in Baghdad and Pasquale survived his injuries, although he spent three days stuck in a Baghdad hospital ward full of flies and short of medical supplies before he could be evacuated.

That evening the lobby was almost empty of Iraqi minders. Peter Arnett asked me to come to his room to record another interview. My sisters in Melbourne had been pestering 3AW for news about us and, knowing just how persistent they can be, I can only sympathise with the radio station for giving in and asking Arnett for an update on us.

It was only now, when Arnett gave me the details, that I learned about the attacks on the Al-Jazeera and Abu Dhabi offices, which meant that within six hours the Americans had hit every foreign media building in Baghdad. Even if they had not been deliberately gunning for the Al-Jazeera office there was clearly a major problem with their targeting practices.

More and more reports were coming in of civilian cars being hit by US tanks. During my interview with Arnett I was careful to try to keep the day's killing of journalists in the context of what was happening all around Baghdad. The foreign press, I said, had suffered a small taste of what many Iraqi civilians had been going through, and members of the press corps had at least had a choice about whether to come to Baghdad.

Arnett's room was well stocked with all sorts of supplies, and he insisted that I take a bottle of gin and more whisky. I don't drink spirits but I knew this would make me popular back in our room. With the war having arrived in central Baghdad this was no time for getting drunk but our nerves were more strained than ever. We had gone from reporters to prisoners, back to being reporters again and now it seemed that we were targets.

One consequence of the war coming to our doorstep was that tempers were snapping in the café, in the corridors and in many rooms. Even Bob and Stuart, who had worked together in plenty of

*Top: Liberation Day. Mohanned al-Jouan is loaded onto
a truck by Marines who found him bleeding to death
in a gutter after being robbed. John witnessed this scene
on 9 April, as the Americans arrived and we later came
across Al-Jouan in a hospital besieged by looters.*

*Bottom: The sun sets on Saddam. All that was left of the
air force headquarters in central Baghdad.* John Feder

dangerous situations, seemed to be getting on each other's nerves. Reporters were so spooked by the attack on the hotel that quite a few defied the minders by draping their balconies with white sheets or sheets marked with black tape spelling out the letters 'TV'. Dozens even spent the night on the lawn outside the hotel for fear of another attack. Sleeping in the open air seemed a rather futile strategy for self-defence, so we stayed in our beds – struggling to sleep and more desperate than ever to get our equipment back.

*

The next day, Wednesday 9 April, John returned from an early sortie to the lobby to say that our minder, Abu Mohammed, had promised we would be able to work from lunchtime. Most reporters expected the Americans to arrive in a few hours anyway. That would mean Taras, who had told us we were all safe in this hotel, had died just a day before it was liberated.

The sounds of battle were now less intense, and regime officials were tacitly conceding that Saddam's rule was over. The lobby was starting to look like a normal hotel, with no minders lingering at all. That suggested that the power balance between us and the hotel management might also be changing.

Until now we had been shrugged off whenever we wanted the power fixed or our sheets laundered. Now we marched downstairs and demanded that if the power to our room could not be restored we had to be put in another room. The man at reception smugly insisted that no rooms were available but when we protested to the duty manager he told the receptionist to give us what we wanted.

Our new room was on the other side of the hotel, with a view north along the Tigris towards the centre of the city. It had water, clean sheets and towels, and even electricity for a bedside light.

The previous day Stewart had found an entire floor of the hotel that was under renovation and had stolen a powerboard and a long extension lead. Today he managed to find a young hotel electrician and slipped him US$20 to come to our room. He told the electrician that we had a powerboard we wanted connected to the wires feeding the bedside lamp. The electrician agreed to do the work but was astonished when he looked at 'our' powerboard.

'This powerboard is not unfamiliar to me,' he said diplomatically, before going ahead anyway and connecting up the powerboard we had stolen from him. Things were looking up. We could now run the fridge, some lights and any work equipment we managed to liberate. I gave the electrician another $40 to perform similar miracles for Steve Martin and Bob and Stuart.

Our big worry now was our equipment. We had to get it back before it and the car disappeared. I wrote a story saying that while the regime had not yet fallen and more lives would no doubt be lost the mood within the hotel had changed as the minders disappeared.

While I was using Steve's phone to dictate that story, Stewart and John were debating whether to break into room 511 to reclaim our gear. They had already been staking out the room, taking turns to keep an eye on it to make sure nobody tried to leave with our cameras, phones and computers. Having initially had an Information Ministry guard staking out our room, we were now returning the favour.

As noon approached, John lost patience. He and Stewart almost dragged one of the hotel managers to 511 and demanded that he open the door. The manager knew it would be unwise to back the old regime but felt he could not open the door without government permission. John took matters into his own hands, breaking the door open while the manager watched. They found all of our equipment except my Thuraya satellite phone. Even the car keys were still there. John was reborn. He raced up to the room and plugged his camera batteries into chargers, then began rigging up the antenna for his satellite phone.

Celebrations were breaking out in some areas of the city, such as Saddam City, a large slum dominated by Shi'ite Muslims. The Shia outnumber Sunni Muslims by more than three to one in Iraq but had been oppressed since long before Saddam designed his regime to favour the Sunnis. Those religious tensions and the claims of the Kurds and smaller ethnic and religious groups had raised fears that the regime's collapse might spark a Balkans-style explosion of violent score-settling. There were also the first signs of looting in the centre of the city.

The foreign reporters had real fears that mobs of hard-line Saddam supporters, or even Saddam opponents blaming the West for having left him in power for so long, might get to the Palestine before the Americans did. By early afternoon it was clear that the Americans were not far away but news crews who ventured into the surrounding streets were returning with tales of a precarious city menaced by snipers, roadblocks and roaming gangs.

I walked out to the front driveway of the hotel and found two Portuguese journalists and a Bulgarian television reporter who had just been beaten and robbed by looters. One of the reporters, Fino Carlos of the public broadcaster Radio Televisao Portuguesa, was still shaking as he explained that they had driven just a few blocks from the hotel before coming across a roadblock of about twenty people armed with semi-automatic rifles and even an anti-tank gun. Someone had shot at their tyres, then they were dragged from their car and surrounded. They were punched and hit with rifle butts as the mob stole their equipment.

'We pleaded with them, saying we were not Americans but they hit us and took everything – our cameras, passports, $25,000 in cash, even my watch and glasses,' he said. 'We were almost lynched. It was very scary and they were getting more violent but then we were saved by some Ba'ath Party people who drove up and told them to behave.'

Stewart was keen for us to take the Pajero out to try to meet the advancing Americans but after the Portuguese team's experience I thought it was too dangerous. None of us had driven in Baghdad or knew our way around at all, and apart from the dangers posed by Saddam loyalists and rampaging anti-Saddamists there was every chance that the Americans would blow away any vehicle they came across.

Bob Graham was standing in the lobby of the hotel telling Stuart Clarke, John and me that we were 'stupid boys' for wanting to go out into the streets. There was a more than reasonable argument for staying put. John and I had always been determined to stay together so that our words and photos matched but in these extraordinary conditions it seemed safer and smarter to split up if necessary to get lifts with other crews who knew their way around the streets.

I saw the BBC's Rageh Omaar and Duncan Stone through the crowd and asked them if they were going out. They said they would be and invited me to go in their van.

155

Stuart had already organised to go out with a crew from Britain's Channel Four News and now he asked them whether John could come along. Cameraman Tim Lambon, a former member of the Rhodesian military, apologised, saying there was not enough space. John was secretly relieved – he did not want to leave the hotel at all – but as he turned to walk back inside Tim felt sorry for him and changed his mind, saying they would squeeze him in.

I walked to the road at the front of the Palestine with the BBC crew to wait for their van. Danahar, their bureau chief, was sticking large 'BBC' stickers on his crew's vests as a rather optimistic safety measure. In what I took to be a gesture of reconciliation after his behaviour two nights earlier he paused then put one of the stickers on my vest.

As we waited for the van, Rageh told me again about the pre-monition he had mentioned earlier of dying in the war's last moments. He was extremely nervous, and just before the vehicle arrived he decided to wait at the hotel for a while longer, asking the van to come back in half an hour or so. The rest of the BBC crew headed out onto the street anyway, promising to return soon. That allowed me to race back and be interviewed by ABC TV in a tele-phone call from Sydney before Rageh and I were picked up by the BBC van.

We cruised slowly south out of Firdos Square towards the advancing Americans, with Duncan hanging out the window filming. Thin crowds lined the street to welcome the Americans. We stopped once or twice, and I had time to jump out and interview a few young Iraqis, who said in halting English that they were delighted to see the Saddam regime fall.

A kilometre or so from the hotel we saw a column of tanks growling towards us, crunching and tearing the road under their tracks. The crowd was cheering and the Americans were enjoying the moment, although soldiers with automatic weapons stood on the back of most of their vehicles scanning the apartment buildings on either side for snipers.

We turned and drove back beside the leading tanks, which had names like 'Dirty Dozen,' 'Carnivore' and 'Death Angel' stencilled on their gun barrels. It was only when they entered the square and parked between the press hotels and the Saddam statue that it became clear that their arrival here would indeed come to symbolise the fall of Saddam's regime.

The first officer to climb down from the tanks was Major Matt Baker of California, the executive officer or second-in-command of the 3/4th Battalion of the US Marines 1st Division. He said the past few hours had seen an end to serious resistance from the Iraqi Army in the capital.

'I think they reached the point today where everybody ran. Up to this morning we had resistance but I think this morning was the turning point,' he told a few of us clustering around him. 'But it's not over – I think there are probably still some pockets in Baghdad and others have fled north. This is a dangerous time because we are doing military action, not police action. Marines are not trained to protect civilians.'

None of us knew quite how right Baker would soon prove to be. From that day the US military's lack of preparation to police the nation – and to some extent its unwillingness – would plague the occupation of Iraq.

As Baker continued to answer questions we got a taste of another theme that would recur in the days ahead. Several foreign peace activists, or 'human shields', had been abusing the Marines from the centre of the square but now an Englishwoman, Uzma Bashir, strode up to interrupt the Major's interview.

'You are a murderer, and Tony Blair is a murderer. You have killed innocent people,' she screamed at Baker.

He turned to face her and said that it was 'very unfortunate that there have been some civilian casualties', then decided he was better off not engaging her in a conversation.

When he strode away Bashir told me she was a 33-year-old university lecturer in social affairs from Hertfordshire in England and she was disgusted that her government had backed the invasion.

'Blair and Bush are dictators. My country is against this war,' she fumed.

John returned excited from his trip in the Channel Four van and ran off to send his photos. I also needed to file pretty quickly. John had already spent some time getting the satellite dish set up but now he was furious to discover that the Iraqis had apparently tried to tamper with his laptop, triggering a security system which required the entry of a new security code.

While John sat at the laptop in our room I set myself up in Steve Martin's room, with one ear stuck to an internal hotel phone to John, and the other jammed against Steve's mobile phone, talking to the help desk in Sydney.

With deadlines ticking closer we went through a sweaty, nervous ordeal for twenty minutes, with the tech guy reading out long series of letters and numbers and me relaying them to John, who responded time and again that they were not unlocking the laptop. Just when we were close to giving up, we realised that one letter was being left out of the codes – suddenly the laptop worked.

Now John discovered that the angle our balcony was facing prevented him from tuning the satellite dish to the appropriate satellite. The biggest story in the world was reaching its climax outside and because we had only just been reunited with our equipment we were having to rush through the technical preparations that others had done at their leisure weeks before.

The satellite problem left us still dependent on Steve Martin's phone. John downloaded his photos into his laptop and rushed it to Steve's room, where we had a frantic hour with John preparing and sending photos and me jumping on the phone when he was not using it so I could file the news and colour stories that would end up on the front page of *The Australian*. We were lucky that Steve did not have a daily deadline but Anton Antonowicz was also using Steve's small room. We were all tired and working frantically, stepping over cables and each other to take turns at the phone. *The Australian*'s news desk had asked for a pile of photos from John for special late night editions and even an 8 a.m. edition that they and some other papers were considering, and he was flat out preparing and sending those photos.

It was hot and noisy but tempers held. Until, that is, we realised the Americans were getting ready to pull down the statue in front of the hotel. The statue that had been standing outside our window all this time was about to become the ultimate symbol of Saddam's fall. The problem was that John had left his cameras in our room and Stewart had disappeared with the key. Having to share a room and a single key between the three of us had long been a pain but now it was a genuine crisis.

John ran off to check our room and came back to say that Stewart was not there. When I had finished filing my story and John was sending his last photos I went and banged on our door again before running out into the square to see if I could find Stewart.

Many reporters do not really care about photos but I was desperate to help John get this photo. Our newspapers would no doubt be able to take a similar image from the wire agencies, which all had cameras down in the square, but if this was going to be the iconic image of Saddam's fall then we wanted that image to be in his camera. He was the only Australian newspaper photographer to have been in Baghdad at any stage of the war and as far as we knew the only one from any country to have moved around the south as a 'unilateral' photographer and then taken photos during the climax in Baghdad, so he certainly deserved to get this historic image. I also felt an enormous debt to him. Everything we had been through so far had been as a team, not just in helping each other with story and photo ideas but in sharing risks and decisions every day.

Down in the square a few hundred reporters, soldiers and Iraqi men who seemed to have come from a neighbouring working-class

suburb stood around as a US military engineering vehicle was backed up to the statue to drape chains around it. The whole thing was a media stunt, as Fordos Square had no strategic significance beyond the presence of the press hotels, but the conquest of Baghdad had reached the point where it was ripe for a symbolic climax.

I hoped that Stewart was interviewing people in the crowd, but feared that he might be just watching a sight that would obviously be remembered for decades. Either way, I figured he would probably be in the square. I pushed through the crowd for ten minutes, then ran sweating back inside. There was still no sign of him and John was furious. We were minutes away from the climax of Saddam's fall and a room key was about to stop John getting the photo.

I tore back into the square and was screaming Stewart's name in the crowd when the statue came down. Two dozen or so Iraqi men jumped on top of it and slapped it with their shoes, chanting 'Crush Saddam underfoot' in Arabic.

A band of those men, in worker's singlets and loose shirts, dragged the statue's head up and down the road, yelling, in Arabic, 'Shame on you, Saddam' and 'Curse Saddam's father'. But Firdos Square and the surrounding streets were certainly not packed with jubilant masses. The crowd in the square was not as big as it appeared in most of the television footage, which tended to show closely framed shots of the men around the base of the statue rather than broader views of the whole square. Even after spending the next few hours talking to Iraqis in the square it was hard to draw any conclusions about why there was not a larger crowd.

Some opponents of the invasion have argued that it showed there was little public enthusiasm in Baghdad for the foreign overthrow of Saddam. The public restraint may indeed have reflected reservations about the new American occupiers and a reluctance to show open support for the invaders for fear that Saddam's regime might somehow survive, as it did after the last Gulf War. But it may also have been because most people in Baghdad had no idea that this 'historic' moment was about to happen and because they were still wary about travelling far from home with looting breaking out around the city. My guess is that it was a combination of all those factors, especially the knowledge that Saddam supporters were still all over the city.

Dozens of US Marines from the 3/4 Battalion, who had fought

their way up through Nasiriyah, stayed in the square savouring this moment of triumph into the evening. Iraqi men of all ages kissed the dusty young soldiers – they had been on the road for twenty-one days without a shower – and placed flowers in their helmets and buttonholes.

Half a dozen men paraded around with a portrait of Saddam upside-down, then theatrically smashed it on the ground. By dusk US officers and their translators were trying to take advantage of the goodwill in the square by asking locals where any Fedayeen were hiding. I heard one translator, Abdul Hassam Mohammed, a volunteer who had been in Coalition uniform for three weeks after being trained in Hungary, interpreting for an elderly Iraqi man who repeated one point at least five times to a Marine captain.

'You say you came here to give us freedom – there is something more important than that: protect us, protect the people,' he said.

Twenty-eight year old Lieutenant Kealoha Stokes, a good-looking surfer from California, barked the occasional order at his men and plainly found it hard to relax in the middle of this celebration. He told me that before his platoon reached Baghdad one Marine, seconded to it from another unit, had been killed and three others were wounded but in the capital itself 'the resistance was not what we expected'.

'We were told it would be real do-or-die stuff but the big, tough Republican Guard that everyone kept talking about just never showed up.'

Stewart found me in the square in the fading light. He had been asleep in the room throughout the excitement. An interior door must have blown shut, muffling the sound of us banging on the door. He had already found John and knew that he was mightily pissed off. To his credit John did not push the point and tried to hide his disappointment over the next couple of days as the falling statue took on iconic status. I knew he was upset and this lost photo remains his biggest single regret about his work in Iraq.

Later in the evening a few human shields stood outside the Palestine holding a placard reading 'Go home, you US wankers', but the Iraqis in the square were still jubilant, often chanting 'USA, USA'. A small crowd almost set fire to the hotel while burning a Saddam portrait which had for years been attached to the front of the building. Hundreds of statues and portraits of Saddam were at that moment meeting a similar fate across Baghdad.

*

That night the British reporters who had helped us so much during our captivity decided to gather in our room to celebrate the fall of Saddam and our own liberation. They arrived with their last stocks of alcohol and wearing their cleanest clothes – Ross was immaculate in his blazer – to discover with a bit of a shock that the three of us were wearing nothing except our tummy-to-knee white bloomers. We were also working away in the middle of the party – John and Stewart had finally got the right angle for the satellite antenna by balancing it on planks of wood sticking out from the balcony, and we had another round of deadlines to meet for a special 8 a.m. edition. But we had amassed a decent supply of grog by now and nothing stopped the party around us, not even the fact that we were still defying Australians' reputations as beer connoisseurs by serving that horrible 'Bavarian' beer.

When the work was finished we briefly interrupted the laughter and boozing to formally thank our new friends for their help during our house arrest and to announce that we would no longer be tying up their phones as we were back in business with our own gear.

They took turns expressing their amusement at having watched us beaver away in defiance of the orders of our Iraqi minders over the past week. It actually felt as if we had been in the hotel forever and had known these journalists for years.

Taras's death, and those of the other two journalists on the last full day of Saddam's rule meant the mood at our little party was mainly one of relief at having survived and gotten the job done rather than one of great triumph.

Anton did manage to sing a few lines of war bravado that I later discovered were from the Gilbert and Sullivan opera *Princess Ida*.

> Oh, I love the jolly rattle of an ordeal by battle, There's an end of tittle-tattle when your enemy is dead. Tis an arrant mollycoddle fears a crack upon his noddle, And he's only fit to coddle in a downy feather bed.

At the time Anton couldn't remember where this ditty came from but that did not stop him singing it again and again ... and again.

Steve told me in a quieter moment that he was slightly worried that Salah had not been to work for three days but he was still not too concerned. Ross Benson's driver and another driver had been dispatched to try to find Salah's house but had not yet tracked him down.

From our balcony well after midnight we could hear machine-gun fire continuing, as one bridge on the Tigris was still being contested. To our surprise we could also see fires burning in the first buildings set alight by looters and vandals.

7

BAGHDAD GETS 'UNTIDY'

The pillage of Baghdad was remarkable. On its first full day in twenty-four years without Saddam Hussein's regime, Thursday 10 April 2003, the city's streets were taken over by cheering looters, cars and donkey-drawn carts piled high with goods taken from burning buildings, as American soldiers uneasily surveyed their own handiwork in the shattered city.

Perhaps the most horrible sight of all was in the middle of the Sinak Bridge, one of the main crossings of the Tigris River in the centre of the city. The charred body of a man was sitting in the driver's seat of a burned-out minibus on the bridge. He had literally been burned to a crisp, carbonised like a blackened anatomical model but was still sitting up at the driver's wheel. Half of his left forearm had crumbled off but what remained of that arm was still cocked out the window in the familiar relaxed driving pose, with the skin and outer flesh burned off and its sinews exposed.

Next to the minibus was the wreck of a jeep containing two more bodies. One was in the back seat while the other lay face down across the front seat, its upper torso still clad in an Iraqi military uniform. The top of the body looked relatively normal but the bottom half had simply been blown away.

We had driven onto the bridge in mid-morning, feeling exposed as we left the riverside buildings behind us. We motored slowly towards several US tanks sitting on the other side of the bridge with their cannons pointed at us. Coils of barbed wire eventually blocked the road, and about thirty Iraqis were lined up along the wire looking at the grisly sight just beyond it. We parked and picked our way through a gap in the barbed wire to the two shattered vehicles, which were two hundred metres short of the Abrams tanks.

A Marine sergeant said later that the vehicles had driven straight at the tanks, which blasted them apart from a safe distance.

'In the end they were attacking us with suicide tactics or suicidal tactics,' he said. 'By suicidal tactics, I mean going right up head-to-head against us with equipment that had no chance of beating us. Most of them just ran away but some, like those guys, really were prepared to die,' the sergeant said before repeating a comment I had heard the day before. 'Frankly we were surprised that the resistance wasn't a lot tougher. We were told to expect real do-or-die stuff in Baghdad, but it was mainly die, not do.'

John began moving around trying to photograph this distressing sight in a way that would be publishable in an Australian newspaper. Al-Jazeera and other Middle Eastern television networks and newspapers were used to showing graphic images of the results of conflict but the media in Australia and other Western nations still tend to shy away from the real faces of death and war. Our readers, or at least our most vocal readers, seem to prefer being shielded from that sort of reality. When I rushed to Holland to cover the assassination of Dutch right-wing leader Pim Fortuyn in 2002, *The Australian* accompanied my description of his murder with a photograph of the tall, elegant academic lying dead in a car park, a bloodied bandage wrapped around his head. The paper was flooded with complaints, forcing the editor to defend himself in a day-long round of radio interviews.

As John circled the vehicles looking for an angle that might capture the situation without prompting similar complaints, two American newspaper photographers, a man and a woman, walked around the same wrecks waiting for the clouds to shift overhead.

'The light is shit now,' the man explained to us. It was not really a time for small talk.

A figure then walked towards us from the tanks. It was an American journalist embedded with the tank unit, who had been asked by the troops to check out what we were doing. As he got closer he recognised the American photographers and when he reached us he had a friendly chat with them. He then stepped close to the burned corpse in the minibus and posed beside it for a souvenir shot, asking the woman photographer to take his photo. As she raised her camera he pretended to interview the corpse.

'Well sir, do you have any comment about what has happened to you here?' he asked, pen poised over notebook as he supposedly waited for a reply.

I was amazed. This display of ghoulish humour, and the stripping of any human dignity from the corpse, was happening in broad daylight in front of us and just twenty metres from the Iraqis watching behind the barbed wire. I stepped up close behind the reporter to read the *Los Angeles Times* business card on the back of his vest. His name was Geoffrey Mohan.

As we walked away John and Stewart looked as horrified as I felt. I regretted not having challenged the guy but I was determined to report about it. The thing that I could not fathom was what he planned to do with such a souvenir photo. Show it to his wife? His family? His buddies in the office?

I mentioned this tacky souvenir photo in a news report that day as evidence that soldiers were not the only people who could be desensitised by war. When I told a few other reporters about the incident Bob Graham was outraged, and he recounted it to an American friend, Craig Nelson of the *Atlanta Constitution and Journal*.

Nelson interviewed me in my room that night, when John and Stewart sat with me to confirm my account and check details on John's photographs.

Nelson tracked down Mohan for a telephone interview and found that he had travelled in a Bradley Fighting Vehicle from the Kuwait border as an embedded reporter with the 2nd Brigade of the Army's 3rd Infantry Division. In the interview Mohan denied that any Iraqis could have seen what he did, a claim that was easily answered – John had photos showing a line of Iraqis watching the shattered vehicles from behind the barbed wire.

In a report published in his own newspaper and several others owned by the Cox company in the US, Nelson said the *LA Times* reporter eventually conceded that his behaviour had been an 'ill-conceived, clumsy, and ill-considered attempt at gallows humor'.

But Mohan also described our interest in the incident as part of an 'agenda against embedded reporters', implying that unilateral reporters were distorting the incident because we believed that 'embeds' were empathising too uncritically with their hosts.

This demarcation had not really occurred to me. I had simply seen his behaviour as an example of how exposure to war could affect reporters as well as soldiers but now that he had raised the issue of embedding it did seem that living and travelling with one army might indeed make a reporter more contemptuous of the other army, and more likely to mock the dead of 'the other'. Nelson told us that in the end Mohan had argued that his actions had to be seen in the context of what he had been through in the war. He had seen horrible things – at one point he was apparently forced to shelter for a lengthy period near the body of a dead Iraqi woman – and he believed those experiences had eventually influenced his behaviour. Which was pretty much the point I had been making.

*

We had driven onto the Sinak Bridge in our own Pajero. Our attempts to flatten its battery and tyres had thankfully failed but we were careful not to go far on our own until we got our bearings. The answer was to hire one of the drivers hanging around the front door of the hotel.

Now that we finally wanted to identify ourselves to Coalition forces Stewart wrote 'TV' on the sides and bonnet of the car in black tape, then we headed cautiously into the centre of town. Shops were boarded up and the upper floors of many buildings had been shattered by missiles. Every few hundred metres we would pass a family car, utility truck or even a horse-pulled cart piled high with stolen office equipment. Plumes of smoke on the skyline showed that at least half a dozen buildings were on fire, and as we drove along we could see that the looting was mainly confined to government buildings.

Gunfire and explosions still rang out along the streets and we had been warned that Iraqi snipers were at work north and west of the hotel, so we wore our flak jackets and occasionally, while driving, even put on our helmets.

One carload of thieves carrying tyres out of a privately owned store had copied the foreign media by taping the letters 'TV' to the side and roof of their car to deter US military attacks. We had seen several family cars doing that in southern Iraq but it was more disturbing to see armed criminals impersonate the press.

After about two kilometres we pulled up on the edge of a central square outside an Immigration Ministry building that was being stripped bare by thieves. Smoke was pouring from upper windows and sixty-odd men were carrying out chairs, filing cabinets and other office fittings to cars, trucks and carts parked around the front doors. One man was casually walking around with a semi-automatic weapon, and another Kalashnikov could be seen lying on the back of a horse-pulled cart, so we were determined to act as if their theft was nothing out of the ordinary.

As we stood on the footpath and in the lobby of the immigration building the type of items being carried past us changed. The obvious items to steal – chairs, computers and fire extinguishers – eventually ran out so attention turned to less obvious loot. Men walked out toting carpets, blinds, light fittings and even ceiling fans and electrical wiring. Many smiled or laughed as if this was all a big party, and when they saw a foreigner watching most would smile and give a thumbs up or say something like 'Ameriki!' or 'Bush Good!'

It all seemed oddly familiar to me. I was in Los Angeles during the April 1992 riots after the acquittal of four white policemen for assaulting the black motorist Rodney King, and the feeling in the Iraqi capital eleven years later was not too different. In both cities the collapse of law and order led to a wave of opportunistic pillage by people who felt they had no great investment in the ruling order.

In LA it was black crowds who laughed and whooped as they ran out of the smashed front windows of small stores with anything they could carry. In Baghdad the looters were scruffy and mainly young to middle-aged men, although there were some family groups. They had obviously come from the city's poorer suburbs, and no doubt included many of the thousands of criminals whom Saddam had released from jail in the lead-up to the war. In both cities the larger crowds had a carnival-like sense of excitement about what they could suddenly get away with, but smaller, hard-core gangs occasionally showed real savagery.

In LA it was random attacks by black gangs on whites. In Baghdad it was revenge killings of Ba'ath Party figures and the occasional murder of people who tried to stop the looting.

The LA Police Department lost control of its city because of the breadth of the race riots over the Rodney King verdict. Baghdad's

Lawless. A mob uses a semi trailer to ram the doors of a bank on Al-Sadoon Street.
John Feder

police and security forces simply disappeared, leaving control to American soldiers and Marines who did not consider policing part of their job.

Driving along Al-Sadoon Street, the major boulevard which ran past our hotel, we saw vivid evidence of the US military's attitude just before noon as some of the looters tired of stealing desks and light fittings. Just two hundred metres short of a US roadblock we passed about twenty men trying to rob the Rafidain Bank. They had smashed the front windows only to be thwarted by bars so one young man was climbing up to the second floor while his colleagues were being more direct. They were calmly guiding a Mercedes-Benz semi-trailer up onto the footpath to ram open the bank's front doors.

We stopped across the road so John could take photographs of this audacious robbery but several of the thieves made angry gestures and started to come towards us. We drove quickly up to the roadblock where I pointed out to two young Marines what was happening right in front of them. One simply shook his head in amazement, while his colleague said: 'Wow!'

'Are you going to do anything about it?' I asked.

'No, our orders are to stop and search any suspicious vehicles,' he said.

US Defence Secretary Donald Rumsfeld angrily attacked the media for focussing on the looting and violence in Baghdad, saying that such behaviour was to be expected after years of repression. The media should stop being so negative and start concentrating on the new freedoms being enjoyed by Iraqis, he said.

'It's untidy – and freedom's untidy – but free people are free to make mistakes and commit crimes and do bad things,' Rumsfeld said. 'Here's a country that's being liberated, here are a people who are going from being repressed and held under the thumb of a vicious dictator, and they're free.'

Yes, it certainly was untidy on the streets. For most Iraqis the first flush of liberty had so far translated into a 'freedom' from any semblance of law and order, as the Coalition's refusal to fill the policing vacuum emboldened the looters, dubbed 'Ali Babas' by Iraqis.

In the middle-class suburb of Sahat Beirut, a few kilometres east of the Tigris, we found anxious-looking groups of well-to-do men standing in clusters every few blocks in the suburb's back streets, which were tidy and lined with large houses.

They were generally members of the Sunni Muslim minority who had done well under the old regime, and they were worried that oppressed and resentful Shias might now threaten their homes. Hussein Khalaf, a 33-year-old criminal law judge standing outside his family home in Palestine Street, was furious. The Americans, he said, had promised to maintain order but had simply washed their hands 'of the crime-wave they have created'.

'I complained to one soldier this morning and he said "I am not a policeman, I am a soldier",' he told us. 'Well, all the real policemen have run away or are too afraid to be on the streets, so who will protect us? We are upset by all this looting of public property. Is the United Nations going to replace this property?'

'At least Saddam gave us electricity, water and food,' he said, echoing the complaints we had heard in southern Iraq about the disruption caused by the invasion. 'How can the Americans say they are interested in the people when they leave us like this? I have seen them with my own eyes shooting civilians, and we just don't trust them.'

Asked where he had seen civilians being shot, he claimed to have seen a US tank positioned in the middle of a road in an outer suburb shooting passenger vehicles which had simply been carrying water and food. Khalaf confirmed that he supported the old regime.

'I am a judge and the law has now broken down. Under the [Saddam] Government people who followed the law were alright – so no, I'm not happy to see Saddam go.'

He complained, like many Iraqis we interviewed, that Washington's favourite exiled opposition leader, Ahmed Chalabi, the head of the US-funded Iraqi National Congress, had been convicted of bank fraud by the Jordanian Government and had little support among Iraqis.

Standing beside him, Khalaf's elderly mother-in-law, Aliya Hussein, chipped in that the US-led attack had 'scared our children, killed people and given us nothing'.

'We have little water, no television to tell us what is happening and no telephones to find out what has happened to our family. Is it right that a lady of my age [about 80] should have this happen to her?'

A neighbour listening to our conversation said that earlier in the morning an ambulance had driven down the street with a loud-speaker asking if there were any doctors who had not fled because there was just one doctor on duty at the nearby hospital.

'I don't care if the regime comes or goes, I'm just worried about the children,' the neighbour said. 'And don't tell me the Americans are worried about us. They are after oil. Next they will attack Syria, Iran and anyone else they want.'

It was not hard to understand their fury about the Coalition's inadequate law enforcement, which seemed to be a clear breach of its obligation under the Geneva Convention to maintain public order in areas it had occupied. The failure to properly police the city was already being seen in many parts of Baghdad as a deliberate attempt to debilitate Iraqi society by allowing billions of dollars of destruction and a terrifying outbreak of lawlessness. The result was obviously going to plague the occupation and reconstruction efforts. If people were too afraid to leave their homes or felt constantly in danger they could hardly be expected to help run schools, hospitals and other services.

At lunchtime we drove back to the Palestine Hotel, where John filed his morning's photos then headed out with Stewart in search of petrol. I stayed in our room to write a lengthy report on day one in post-Saddam Baghdad and catch up with the radio news. The Kurds had taken Kirkuk in the north and prominent Shi'ite clerics had returned to southern Iraq from exile in Iran, where Shia dominate government and make up a clear majority of the population.

Many of these clerics had sought refuge in Iran over the years and they returned as potent players in Iraq's future with a gratitude to Tehran that left Washington distinctly uncomfortable.

After lunch we set out to see how the city's hospitals were faring. When we approached the major Kindi hospital a gunfight was underway between looters and armed defenders. The gangs had stolen drugs and sophisticated medical equipment, and staff had already been forced to evacuate patients to other hospitals.

Not far away, at the smaller Ibn al Nafis Hospital in the suburb of Sahat al Andalus, we found local residents armed with semi-automatic weapons guarding the hospital from behind a large iron gate. The only doctor on duty, Dr Fars Shaja, was bewildered by the violence.

'These people are stealing medical monitoring equipment, which has no value to them at all,' said the portly, softly spoken doctor. 'What are they thinking? They must know that taking that equipment will kill people.'

'We need security first,' he concluded. 'People can talk about democracy all they want but first we must have basic security so that everyone can think clearly.'

He took us on a stomach-turning tour of the hospital's wards, which were already filled with the stench of the dead and dying. One body had been left in a bed with a sheet crumpled over its head, and most stretchers were caked in flies and dried blood. Most support staff had been too scared to leave their homes so the medical staff were trying to cook for patients in the corridors, where puddles of bile, blood and human waste lay on the tiles.

Moans and cries echoed from ward to ward. Dazed men lay with holes in their sides or mangled limbs, usually with just a bandage or two covering their wounds and not even an intravenous drip in sight. John recognised one patient, a young man named Mohanned al-Jouan. He had seen the man's life being saved the day before by a group of Marines.

Al-Jouan and a friend had been driving in the city when they were stopped and robbed by a gang armed with assault rifles. Not satisfied with taking his car, the thieves had shot Al-Jouan in the abdomen and his friend in the neck. The Marines found them bleeding to death in the gutter.

John, who was scouting the streets in the Channel Four van, photographed the pair being loaded onto the back of a truck to be taken to hospital. Now Al-Jouan's life was again in danger from looters attacking the hospital. Gangs had been fought back twice that morning from the hospital's gates.

Dr Shaja was depressed about what that level of violence held for the future.

'This looting will end soon, God willing,' he said. 'But then what happens?'

Dr Shaja asked us to call his sister in Canada to tell her that his family was OK. We took her phone numbers and called her as soon as we got back to the Palestine just ahead of the 6 p.m. curfew, making more than a dozen similar calls for people who had begged us to let relatives know they were OK. Before long Iraqi opportunists would appear on the streets selling access to satellite phones for an extortionate US$10 – a month's salary for many Iraqis – a minute.

Back in the hotel, we found we were not the only ones to have seen a bad first day in the free Iraq. Bob Graham and Stuart Clarke were upset by what they had seen that morning in an alleyway in the northern residential area of Adhamiya. Pinned down for three hours by crossfire between a large force of Marines and a number of Fedayeen sheltering in ordinary homes, they watched as a US sniper shot dead Tariq Al-Amari, a 47-year-old father of five, while he was waving a white flag on his own balcony.

Al-Amari had taken the risk of venturing out onto his balcony to investigate the screams of a five-year-old girl who was lying wounded in an old Volkswagen outside his apartment block. Zahra Samir and her family had been fired upon by the Americans while trying to drive out of the street to escape the fighting. Zahra was left on the back seat with a head wound and her aunt, Hanna Yassin, was shot through the back and buttocks. They were bleeding forty metres from the US position as the fighters on each side stayed in their firing positions, trying to pick off anybody who broke cover.

Bob and Stuart, their translator Mohammed Fatnan and the three-man crew from Channel Four listened to the screaming until Mohammed risked his life by walking into the open, picking up the wounded girl and carrying her to the American position. He then went back and did the same for her aunt. The wounded were treated – reluctantly, according to Bob – by US medics and the young girl was sent off to be evacuated to Kuwait for treatment. Several hours later Bob and Stuart were both pale and shaking their heads in amazement at the attitude of the Americans and the bravery of Mohammed.

'I have learned a lot about myself in the last few weeks – what I believe in and what I'm capable of,' Bob said quietly. 'That was one of those learning experiences. I know for a fact that I could not possibly have done what Mohammed did – it was just sheer bloody courage.'

Stuart was showing real physical effects of his gruelling month in Baghdad. Like the rest of us he had not had an ideal diet but he is diabetic and had not been able to properly manage his insulin injections. Already lean, he had lost more than seven kilograms. There had also been a mental toll, after repeated visits to hospitals photographing disfigured children. Reporters can look away at the worst moments but photographers have to stare straight down their lenses at some of the most gruelling sights in the world.

Reporters can even stay away from the more dangerous and disturbing events – we can sit comfortably inside our hotels, interviewing people later or perhaps drawing information from the Internet to reconstruct events on the street. Camera operators have no such luxury, as the only way they can record an event is by being there at the time. As a result many photographers are even more hardened than experienced reporters but Stuart and John Feder were both unusually sensitive and compassionate men for this line of work.

Two weeks earlier Stuart had found in a corner of the Yarmouk hospital a seven-year-old girl who had been burned from head to foot. She was naked, covered in white cream and screaming in pain. As he looked through his lens at her he could only see his own daughter Grace, who was the same age.

'I broke into tears and had to go outside and sit on a kerbstone for a while to get my act together,' he told me quietly.

After I spoke to them Bob and Stuart heard – wrongly, it turned out – that Zahra, the five-year-old girl who had been wounded that day, had died. Stuart 'lost it', in his own words, and declared that he would stay only a few more days then leave Baghdad. Worried by his weight loss, Bob urged him to go home. With hundreds of other reporters and photographers now flocking into Baghdad, Stuart decided it was indeed time to go.

Few of us felt like celebrating after that first day on the 'untidy' liberated streets. After twenty-four years of Saddam, the grievances and tribal hatreds that could be unleashed across Iraq seemed to be at least as strong as the forces that destroyed Yugoslavia when dictatorship ended there.

And Iraq had no Nelson Mandela or Vaclav Havel, not even a Boris Yeltsin to step into the leadership vacuum, leaving its twenty-five million people facing a precarious journey to some sort of self-government.

Saddam had been ruthlessly efficient at stopping the emergence of alternative leaders or rival centres of power in Iraqi civil society, and the leaders of exile movements like Chalabi may have been favoured by Washington but they had little legitimacy within Iraq. Even Saddam's opponents within Iraq felt that exiles who had lived comfortably abroad for decades should not return to rule people who had suffered through the nation's sanctions, wars and dictatorship.

Oppressed ethnic and religious groups, including the Kurds in the north and the Shi'ite majority, were already setting high demands for the new Iraq, while her neighbours, from Syria and Iran to Turkey and Saudi Arabia, could easily interfere in the country's internal affairs to protect their own interests.

Washington's promise of a new Iraq introducing democracy to the Arab world was welcomed by few of Iraq's neighbours and could face external sabotage. Turkey had already demanded US action to restrain the aspirations of the Kurds. Syria, where Arab nationalists first formed the Ba'ath Party, felt directly threatened by the invasion of Iraq, and Iran's clerics were nervously considering their own status as the third member of George Bush's 'axis of evil' alongside Saddam's Iraq and North Korea. Even Washington's once-loyal allies, the Saudi royal family, were less than keen to see a viable democracy that could lead to calls for democracy within Saudi Arabia.

Iraq had important assets, like huge oil reserves and a well-educated population, to encourage some optimism about its long-term prospects. But those in the Bush administration who believed, like Deputy Defence Secretary Paul Wolfowitz, that simply removing the dictator would lead to the sprouting of democracy were being optimistic at best.

Resentment of the US and its allies had been built up among Iraqis by a decade of crippling UN sanctions and by Saddam's propaganda machine, and was now being fed by the Coalition's poor handling of the breakdown in law and order. Washington's unrelenting support for Israel in its conflict with the Palestinians was also resented across all ethnic, religious and class divides. Ordinary Iraqis kept insisting, in interviews on the streets, that the invasion was motivated by Zionist plots and US schemes to subjugate all Arabs and Muslims.

To achieve anything, the Americans would have to stay in Iraq long enough to break the grip of a Ba'ath Party which had put its stamp on generations of teachers, policemen, soldiers and bureaucrats. But just one day into the occupation the US forces were already facing demands to leave straight away, with some of the more hard-line Iranian-backed Shi'ite clerics warning that their supporters would attack American forces if they did not quickly hand power back to Iraqis.

The challenge, I thought, would be to hand power as quickly as possible to a government overseeing some sort of federation based on geographic regions rather than ethnic groups, giving the Kurds and others autonomy but neither the means nor incentive to pursue ethnic cleansing.

*

Breakfast at our hotel on Friday 11 April was like an informal news seminar. Reporters who were about to plunge out into the streets swapped tips and story ideas, safe in the knowledge that sharing their latest brainwave or piece of information with somebody from another country would not hurt any competitive edge they might have in their own markets. Several reporters said at breakfast that they had been into the presidential compound the previous day, so we decided to head there for a look.

We hired the same driver again to take us there and wait for us at the main gate to the compound holding Saddam's various palaces, an enormous arch dubbed Assassin's Gate. Under Saddam, locals had been scared even while driving past because his guards would chase down a car if they thought the driver was behaving suspiciously or disrespectfully.

Assassin's Gate would soon be heavily guarded once again because the occupation administration was planning to use the compound as its own headquarters. But today the gate was completely unattended and we strode through onto a leafy boulevard stretching more than two kilometres in front of us. On both sides of the road were manicured gardens and groves of trees set around monumental buildings, or what remained of them. There were several grand palaces for Saddam and his sons and presidential buildings used for administration and hosting state visits.

As we trudged along in the morning heat we were passed by US military vehicles but nobody seemed to pay us any attention. Spent ammunition was sprayed over the road, and every now and then a cache of live ammunition or even weapons would be sitting in a neat pile beside the road or in one of the small dug-outs where it had been stored by the Republican Guard.

More than once we came across the sickly smell of a dead body and could follow the smell to the remains of an Iraqi soldier among the trees.

Stewart said he wanted to take home an Iraqi helmet as a souvenir if he found one beside the road and I said I thought that would be bad taste.

'Well it would be if it's got a hole in it,' John said.

'Even if it hasn't got a bloody hole in it somebody probably died in the thing,' I said.

John agreed but Stewart still had his souvenir when we left.

We stopped at a parked Bradley to chat to its commander,

Sergeant Eric Wright, who said his vehicle had been the first to arrive at Saddam's main palace.

'It was pretty amazing just to go to his front door, then we actually took the palace,' he marvelled with a shake of the head. He said his three-man crew, backed by six soldiers in the back of the vehicle, had found the resistance half-hearted at best.

We wandered through the largest of the shattered palaces. Despite the bombing we could still see that the décor had been faux grandiose. Saddam had built to impress and had obviously not been restrained by either sanctions or any discernible good taste. He had been striving for Versailles but ended up with Las Vegas – enormous rows of mirrors, lashings of gold paint, huge chandeliers, and fake baroque furniture. A row of grand, gilt-edged chairs was covered in rubble and bits of broken chandeliers. Amid all the rubble there was a sense of dynastic collapse and history being made, and John took photos of Stewart and me sitting in one of the chairs.

We kept an eye out for small souvenirs but were less ambitious than some. Benjamin Johnson, a 27-year-old Fox News technician who had been embedded with US troops, was hit with criminal charges two weeks later and sacked by Fox for trying to smuggle into the US a dozen large paintings of Saddam and Uday Hussein that he took from Uday's palace. Quite a few other soldiers and reporters were caught trying to take home valuable artefacts. Five soldiers stationed in the palace complex were accused of grabbing an even better souvenir – $900,000 in US banknotes from a $600 million stash found in the palaces.

The three of us were certainly not looking to emulate the plot of the 1999 movie, *Three Kings*, about American soldiers smuggling billions of dollars of gold bullion out of Iraq after the 1991 Gulf War. The only thing I had collected in Iraq was a worthless portrait of Saddam that I had found under rubble in the Ba'ath Party office in Umm Qasr. It had been painted straight onto plywood and was broken in two when the party office was trashed. In a reception room of the palace I noticed a bookshelf lined with cheap, plastic-bound books that Stewart said were about Arab legends. They were modern colourful books of no special value so we each took one, stopping on the way out to press a few petals from Saddam's rose garden between their pages.

After another ten minutes' walk we came to the biggest and most eye-catching building in the complex, a vast thing topped by four huge busts of Saddam's head, each about eight metres high. It had deliberately been left untouched by the weeks of Coalition bombing and had already been earmarked as the headquarters of the new administration, the 'Coalition Provisional Authority'. A 400-strong army task force was occupying it, with a few dozen camped out on its front lawns and some sleeping inside, enjoying their first rest under a fixed roof in weeks.

The Marines were in control of the other side of the river, where our hotel was, but the 4/64 Battalion of the Army's 3rd Infantry Division was using the palace as its new base. Two sleepy, painfully bored sentries at the front gate eventually summoned Sergeant Robert Zlotow, an earnest twenty-four year old from Chicago, who agreed to give us a tour.

Having passed through plenty of poor villages on their march through southern Iraq the Americans were keen to expose the lavish spending on Saddam's palaces, so Zlotow marched us down enormous, ornate corridors into a series of ballrooms.

'Was it "Oil for Food", or "Oil for Chandeliers"?' he asked over his shoulder in an obviously well-rehearsed joke about the UN's administration of Iraqi oil sales during its decade of sanctions.

The three-metre high ceremonial front doors of the palace were inlaid with gold, and there were literally kilometres of corridors lined with marble and parquetry floors. Room after room had soaring ceilings, five-metre high mirrors and gold-painted bathroom fittings.

The palace was almost brand new, and most of the rooms seemed not to have been used. Sergeant Zlotow lost his way once or twice as he led us up and down stairs and corridors. 'It's very easy to get lost,' he said. 'Some of our men have already found that you don't want to go walking or looking for the bathroom at night without a flashlight or you could be gone a very long time.'

Part of the problem with navigation was the lack of electricity for lights. 'The place is so big that we have not even been able to find the generators yet,' Sergeant Zlotow said.

In front of the palace was a fountain almost the size of an Olympic swimming pool. Out the back we found another pool and a double diving board, set among hectares of gardens crammed with fruit trees, palms and rose bushes. A dozen soldiers poked around in the pool house, where specialist Randy Wilkinson of Florida inspected part of Saddam's personal gun collection, including a hunting rifle presented to him by the Iraqi Army in 1975 when he was vice-president.

Similar trophies were being found all across Iraq and some US soldiers succumbed to temptation. A week later one would be arrested for trying to ship an AK-47, a rifle and a pistol – all gold-plated – to a US military base via Heathrow Airport.

I had been surprised while covering previous US military operations in Haiti and elsewhere by the willingness of American soldiers to express their personal views about the operations they had been sent on, a striking contrast to most Australian soldiers' reluctance to say almost anything for fear of punishment. This American openness has a simple logic – when US soldiers are asked to fight and die for their country's values, high among those values are their own democratic rights and free speech.

Most of the soldiers in Iraq – both American and Australian – behaved as I had expected in this regard. While the Australians were generally scared to talk on the record, five minutes with an American would almost always yield some pretty strong opinions. Standing by the pool, Sergeant Darren Swain of Talladega, Alabama, told me he was not happy to be fighting for Iraq.

'We swore to defend our country from its enemies, foreign and domestic, but that is not what we are doing here. I don't want American soldiers dying for the whole world,' he said bitterly.

While Captain Stefan McFarland fooled around on Saddam's diving board, other soldiers showed us the Iraqi military insignia and emblems they had souvenired. But our most important exchange of the day came when Zlotow led us to a second-floor room in the palace which had been converted into the battalion's command room.

The commanding officer, Lieutenant-Colonel Phillip DeCamp, was hunched over a map when we entered but he swivelled in his chair, chewing a cigar, to exchange pleasantries. I took the chance to ask whether his unit had been involved in the attack on the Palestine Hotel and he nodded emphatically, saying it had been the work of 'my boys'.

'What was that about?' I asked, with a mystified look.

'Well, there's a few things you have got to realise,' he said, leaning back in a pugnacious picture of confidence. 'It was dark, very dark ... there was poor visibility.'

I had looked at my watch seconds after impact, and the attack had happened at precisely noon on a clear day. I kept my mouth shut so he would keep talking.

'Second, they were coming under heavy RPG [rocket-propelled grenade] fire and the crew thought they could make out a spotter on that building.'

This was an important departure from the official explanation, which was that the tank was actually being fired on from the hotel. General Buford Blount, commander of the 3rd Infantry Division, had issued a statement that 'the tank was receiving fire from the hotel, RPG and small-arms fire, and engaged with one tank round. The firing stopped.'

A statement from US Central Command backed up that claim, insisting that 'significant enemy fire' had been coming from both the Palestine Hotel and the Al-Jazeera building earlier that morning, and that in both cases the US forces had 'returned fire ... consistent with their inherent right of self-defence'.

'These tragic incidents appear to be the latest example of the Iraqi regime's continued strategy of using civilian facilities for regime military purposes,' CentCom said.

That was simply implausible. The effective range of an RPG is three hundred metres for moving targets and five hundred metres for stationary targets. The Palestine Hotel was 1.7 kilometres from the tank that fired on it, a distance that would also render any sniper fire ineffective against the tanks. And journalists watching from dozens of balconies had heard no firing at any stage from the hotel.

But now the explanation had changed, in this version I was getting from Lieutenant-Colonel DeCamp. The tank crew had not believed that the hotel was being used as a base for firing but as a vantage point for a spotter guiding the RPGs and smaller weapons.

The glint of a TV camera's lens could indeed be mistaken for a spotter's telescope or binoculars but the two would never have been mixed up if the crew had simply been told what millions of television viewers around the world already knew – that hundreds of journalists and dozens of TV cameras were in that building.

'But why would they fire at a press hotel?' I asked DeCamp. 'Everybody in Baghdad and people all around the world knew that building was full of foreign press.'

DeCamp sat forward, less comfortable now, and said his men had not been briefed on the presence of reporters in the Palestine and Sheraton hotels, the two biggest buildings on Baghdad's skyline. My sceptical silence elicited a final explanation from the Colonel, the one that rang most true with me.

'And the other thing is, one of our commanders had just been shot – in the throat,' he said, jabbing a finger at his own neck. 'And they don't like it when one of their guys gets hit, I can tell you.'

This last line was delivered with a brisk shake of the head, as if to say 'No siree, you don't want to fool with us'.

So there was the explanation that was subsequently supported by inquiries conducted by media industry bodies in the absence of any public inquiry by the Pentagon. The tank crew were blasting away in a heavily populated city after some of their own men had been shot, and had not been given basic information about the presence of hundreds of non-combatants, journalists, in the biggest buildings facing them.

An investigation by a US-based media industry group, the Committee to Protect Journalists, found that Associated Press reporter Chris Tomlinson happened to be embedded with DeCamp's battalion at the time of the attack and overheard crucial evidence while monitoring radio exchanges. Tomlinson was in DeCamp's command centre listening on a military radio to conversations between tank commanders when some of the battalion's tanks on the west, or palace, side of the Tigris came under heavy fire from across the river. Colonel David Perkins, DeCamp's commanding officer, did know that the Palestine Hotel was full of journalists and had been trying to identify it to prevent it from being hit by US air strikes, Tomlinson said.

Around the same time, Sergeant Shawn Gibson was manning a tank on the Jumhuriyah Bridge. His company had been under fire all morning and was trying to locate a spotter or 'forward observer' coordinating the Iraqi attacks. When he saw a glint of light reflecting off what he thought were binoculars on the balcony of a tall building across the river, he asked his company commander, Captain Philip Wolford, for permission to fire, and got it.

'The fire was arriving with no let up,' Wolford told the French magazine *Nouvel Observateur* a week after the incident. 'I returned fire without hesitation. That is the rule. It was the strongest resistance I encountered in Baghdad.'

Gibson and Wolford both said later that they had never been told that journalists were in the Palestine Hotel, which could be clearly identified by a large English language sign visible from where Gibson was on the bridge. The hotel had not been marked on the maps distributed by their division headquarters, and they were not told to avoid firing on it. The tank fired a 120 millimetre HEAT round, an incendiary shell that is intended to kill people and not destroy buildings, which explains the limited damage to the hotel.

Chris Tomlinson, the Associated Press reporter, told the inquiry by the Committee to Protect Journalists that Wolford's commanding officer DeCamp then started screaming over the radio at Wolford: 'Who just shot the Palestinian [*sic*] Hotel? Did you just fucking shoot the Palestinian Hotel?' Tomlinson said that at first Wolford was not sure what he had hit but after some minutes he said 'Yes, yes. We had an observer up there.'

'And DeCamp says, "You're not supposed to fire on the hotel." And then there is a brief discussion about what he did see and why did he fire because this was very serious. They weren't supposed to shoot at the Palestine Hotel.' Tomlinson said DeCamp ordered Wolford to cease firing, then drove his own tank to meet Wolford, apparently to have a private discussion. Having heard all this, Tomlinson went to Colonel Perkins, DeCamp's commanding officer, to tell him that his effort to locate the Palestine Hotel was too late.

'I know, I know,' Perkins said. 'I have just given the order that under no circumstances is anyone to shoot at the Palestine Hotel, even if they are taking fire, even if there is an artillery piece on top of the roof. No one is allowed to shoot at the Palestine Hotel again.'

After heavy pressure from media groups, and an unsuccessful attempt by the family of the dead Spanish cameraman Jose Couso to extradite DeCamp, Wolford and Gibson to Spain on war crime charges, the Pentagon eventually conducted an inquiry, although it was not open to the public.

On 12 August, four months after the attack on the hotel, the military's Central Command issued a statement concluding that its officers had acted appropriately. The tank crew 'properly fired upon a suspected enemy hunter/killer team in a proportionate and justifiably measured response,' the statement said. 'The action was fully in accordance with the (US military's) 'Rules of Engagement.'

But the inquiry failed to explain why the tank crews were not told that the Palestine was a press hotel, information that DeCamp and Perkins did have. The Pentagon had spent months preparing for the invasion of Baghdad, carefully planning the assault with satellites and human intelligence sources providing detailed targeting information. And yet – through either an oversight, an accidental breakdown of communication or a deliberate decision – when the tanks were finally sent into the city, officers like Wolford who were making targeting decisions were apparently not told about the whereabouts of hundreds of foreign journalists or, for that matter, the Al-Jazeera office.

The Pentagon's public attitude is that the journalists knew that a war zone was a dangerous place and they had been advised to leave Baghdad. The Pentagon is also adamant that it will not conduct public inquiries into this or many other incidents in which civilians were killed during or after the war.

Paul Pasquale, the Reuters cameraman injured with Taras, makes the point that he was never contacted by the US military, either with an apology and explanation or to ask him to give evidence to its inquiry.

'What sort of inquiry did they conduct if their whole case is that the tank believed there was a spotter in our hotel but they never even asked me, the only survivor from the point of impact, if there was any spotter there?

'Where is the accountability? When I was in the [British] army we had to account for every bullet we fired. And if you were after a spotter you called in the snipers, or outflanked it. You didn't just blast an unidentified civilian building with a bloody tank. I think the problem is they saw every single Iraqi as a hidden enemy.

'It puts what was happening to the Iraqis in perspective – if it was just a mistake that they hit us, then how many other civilians and civilian buildings did they hit?'

A few hours after my chance meeting with Lieutenant-Colonel DeCamp, Anton Antonowicz of the *Daily Mirror* got a distressing phone call in his hotel room from Zubaydah, the wife of Steve Martin's driver, Salah.

She was in the lobby of the hotel wanting to know where Salah was – she had been hoping all week that he had been trapped in the hotel by the fighting. Anton, who had hired Salah before Steve, went down to the lobby. Salah's son, sixteen-year-old Ali, who would occasionally ride along with his father on assignments, ran up asking: 'Mr Anton, Mr Anton. Where's my Dad?'

Anton explained that Salah had been working for Steve, so they sat down in the lobby to wait for Steve to return from his day's work. When he did get back to the hotel Steve was too embarrassed to invite them up to his room, which had not seen a cleaner in weeks, so he sat with Zubaydah, her elder son and her two daughters on a set of couches beside the Palestine's front door, where they shared the horrible realisation that Salah had indeed gone missing between home and work.

'The hardest thing I have ever had to do as a journalist was to tell that woman and her kids that I hadn't seen Salah,' he told me later.

The family left, hoping that he might have been injured or perhaps even arrested somewhere in the city's pandemonium. But Steve could not kid himself.

'I went upstairs and just stayed in my room alone for a couple of hours. I called London to tell the office what had happened and did my best to get my head together. I was in a state of shock in many ways and it's all such a blur.'

He sat wrestling with the realisation that Salah, diligent and considerate Salah, had only driven through those dangerous streets because he wanted to tell Steve in person that it was not safe for him to keep driving.

From our room that night more than a dozen public buildings could be seen burning on the skyline, and the destruction was still spreading.

*

Stuart Clarke left for Jordan early on Saturday 12 April with Anton Antonowicz and Ross Benson. Bob was now alone so there was room for him in the Pajero as we looked for more stories in post-Saddam Baghdad.

In the hustle and confusion of the war it had been hard to convey the everyday despair that Saddam had wrought but now we could see clearer glimpses of it as ordinary Iraqis began to react to the fall of the regime.

One of the first responses to the government's collapse was a passionate rush to find out what had happened to the hundreds of thousands of people who had gone missing under Saddam's rule. One answer was already being unearthed in scores of mass graves around the country, which were believed to hold hundreds of thousands of Saddam's victims.

Other answers about the missing were locked in Saddam's prisons, or so thousands of relatives hoped. As soon as the regime's leaders had fled Baghdad many relatives began making their way to the prisons in the hope of finding survivors. Rumours were spreading of underground cells packed with prisoners. By now most of the officials of the old regime had been gone for at least four days, and if any survivors really were hidden away in prison cells they had been without food and water for at least that time.

We drove to the capital's north-western suburbs, to the headquarters of the Istikhbarat secret police, which specialised in suppressing potential anti-government movements. The main office block was a large building set on a few hectares of open ground. It had already been thoroughly looted but its basement floors and the ground around the building were now being scoured by dozens of relatives looking for underground cells. Bob had been here the previous day to see British troops do exploratory digging which did not detect any sign of such cells.

Fired by rumours and pure hope, relatives had returned today to take matters into their own hands. They got down on their knees to listen to the ground, lifted trapdoors and banged on pipes and granite tiles to try to elicit a response. Every now and then somebody would claim to have heard banging from underground, so a few dozen people would rush off to try to dig up that spot.

Kathim Mohammed Hameed, a labourer from Basra, said he had made the hazardous trip from the south to search for two cousins who had been arrested in 1979. I asked him whether he really thought the regime would have kept prisoners alive for so long and he shrugged. 'We have to hope, we have to hope,' he said.

One man who conceded that his relatives were probably dead was baker Kasim Finjan Saleh. 'But we have to know, and there is always hope,' he said as we stood in a small crowd outside the gutted secret police headquarters. Kasim and his sister Jamila had travelled from the Shi'ite suburb of Shu'ala in north-west Baghdad because two of their brothers had been brought here twelve years before.

They knew their brothers were dragged here because Kasim had been arrested, beaten and interrogated with them, and he last saw them in cells here before he was released. Their eldest brother, Abu Mohammed, was killed at the age of thirty-four while fighting in Saddam's army in the 1991 invasion of Kuwait. In the wave of anger against Saddam after that war his funeral had turned into an anti-Saddam protest.

Searching for their lost brothers. Kasim Finjan Saleh and his sister Jamila scoured a secret police building in the hope that two brothers arrested in 1991 had been kept alive by Saddam's regime. John Feder

'They took our two other brothers, Amer and Jassim, on the day of the funeral,' said Kasim, who was a 24-year-old soldier in Saddam's Republican Guard at the time. 'I was not at the funeral but they arrested me the next day and brought me here.' Amer was a hotel waiter and Jassim a student, both in their twenties, when they were dragged here.

'I heard them being beaten and tortured in the room next to me, and screaming in the night,' said Kasim, whose face was lined with twelve years of painful memories. 'After two weeks they interrogated me and right at the start they dragged Amer in and dumped him on the floor in front of me as a warning.'

After several beatings and twenty days in captivity Kasim was released because two witnesses swore that he did not attend the funeral.

'But we have never seen them again,' whispered Kasim, almost in tears.

Jamila said her surviving brother had been traumatised and deeply depressed for years after his release.

'He was closed up within himself for a long, long time. We all suffered – our parents have never recovered.'

The family could not even complete the usual Shi'ite funeral rituals for Abu Mohammed, which call for a second round of ceremonies a few weeks after the first funeral.

'People were too scared to come to our house because the secret police were sitting outside. For a long time nobody would even think of knocking on our door,' she said.

When I asked Jamila what effect the tragedy had had on her own life she was embarrassed to admit her own suffering.

'Losing my wonderful brothers has ruined my life, too,' she said. She had spent years caring for their distraught parents, and was now unmarried at the age of forty-two.

The search of the prison was complicated by the distrust and suspicion that flourished under Saddam. As we had seen with the various species of minders at the Palestine Hotel, regime operatives tended to keep details of their work secret from their colleagues and nobody had openly confirmed the location of the prison cells.

We decided to drive on into the Saddam City district but it was a nervous drive. Even before the breakdown of law and order, Iraqis had been heavily armed and now residents had formed vigilante groups and home-made roadblocks to try to protect their own streets.

Saddam City was a vast, low-built area of more than a million people which had always received much less than its share of electricity, sewerage and other public services. The Shi'ite clerics exercised enormous influence over their followers without ever being allowed to hold political office or military power. Yet, when we reached the Saddam City Hospital, the front gates were being guarded by a militia overseen by clerics. Six AK-47s could be seen in the hands of plain-clothed volunteers as we made our way through those gates into a courtyard full of noise and activity.

In one corner a man beat his forehead and cried over the body of a younger man on a stretcher at his feet. Two women pushed through the crowd with a small girl lolling lifelessly between their arms. Men in white medical coats rushed about, and several clusters of people gathered around black-robed clerics who yelled instructions above the din.

We found an Imam, Sayeed Saad, who said they had been forced to take up arms to protect the hospital.

'The Fedayeen are trying to break into the hospital warehouses and even kill patients, right now,' he said. 'It is residents who are protecting the hospital, and that is why it is the only big hospital in Baghdad that has not been looted or forced to close its doors. The religious leaders are helping by getting people to settle down and abide by the law. We have put together an armed militia just to protect the hospital.'

He stressed that the residents had never before formed a militia, and he did not disagree when I suggested that the experience of banding together to take up arms in defence of their community could be a turning point that the Americans would come to regret.

The Shia would gain confidence from this experience, he said, leaving them more likely to stand up for themselves against 'the American invaders' as well as against Saddam's supporters. 'We do not want trouble with the Americans but we are against Saddam Hussein and against America. They are of the same currency. The people just do not believe the Americans have come here to help the Iraqi people – they came here for their own good.'

Saddam City Hospital. In the first sign of Shi'ite militia activity in Baghdad, clerics filled the law-and-order vacuum left by US troops by organising their own force to protect young Ali Abbas and other patients. John Feder

Ahmed Chalabi and the other exiles being groomed by Washington to rule Iraq were not acceptable national leaders, he said, as they had no connection with 'ninety-nine per cent of the Iraqi people'.

A younger cleric, Sheik Kathim al Fartousi, said the Americans should be protecting all of Baghdad's hospitals. 'The hospital has its own generators but what we need from the Americans is military protection. A lot of doctors have not been turning up because of fear of the Fedayeen,' he said.

He and the other clerics offered angry denials when I suggested that people from Saddam City seemed to have been involved in much of the looting. But within weeks the long stretch of public land running through the centre of Saddam City would become the site of the biggest outdoor market of second-hand office furniture in the Middle East, row after row of stolen desks and filing cabinets lined up next to hundreds of looted air conditioners and office fans.

We asked to see the director of the hospital, and Dr Mowafak Gorea eventually came out into the courtyard. A short, bespectacled and obviously tired man, he was driven by determination and a manifest pride in his own achievement in keeping the hospital open.

'I have not left the hospital even for a minute for twelve days,' he said in English. 'I have not seen my family for two weeks and don't know what has happened to them. Every other major hospital has had to close because of the law-and-order situation, but we have had the courage to stay put and now we are being backed by the local holy men and their supporters. We are receiving patients from all the other hospitals.'

A Christian who used the name Gabriel, he was extremely proud of the support he had won from the Shi'ite community.

'The most important thing was we held together tight for one day. The staff ran away from the other hospitals but I did not and my staff did not and when they saw that, the local holy men decided to help. The people here are poor and not educated but they follow the holy men.'

From a normal staff of 500, a skeleton team of 22 doctors and 100 to 150 support staff had stayed at work. Like the clerics, Dr Gorea was angry with the lack of protection being offered by the US military.

'It would be a simple thing for them to protect our hospitals if they wanted to but they don't seem to be interested.'

By now it was late afternoon and the curfew was approaching, so I wanted to get back to our hotel. But when Dr Gorea invited us to tour the hospital wards we were trapped. Saying no would have been rude as it would have suggested we were not interested in his patients.

8

ALI'S EVACUATION

I was a little annoyed to be dragged around the wards of the Saddam City Hospital. I already had plenty to write about and my main interest at the hospital was the fact that the Shi'ite clerics were forming their own militia.

We had already seen enough despair for the day, when we interviewed families searching for jailed relatives who were obviously dead, and these wards would certainly be packed with horribly injured patients. It had been heavily reported, for instance, that this was the hospital caring for Ali Ismail Abbas, the young boy who had lost both parents and both arms in the missile strike on the little hamlet of Zafaraniya. Many of the other 200-odd patients were bound to have war wounds that were less cruel than Ali's but still terrible.

A doctor with a very bad toupee led us through several dimly lit wards, while Stewart translated questions from Bob and me, and John took photos.

Ali had already received an enormous amount of publicity, especially in Britain, and my instinct was to focus on other victims. We spent some time talking to the parents of two little cousins who had been playing together three nights earlier when a US bomb had hit their home, injuring eleven members of the family. Five-year-old Ahmed Farhan still did not realise that he had lost his left foot. He was conscious but the bottom of his left leg was propped up on pillows in a way that hid it from his view, and his parents had not yet tried to explain the enormity of what had happened to him.

His cousin and playmate Haider Mutasha, seven, was in the next ward with a broken leg and small cuts all over his body. Like Ahmed, Haider was surrounded by half a dozen family members, who sat on the floor beside his bed or stood stroking his hair and reassuring him.

The doctor in the toupee then asked if we wanted to see Ali. I was in two minds but Bob felt we should. To try to stop his huge open burns from becoming infected the twelve year old had been put in a room of his own in a supposedly sterile environment. It was barely clean, let alone sterile, but the doctors insisted that we would have to put on gowns and white gumboots to go to his bedside, and only two people at a time could enter his room.

It made sense that Stewart and John should go in – Stewart to speak to him in Arabic and John to take his photograph. As they braced themselves and put on their gowns I gave Stewart a few questions to ask Ali. Bob and I wandered around the corridor while they climbed into their boots. Suddenly I found myself looking through an open door straight at Ali, who was holding my gaze.

He was lying on a bed about eight metres away, with his head and shoulders protruding from what appeared to be a little tent over his body. Our eye contact caught me by surprise, and I instinctively nodded hello with a sympathetic smile and threw my right hand up a few inches in a little wave. He reacted just as instinctively, nodding back and lifting the bandaged stump of his right arm, which was just a few inches long. He turned his face back towards the ceiling.

I felt like an idiot. Without thinking, I had given a wave of all things to a child who could not wave back but would naturally try. I was overcome by the awkward remorse of the well-meaning but clumsy, those of us who do not know quite how to behave around the disabled. Offer a handshake to a person missing a right arm and he or she will generally just smile and shake with their left but it is the awkward embarrassment of the rest of us that can be so excruciating.

Ali was lying under a metal frame in the shape of a semi-circle designed to keep his polyester blanket off his torso. From the corridor I could see that he had an unblemished face and large, dark eyes which simply accentuated the mess of his torso. Small bandaged stumps protruded from each shoulder and his chest seemed to be covered by a black vest or paint, with splashes of white around the edges. Beside his bed stood his father's sister, Jumeira, bringing an air of mourning with her heartbroken expression and black robes and headdress.

The publicity about Ali, especially in Britain, had already been enough to make him the 'poster child' of this conflict. Every modern war or famine seems to produce one, like the napalmed girl running along a road in Vietnam, the boy as thin as a stick figure during the Ethiopian famine, and the green-eyed Afghan girl on the cover of *National Geographic*. The deaths of five hundred anonymous children might be shrugged off by people on the other side of the world but the sheer cruelty of this one child's plight was something that would touch anybody.

We had heard from reporters in the Palestine Hotel that British newspapers were organising Ali's evacuation and, while trying not to be callous about it, I felt that he was the one victim in the whole country who did not need more publicity to bring attention to his case. I was also a touch cynical about the tendency to focus on one child. Creating and then saving a poster child could be a false balm to Western consciences, allowing us to feel better about ourselves as we ignored the thousands of other victims of the war.

Having gone without regular access to the Internet I may have known less about Ali's case than any other foreign journalist in Baghdad. Bob told me in the corridor that Ali had already told reporters over the previous week that if he didn't have his arms he wanted to die because he had no parents to look after him. Normally a cheery fellow, Bob shook his head with an observation that would have sounded trite in any other circumstances. 'Nobody to hug and no arms to hug with.'

We asked to speak to Ali's nurse and were introduced to Fatim Mohsin Sharhan, a thirty-two year old with five years' nursing experience who specialised in burns. Since Ali's arrival she had spent most of her time with him. He had become a special case for her and everyone else in the hospital, even for the other patients, she said. Doctors at the Kindi Hospital in central Baghdad had amputated what was left of his arms and given him anaesthetics; then, after eight days, he and other patients had to be evacuated here to escape attacks by looters.

'But if he stays here with us, he will die,' she said simply. 'He's stable now but our hospital is not sterile enough, and before long he will get blood poisoning here. We want him to be taken to special facilities overseas so he will have some chance. Here we could lose him at any moment.

'Ali says he wants to go overseas, go anywhere to get treatment.

Some journalists have told him that they are going to take him over-seas tomorrow to get treatment so he is waiting for that.'

A doctor standing nearby in the corridor confirmed her gloomy judgment.

'He needs a much more sterile environment because he's going to get blood poisoning here. We are doing our best but there are spe-cial rooms for burns victims [overseas] where they reduce the temperature and the bacteria in the air.'

The Saddam City Hospital also lacked the proper anaesthetics to reduce his agony, especially when his nurses and relatives needed to clean his wounds.

John and Stewart were subdued when they came out of Ali's room. John caught my eye, then closed his eyes and shook his head without saying anything. Stewart's eyes were red and he was blinking back tears. Looking for something to focus on, he made a show of flicking through his notes but he did not need them to remember his conversation with Ali.

'I asked whether he was in pain but he just looked at me and said "My mother died, my father died, my brother died",' said Stewart. 'He didn't talk about his own wounds at all. I wanted to tell him he would be OK but what could I say? He asked if anyone was going to help him and I told him yes, that people were coming to help him, then he started to cry.'

'He said "Who will help me? What will they do? When are they coming to help me?"'

What had looked like a black vest on Ali's chest was actually his charred skin. He had second and third degree burns to thirty-five per cent of his body, covering the front of his torso from his neck to his scrotum, and reaching around onto his back. Third degree burns are deep enough to destroy nerves, so the worst pain would be coming from the second degree burns around the edge of that charred flesh.

John did not say anything, using the small viewing screen of his digital camera to show me the close-ups of Ali. I cried as we walked quietly along the dark corridors, blinking my eyes dry as we reached the sunlight of the courtyard.

The hospital director was still in the courtyard and nodded with satisfaction that we had seen his patients. He said moves were underway to get Ali out of Baghdad. Dr Gorea had a sister who had been living in Sydney for twenty years, and he asked if we had a satellite phone so he could tell her their family was OK. I said he was welcome to use it if he could get to the Palestine Hotel. The doctor said he had a meeting there the next day so he would come to my room afterwards.

Trusting me more after this offer of a personal favour, he gave me his more frank assessment of the security problems at the hospital and elsewhere in Baghdad.

'The Americans are behind this. They are doing it deliberately,' he said. 'They could easily protect us and all the other hospitals but they want us to be dependent on them. I don't care – here we can look after ourselves.'

I suspected by now that he was at least partly sustained by a pugnacious pride in his own abilities but I was surprised by his cynicism towards the Americans. If a Christian hospital administrator with family in the West was seeing conspiracy theories, how were the more sceptical Muslim leaders likely to view the actions of a 'crusading' president and a superpower which they had for decades seen as Israel's unfair patron?

When the armed guards opened the hospital gates amid much yelling to usher us out, I expected never to see Ali again. There was little conversation in the Pajero on the drive out of the clogged streets of Saddam City. John fiddled with his digital camera, looking back over his day's photos, while Bob and I sat quietly in our own thoughts, studying the people, bustle and traffic on the streets.

We passed more burning public buildings, where smoke poured from upper windows while looters filed in and out of the front doors. One glaring exception was the Ministry of Oil, a large brick complex on Palestine Street which had been deliberately spared Coalition bombing and was now escaping looting and vandalism.

The reason was obvious: US troops stood guard at the front gates and in sentry boxes on the high walls ringing the complex. In the fifteen seconds it took us to pass the complex, a convoy of about ten US armoured personnel carriers drove out of the ministry grounds. This heavy protection was a striking contrast to the way Dr Gorea's hospital and other public buildings had been left unguarded by the Coalition. I wanted John to capture this contrast in photographs and we were quite excited about the idea but the curfew was almost upon us so we resolved to come back the next day.

By now literally hundreds of reporters were pouring into Baghdad, and when we got back to the hotel Ian McPhedran had arrived from Jordan. Rooms were still rare so he shifted into Bob's room, taking Stuart Clarke's bed.

Ian knew John well and was concerned about him when he saw how drained he was by the experiences of the past few weeks. Ian had never met me but thought I looked 'bloody ordinary' as well. I had been averaging less than four hours' sleep a night for three weeks and we had run out of razor blades so by this stage the stubble on my face was about as long as my super-short hair. For the first time in my life there were shades of grey in those whiskers.

Indeed, we had just about had enough of our little road trip through Iraq. In nineteen days we had been arrested at gun point, driven through a tank battle, kept under 'hotel arrest' and constantly kept awake by nearby artillery exchanges and small-arms fire. Never knowing when we might get caught up in that fighting, we had lain awake at night worrying about the stress our families and partners were suffering, and we had seen some haunting sights, including watching a new friend die in front of us.

In the process we seemed to have been the only news crew from any country to have reported independently from the real battle-zone during the first part of the war, in southern Iraq, and then to have reported from Baghdad on the climactic days of Saddam's regime.

By this stage John and I wanted to do a few days of post-Saddam stories then get out. Ian was fresh after his time in a decent Amman hotel and had plenty of his own story ideas, including checking on people he had dealt with before the war, so we agreed that John would split his time between projects for Ian and projects for me in our remaining days here. There would be plenty of stories to keep two reporters busy in Baghdad, and we still had Catherine in the north, while Rory was now in Basra.

Frustrated by the lack of information being released in Doha, Rory had flown with a few other reporters to an Australian Navy ship, the HMAS *Kanimbla*, where they were offered a helicopter ride to Umm Qasr for a one-night stay. When he reached the docks there he set up camp in our abandoned tent and refused to go back to the ship the next day.

Phil Pyke, the army public affairs officer who had helped us in Umm Qasr, had packed away our tent and supplies of food and water and he helped Rory enormously during his stay on the docks. Rory eventually hired his own car and driver to visit Basra. The British had taken the city by then but it was still unstable enough for Rory's car to be stolen, forcing him into awkward negotiations with the owner over how much News Ltd should pay to replace the car.

The influx of new media teams, including Australian TV networks, outweighed by more than three to one the exodus of exhausted journalists who had spent the war in Baghdad. Among the new arrivals was Phil Coburn, an Irish photographer from Steve Martin's *Sunday Mirror* who was already worn out by spending the entire war trying to get into Iraq from Amman. Twice he had been in convoys heading for the Iraqi border when his head office had called from London to order him to turn around because they felt it was too dangerous to drive to Baghdad.

Ian had brought a large supply of food, toiletries and cash, and we felt spoiled by things like decent soap and toothpaste. Ian also had some of those famous Australian camping skills that John and I lacked. On Bob's small gas plate he cooked up a stew he called a 'train smash', which we savoured with a glass of red wine as if it was a gourmet meal.

We were getting ready for bed when there was a knock on the door. A tall, bulky Australian, almost as big as Ian, was standing there with some luggage and a sleeping bag under his arms. 'I don't suppose you have seen my flak jacket?' he asked with a smile.

I had never met Rory. He was even more surprised than I was when the door opened. He said later that he was taken aback to be greeted by an unshaven character naked apart from what he called 'big, weird, white Y-fronts'. He could see over my shoulder that John and Stewart were wearing the same thing as they lounged around our already crowded room.

Rory had hitched a lift with some American reporters, shoving most of our gear into a CNN truck heading to Baghdad. We were desperate for our stuff, especially Stewart's passport, but the CNN convoy had to abandon one truck on the way north and it was a nervous couple of days before the passport turned up in Baghdad. We were peeved that Rory had not put Stewart's passport into his own pocket for safekeeping but he did get almost everything to Baghdad.

The hotel was full with all the new arrivals so Rory slept on the floor, making four of us in a room that probably would have been comfortable for one.

On Sunday morning, 13 April, Louis Valdovinos, a Marine lance-corporal on sentry duty at the Oil Ministry did not understand quite why we were so interested in the security he was helping to provide. He answered my questions anyway and agreed to be in a photograph. About seventy Marines and a large number of military vehicles were protecting the ministry, he said. We spent the next few hours driving around the city so that John could shoot seven devastated public buildings to contrast with the pristine Oil Ministry.

The looting and burning had already caused damage worth hundreds of millions of dollars and was far from finished. Traffic in downtown Baghdad came to a stop at one point as the smoke from burning buildings became so thick that car headlights could penetrate only twenty metres.

At the Kindi Hospital we found that the increasingly confident Shi'ite militia from Saddam City had sent armed volunteers here, as well as to other hospitals, to help and was planning to send them out into the streets a day later to set up security roadblocks in Shi'ite suburbs.

One of the volunteers at the Kindi was Hayder Daoud Salman, a television repairman who cradled a semi-automatic weapon and shook his head as he spelled out the public relations disaster caused by the Coalition's choice of public buildings to protect.

'People only have to use their eyes to see what the Americans are really interested in,' he said with a shrug. 'Everyone is looking around at what the Americans are protecting and what they are leaving to the Ali Babas, and knowing why they came here.'

'I spoke to an [American] officer and asked them to secure the hospital and he said "I am not allowed to protect you". I said "Can just one tank stay so everybody can see it and they will leave the hospital alone?" and he said "I'm following orders, we can't do that". Yesterday the soldiers came for two hours, today nothing.

'Instead it is only the Ministry of Oil they protect. I think it is a message that their only interest is oil. They are showing us the truth. My personal opinion is there is a message here for other countries that America is interested in something bigger [than Iraq].'

When we got back to the lobby of the Palestine Hotel a small number of harassed US military spokesmen were trying to cope with questions from packs of journalists. So many reporters were flooding into the city that the military's PR machine was struggling to cope.

Major Paul Konopka, a spokesman with the US Marines 1st Regimental Combat Team, defended the high-profile protection of the Oil Ministry, insisting that the military had no regrets at all about how it had handled the law and order challenges in Baghdad.

'Our military presence, given the size of the city, is very small. It was appropriate to the size of the military force we faced but it is very small in terms of protecting the whole city,' he said.

'So when you had the looting, we could only protect so much of it. In that situation it's like first aid. You have to set priorities and stop the bleeding, then you can do other things later. The first priority was things like water, power and sanitation, things the Iraqi people told us they wanted.'

So why would the Ministry of Oil rank above basic services, such as hospitals?

'The answer is obvious. Oil fuels everything – it fuels hospitals, trucks that deliver food, everything.'

When I pointed out that the Oil Ministry handled multi-billion dollar oil exports and related policy issues rather than deliveries of fuel to hospitals, Major Konopka conceded that the US decisions were not really about Baghdad's short-term needs.

'One of Iraq's greatest resources is oil,' he said. 'That's going to help rebuild Iraq into the democracy it wants to be and that is why it needs to be protected.'

The oil industry would indeed be crucial to Iraq's long-term recovery. The problem was not the protection of that industry's nerve centre; it was the failure to protect the other public assets that provided precisely the services that Major Konopka had listed, like health and sanitation.

The foreign press was already reporting with outrage on the

failure to protect the National Museum, where fortunately the losses turned out to be a fraction of what was initially reported. The people of Baghdad were concerned about the treasures of their history but right now they were much more worried about the attacks on their hospitals, as they should have been.

Dr Gorea from the Saddam City Hospital did not come to our room after his meeting in the Palestine Hotel that day but he had given me a phone number in Sydney for his sister, Fatim Gammo, so I called her to say that her brother had survived the war. She cried with relief and gratitude, saying 'God bless you' five or six times. She said she had read every word I had filed from Iraq, and promised through her tears to pray for me.

*

It occurred to me that if the Coalition was not protecting most public buildings they might not have secured buildings like the Foreign Ministry, which were full of potentially newsworthy documents.

While John went out with Ian on a story, Stewart and I went to the Foreign Ministry to spend a few hours poking through rooms full of ash and singed papers.

Only twenty or so looters were still at work there and the building was still smouldering from fires which had devastated most of its ten storeys.

We first went into the smaller protocol building next door, finding its polished stone floors about fifteen centimetres deep in a mess of documents. To steal the office furniture and filing cabinets the looters had simply tipped out thousands of files. After thirty minutes we could tell that all the papers lying around in that two-storey building were boring bureaucratic forms and passport applications.

The main building had been hit by a missile and then torched by looters. The elevators and wiring had been destroyed by the fires, and the unlit stairwells and corridors were dangerous to navigate. In one dark corridor on the second floor I slashed my forehead on a thin piece of steel jutting down from the ceiling.

We eventually found our way to the main archive room. Long metal shelves were stacked with thousands of files that had been carefully maintained by Saddam's bureaucrats – like most totalitarian regimes this one loved paperwork – but those files were now endless rows of white ashes, ready to dissolve into little piles at the slightest touch. It was hard to believe that the Americans had not rushed here and to the other sensitive government buildings in Baghdad to protect the files and accumulated intelligence of Saddam's diplomacy.

A small office off that archive room was knee-deep in documents that had not been burned. They had been thrown out of filing cabinets by looters looking for valuables and hidden safes behind the cabinets. Stewart was as intrigued and excited as I was. We were clearly the first people to enter this or the main archive room with any interest in the actual documents, none of which had been picked up or stacked in such a way that they could be read.

Sweating in the gloom and smoky air we looked for files relating to Australia, holding them up to read them by the occasional shaft of dim sunlight making its way through the smoke and gloom. I burrowed away looking for English writing, which was rare, and after a while I got Stewart to write out the Arabic script for Australia so I could help him go through the piles of files, handing him anything in Arabic that looked interesting. Stewart read the covers of hundreds of files and eventually found a cardboard folder with cables relating to the Australian mining firm BHP.

When translated and investigated back in London that file would reveal some embarrassing contacts that the Australian resources giant BHP had had with Saddam's regime in an attempt to win business during the UN sanctions era. The minutes of one of those contacts, a private meeting with Iraq's senior diplomat in New York in February 1999, showed that it had been organised in the name of the former British Foreign Secretary, Sir Malcolm Rifkind, a BHP consultant who had publicly vowed to have no business dealings with Saddam's regime.

Sir Malcolm told me later that his BHP colleagues had mistakenly used his name to organise the meeting but he had refused to attend because he was determined 'to give no succour to that regime'.

Another BHP Petroleum executive, Norman Davidson Kelly, did attend and according to the Iraqi record of the meeting he told the Iraqi diplomat on behalf of BHP that the Australian Government's tough attitude towards the old regime had only limited support among Australians and was simply an attempt to curry favour with Washington and ensure US military support at a time when Indonesia was an unstable neighbour.

That night we were trying to shuffle beds at the Palestine Hotel. Journalists were no longer obliged to stay there or in the Sheraton so Rory found a room in a smaller hotel across the road. He visited us for dinner and a drink, though, and ended up stuck in our room again because an outbreak of shooting right beside the Palestine late in the evening made the short walk to his hotel precarious.

There was no need for us to have three reporters in Baghdad, so Rory had lined up a car and driver to head north the next day to Tikrit, Saddam's home town which had not yet been taken by the Coalition.

*

Having our own satellite phone meant the luxury of Internet and e-mail access, and on Monday morning, 14 April, I received an e-mail asking me to call Deborah Jones, a deputy editor on *The Australian*. She told me that a wealthy Perth reader of *The Australian*, named Tony Trevisan, had telephoned to say he had been so moved by my report on twelve-year-old Ali, and John's accompanying photograph, that he wanted to know how he could help him.

I had actually not written that much about Ali, as he had not been the main focus of our visit to the Saddam City Hospital. The story ran on page 15 under the headline 'Shi'ite militia protects last hospital from mobs', which accurately captured the thrust of my report. I only mentioned Ali in the middle of the report – just six of the twenty paragraphs were about him. It was accompanied by two photos – one showing Dr Gorea standing in the courtyard, the other showing Ali in bed with his aunt standing behind him. What had touched Trevisan and many other readers was John's shot of Ali, his hair stuck to his forehead with sweat, dark eyes looking straight into the camera.

I told Deborah I was sure that Ali was already being looked after, as several British journalists had apparently promised to organise an evacuation. But if some rich guy wanted to send money

John Feder's photograph of Ali, published in newspapers around Australia, which moved a Perth property developer to offer money to try to save Ali. That got us involved in Ali's case.

I was happy to find out where he could send a donation. There were no working telephones at the hospital so that meant spending a few hours driving to and from Saddam City, about a forty-minute drive through streets on which there was plenty of shooting and no police. John was going on another job with Ian but I had no appointments that morning so I decided that Stewart and I might as well drive back to the hospital.

Sitting in Dr Gorea's office we were surprised to find that he had angrily given up on the idea of Ali being evacuated. His meeting at the Palestine Hotel the previous day had been with the American military to try to organise Ali's evacuation but it had obviously not gone well.

'The Americans are not interested in helping Ali so we will look after him here – we don't need their help,' he fumed. 'Everyone in the world promises to help Ali but nobody has done anything. We have got lots of promises and no action – the Queen of Jordan said she would help Ali, the English newspapers said they will help, the Germans were going to help, the Swedish were going to help. And he is still sitting in his bed upstairs.'

Remembering his scepticism about the Americans and his prickly pride in his ability to cope without their help, I pressed him on whether the hospital really would be able to look after the boy. He eventually conceded that he shared the opinion of Ali's nurse and other doctors – without a quick evacuation he would almost certainly die.

The meeting with the Americans had apparently been organised with the best of intentions by a freelance journalist working for *The Times*, Janine di Giovanni, and the proposal had been to take Ali to a US military hospital ship.

'But now they don't want to take him,' said Dr Gorea. 'It is a bad idea anyway. I told them that the deck of a ship is a bad place for an injured boy. There is infection everywhere.

'In any case his family could not visit him on a ship. He has lost his parents so he needs to be close to his remaining family.'

'What about sending him to Kuwait or Jordan?' I asked. As we discussed the options Kuwait seemed the best bet. Having come into Iraq through Kuwait I knew how desperately keen the Kuwaiti Government was to improve its image in Iraq and the rest of the

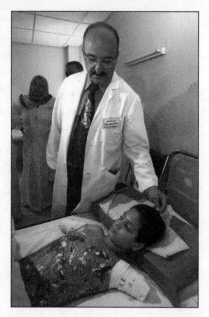

Left: Ali and his aunt during our first visit to the hospital.
Right: Ali with Dr Mowafak 'Gabriel' Gorea, the hospital director,
when John and Stewart returned to the hospital. John Feder

Arab world after being the only Arab state actively to support the US invasion. The Kuwaitis were rich, had first-rate health facilities and had been sending aid convoys into Iraq from the first opportunity.

'Can you organise for the Kuwaitis to take him?' the doctor challenged us, expecting that to end the discussion.

But I knew that the answer could be sitting right next to me – Stewart J. Innes, the one-time embassy trade consultant turned part-time war tourist and full-time savvy translator, who had already proved himself a more than handy 'fixer'. He had lived in Kuwait since 1994, had been working at the Canadian Embassy since 1997 and was just the sort of charmer who would have a lot of connections in Kuwait City.

I looked at Stewart and he nodded vigorously.

'I think they would – how could they say no?' he said to the doctor before turning to me and adding: 'I could make a few calls, anyway.'

'If the Kuwaitis did agree would you allow Ali to go there?' I asked Dr Gorea.

'No – you would still need to get the Americans to provide a helicopter. That boy is not going anywhere in an ambulance. It is eight hours by road to Jordan or Kuwait and the trip would be too painful. It would kill him. He has to go in a helicopter, so only the Americans can help and they are not interested.'

Ten minutes earlier we had been ushered into Dr Gorea's office hoping to find a bank account to which a property developer from Perth could send money for Ali. Now, somehow, we were cajoling the hospital director into letting us try to get the boy out of the country. Blurring the lines between journalist and aid worker on a project like trying to shift Ali had never crossed my mind but now that a reader's telephone call had landed us back in Dr Gorea's office taking a fresh look at Ali's case, my motivations were not complicated.

An evacuation of Ali would obviously be a good story but that was not my main interest. Getting the kid out of Baghdad would be the top priority, and if that was threatened at any stage by our desire to report on it then Ali's interests would come first. There were plenty of other stories in Baghdad for our readers.

I suspect that if we had just arrived in Baghdad we might have moved on to other stories rather than getting bogged down in Ali's case. As it was the three of us had just about done our work in Iraq, and trying to help Ali was a challenge that might put a more positive note on what had been a pretty gruelling, even disturbing, few weeks.

I assumed that a helicopter would be impossible to organise, so I argued with Dr Gorea for some time about the merits of moving him in an ambulance, saying the risks and discomfort would still be better than waiting upstairs for his wounds to fester.

'If the Kuwaitis did agree to take him, and we got either a special ambulance or a helicopter would you let him go?'

'Maybe,' he said. 'Because he will die here.'

As we drove back to the hotel Stewart and I were happier and more motivated than we had been for days. After seeing plenty of death and tragedy we might just be able to do something constructive before leaving Iraq.

Stewart went straight up to the hotel room to call Kuwait while I tried to find a US military doctor to see if there was any possibility of organising a helicopter or ambulance. I spent two hours in a noisy queue at a civil affairs desk that had been set up in the Palestine Hotel's lobby. Behind the desk was a corridor running to the conference rooms where the Iraqi Information Ministry had held its press conferences. Those rooms now held an undermanned team of 'civil affairs' specialists from the US military who were trying to organise the revival of Iraq's police force, electricity system, hospitals and dozens of other services.

I was eventually told I needed to see someone called 'Doc Martin', who was tied up in meetings. The whole operation was chaotic and most reporters who were waiting in the same queue for information or interviews gave up and left. I waited because I was no longer working to a newspaper deadline – if pursuing Ali's case swallowed up most of my remaining time in Baghdad then so be it.

Eventually Petty Officer Ed Martin, a red-headed navy medical officer in his twenties, came out to see me. He was not a doctor – because of a popular shoe brand, 'Doc' was a rather obvious nickname for a medico named Martin. He happened to be the American official who had met Dr Gorea the previous day. He was exasperated with the hospital director, sceptical about my involvement in Ali's case, and generally less than friendly.

'Look,' he said, 'I have dealt with other journalists about this case and already wasted a bit of time on it. I don't really want to deal with that doctor again . . . I don't think we can help.'

Martin said the proposal that had been put to him at the meeting with Dr Gorea was to take Ali to a US hospital ship, but, he said now, this was 'not a viable solution'.

'Those ships are designed for American military casualties. This kid doesn't speak English and we don't have translators out there for him and his aunt. We also don't have paediatricians on our ships.

'And this kid has not just got life-threatening burns, he has lost his arms – he needs long-term care, with plastic surgery, rehabilitation and prosthetics and we can't just take him back to America. What we could do on a ship is prevent infection and keep him alive through the danger period of the next few weeks but then we would basically be dropping him back into a Baghdad slum.

'I just don't think that is a real solution for this kid, and we have got an awful lot of other medical problems to deal with.'

What if the Kuwaitis agreed to take him, I asked? Would the Americans allow an ambulance from Kuwait to enter Iraq and come to Baghdad to get Ali?

'You go and see what the Kuwaitis say. I can't promise anything but come back to me if you have got them on board,' he said before marching away. Like Dr Gorea, Doc Martin was highly sceptical that we would deliver any Kuwaiti involvement. And like Dr Gorea he was challenging us to show our own bona fides by proving we would stick at the case.

Stewart had called Bassima Dalle, a workmate at the Canadian Embassy in Kuwait City, and asked her to contact Kuwaiti government officials and charities. She got to work ringing around Kuwait City.

A few minutes after I returned to our room Stewart received a call on our satellite phone from Dr Abdul Rida Abbas, an assistant director of emergency services at Kuwait's Ministry of Health. Stewart ran through the details of the case with him. Dr Abbas said that if they did get involved, the Kuwaitis would need to be certain that the Americans would meet an ambulance at the border and protect it while it was in Iraq.

Picking up on the points made by Ed Martin, I told Stewart to stress to Dr Abbas that we needed Kuwait to commit to Ali's long-term care. We were not interested in letting them have a short-term public relations coup only to send Ali back to Iraq without all the treatment he needed.

Dr Abbas said he would call back later that day. About an hour later he rang to say the Kuwaitis had agreed. Officially the decision would be made later by a member of Kuwait's ruling family but in reality it had already been made. Stewart hammered home the point about Ali's longer-term care and was assured that Kuwait knew it was taking on a lengthy commitment.

When Stewart got off the phone and told me what had been said we hugged each other. This really could work. I ran back to the lobby and after another lengthy wait I got to talk to Doc Martin again. He was surprised that we had delivered, and his attitude changed dramatically. He told me later that this was the moment when he stopped seeing me as just another reporter chasing a story and decided we were serious about helping Ali.

I told him of the Kuwaitis' concerns about getting an ambulance across the border and needing a military escort but he said not to worry about that. If I could deliver a few more things he would probably be able to provide the helicopter that Dr Gorea wanted.

For one thing he needed a guardian, probably Ali's aunt, to travel with him. He also wanted some form of written consent from Ali's family or legal guardian that they approved of him being taken to Kuwait by the US military.

'We can't just kidnap the kid – we have to have a legal basis for taking him.'

The hospital would have to be willing to hand over all of Ali's medical records. And Martin already knew about the Shi'ite clerics' role at the hospital. The US military was generally staying well away from that part of Saddam City, and he had to be absolutely certain that the clerics were comfortable with US troops entering the hospital and taking Ali away. Finally Martin wanted my assurance that Dr Gorea was definitely on side and would not change his mind at the last minute.

Martin was as pleased as we were that this just might be pulled off, and he said an evacuation might be possible as soon as the next day.

While he had wanted all along to help, Baghdad was still a dangerous and inconvenient place to operate and Martin had had neither the time nor the freedom to run around negotiating with all the parties to make something happen for Ali. It was still too dangerous for aid agencies to operate in the city, and we were providing the wheels, phone and time to get things moving.

It was now late afternoon but we decided there was time before dusk for another return trip to Saddam City. With each passage through the area we could see it changing as its Shi'ite identity was asserted with a new confidence. Black 'martyr' signs with gold and white lettering were now draped on many buildings to list the names of family members killed by Saddam's regime.

Volunteer roadblocks had been erected that day to assert Shi'ite control, and graffiti had already appeared renaming Saddam City as Sadr City, after the Shi'ite Ayatollah Mohammed Sadeq al-Sadr who was murdered in 1999 on Saddam's orders. When we arrived at the hospital it too had been renamed – it was now Hussein Public Hospital after another Shi'ite cleric, whose photograph had been stuck over the old sign at the front gates.

Dr Gorea had left his office to catch up on sleep. His deputy woke him by telephone so I could explain our progress. He was as surprised as Ed Martin that we had followed through, and said he would do whatever the Americans wanted.

The deputy sent somebody to find Ali's family, who were staying near the hospital. While we were waiting outside in the late afternoon sun Sheik Fartousi, the young cleric we had met on our first visit, appeared, demanding to know about this rumour that the Americans were taking Ali.

Stewart began to explain in Arabic but Fartousi, who seemed more arrogant now about his power around the hospital, began berating him. A dozen or so people gathered as Fartousi, an intense bearded figure in white headdress, black robes and grey tunic, lectured us with a patronising manner and dismissive hand gestures. Suddenly Stewart angrily cut him off, to the surprise of Fartousi and his audience. Stewart told me later that Fartousi had declared that the Western press was full of wind and empty promises.

'You people have been making these promises for more than a week but you have done nothing. We are sick of your lies ...' he said, before Stewart's temper took over.

'Don't say "you people" have been doing nothing for a week! You had never even seen us until the day before yesterday. I don't care what anyone else has said or done – we have told no lies, and we WILL get Ali out of here as long as you don't ruin things.'

This angry blast was in Arabic, and while it was some time before Stewart got a chance to translate it into English for me, I got the drift from the way he was jabbing his finger in Fartousi's face. The wide eyes of the people standing around made it clear that they had never heard Fartousi spoken to like this. The cleric's own sullen glare gave the same impression.

Stewart went on more quietly to say that the Americans would not take Ali unless a guardian went with him, so we needed to speak to his aunt. Keen to regain the offensive, Fartousi saw a new line of attack.

'We will not send an Iraqi woman away to Kuwait! Her place is with her family. Iraqis do not traffic in their women.'

The deputy director of the hospital had listened to the whole exchange and now he came to our assistance. He shrugged his shoulders as if there was no problem and said 'Fine, so we will send the uncle.'

Fartousi was deflated but then decided he could pretend he had imposed his will. 'Very well,' he said. 'If you abide by my conditions I will approve this thing.' With that he turned and stomped off, looking like he was not quite sure whether he had come out on top.

A few minutes later a man described as Ali's uncle arrived. Mohammed abd Hamzah al Sultany, the man who had helped pull Ali and his sisters out of the wreckage of their home, was technically not Ali's uncle. He was in fact a cousin of Ali's father, and the brother of his first wife but the extended family had designated him as Ali's guardian.

A bespectacled man whose greying hair made him look a decade older than his thirty-seven years, he had a gentler and more thoughtful manner than was typical in the tougher suburbs of Baghdad. He placed his open hand on his heart to show his gratitude for our involvement then nodded silently as Stewart briefed him.

He agreed instantly to travel to Kuwait with Ali, even though we had no idea how long he would be away. He and his wife Shetha Majid Fahad Hamza had five children of their own and had already accepted responsibility for Ali, his half-brother and the five of his six half-sisters who were unmarried. Mohammed, or Hamed to his friends, normally supported his family by working as a carpenter and irrigation pump repairman but his own brothers and sisters would look after his family while he was away caring for Ali. We told him that he and Ali should be ready to go the next day.

It was dark and well past curfew by the time we got back to the hotel. I found Doc Martin again and he said he would come to my room early in the morning to use our satellite phone to call the Kuwaiti authorities to work out details of Ali's transfer – surprisingly, the US military was short on phones.

Martin was busily trying to reward us by somehow ensuring that we would have exclusive coverage of Ali's evacuation if it went ahead. I was surprised and told him that it would be great but it was not our priority. I said it would be impossible anyway because British television cameras had been constantly hovering beside Ali's bed, their reporters at times leaning over the boy to be filmed talking to him.

The plan was to have a military ambulance go to the hospital late the next afternoon but at one point Martin, who was thinking out loud about the options, suggested that it could be delayed until very early the next morning so there would be no other journalists at the hospital. I reminded him that the whole point of the exercise was to get Ali out as quickly as possible, so we stuck to the existing schedule.

Martin then suggested that John and I, or perhaps just one of us, could fly in the chopper with Ali. We discussed it but decided it could be an unnecessary complication. We naturally wanted to document his evacuation but the main goal was to ensure that it went ahead as quickly and as smoothly as possible.

Martin decided that he would tell the ambulance convoy about our role and tell them to let us accompany them to the airbase where Ali would be transferred to a helicopter. He could not tell us the location and name of the airbase as that was still secret so we had to follow the convoy and make sure we did not lose it.

British television crews had rushed to the hospital that afternoon after Prime Minister Tony Blair had commented on Ali's case. Steve Martin had written a report, published on the front page of that morning's *Daily Mirror*, in which Ali's nurse pleaded for Britain and the US to help the boy. Blair was asked about it in the House of Commons and gave a non-committal response, noting that Baghdad was controlled by the Americans, not the British.

'We are in touch with the authorities in respect of cases such as this, which are not in our zone of control,' he said. 'We will do whatever we can to help him [Ali] and to help others, because there are others in a similar position.'

I called Tony Trevisan in Perth that night to speak to him for the first time and tell him what had happened as a result of his offer of help for Ali. He was delighted, confirming John's photograph had moved him deeply.

'It was a cruel photo to see, with those injuries and his beautiful brown eyes, but it was one of the most compelling photos I have ever seen.'

I told him no money would be needed to get Ali out of the country as the US military would be footing the bill. Instead Trevisan offered to send US$5000 to support the uncle in Kuwait and I promised to find out if that was necessary.

The next morning Doc Martin was late in coming to our room, so while I waited for him Stewart and John went to the hospital to let the doctors and family know that everything was on track for a late-afternoon pickup of Ali.

Doc Martin and Colonel Kevin Moore, the chief surgeon of the 1st Division of the US Marines, eventually arrived to use our phone to speak to the Kuwaiti officials about the details of the evacuation. This was their first contact with the Kuwaitis at all, and they needed to arrange exactly where Ali would be flown and what facilities would be on hand for his arrival. After several conversations with Kuwaiti government officials Colonel Moore confirmed that Ali would be picked up late in the afternoon.

While the colonel was on the telephone I told Doc Martin about Blair's suggestion in the Commons the day before that the British Government might be taking an interest in Ali's case, and asked whether there had been any such British intervention. He said that if there had been any contact between the British and US governments about Ali it had had no impact on what was happening on the ground. The helicopter had been initiated by Doc Martin with per-mission from Colonel Moore, and they had heard nothing about Ali from their own superiors, let alone any impetus from London.

'If they [the British Government] did get involved they might have got something going in a few days but this is only happening now because of what you guys have done,' Moore said.

While I waited for John and Stewart to get back from the hos-pital I wrote a 'holding story' for the first editions of our newspapers. A holding story is one which anticipates an event in order to get the paper through an awkwardly timed first edition, until later editions can confirm that the event has actually taken place.

The six-hour time difference to Australia meant that Ali would probably be leaving the hospital just as our first editions were printed, in the late evening. If anything went wrong with the evacu-ation I would need to borrow a phone and ring in with changes to the story.

The story began like this:

'Ali Ismail Abbas, the Iraqi boy who lost both arms and both parents to an American rocket, was finally being evacuated last night from the Baghdad hospital where he faced certain death from his injuries.

'Twelve-year-old Ali was being taken by the US military to Kuwait City, where the Kuwaiti Government has agreed to treat the burns which cover more than a third of his body.'

The report explained our involvement:

'His rescue was organised by *The Australian* after a Perth reader, Tony Trevisan, telephoned the newspaper to ask if he could help after reading in Monday's newspaper that Ali's nurse and doctors believed he could die any day from blood infections . . .

'Stewart Innes, a Kuwaiti-based Briton who has been working as *The Australian*'s Arabic translator during the war in Iraq, then used his contacts in Kuwait City to approach health and charity officials there.

'Within hours an assistant director of the Kuwaiti Health Ministry, Dr Abdul Rida Abbas, had agreed to provide immediate help to save Ali's life and the longer-term care he desperately needs . . . '

An important complication was that we were working for all News Ltd newspapers, not just *The Australian*. They had all shared the expense of having us in Baghdad, so anything we did there was also on their behalf. I sent an accompanying message to those newspapers saying that when referring to our team in Baghdad they should substitute references to *The Australian* with 'News Ltd' or their own masthead name.

Similarly, when we were arrested the *Adelaide Advertiser* had reported that its team had been detained, while *The Australian* said its team had been detained – it was always quite clear to anybody who read both papers that it was the same team. That is standard operating procedure when correspondents are shared by two or more papers. If a newsmaker speaks to a correspondent shared by the Fairfax papers, for instance, the Melbourne *Age* will say that he or she 'told the *Age* . . . ', while the *Sydney Morning Herald* will substitute 'told the *Herald*.' Nevertheless the News Ltd newspapers would later be accused in the Fairfax press and on the ABC of wrongly claiming credit for Ali's evacuation for each newspaper.

John and Stewart came back from the hospital exasperated, saying it had become a media scrum. Fearful that they might miss some twist in the story, some reporters had staked out Ali's room, ignoring pleas from his doctors for them to leave the already unsterile room.

Stewart was especially steamed up, having got into an argument with a producer from the British commercial network ITN. ITN was running especially hard on the Ali story, repeatedly broadcasting footage of their own reporter/newsreader at Ali's bedside and doing their best to 'own' the Ali story. They would later broadcast a thirty-minute prime-time special on Ali which focussed largely on their reporter/newsreader's relationship with him.

Their producer overheard Stewart talking to Dr Gorea about the planned arrival of the ambulance to take Ali to an airbase and interrupted to declare that she 'would not allow' Ali to leave the hospital in an ambulance as she believed it would kill him. Stewart, who had never come across the more thrusting elements of the British media, was nonplussed, and told her to mind her own business. Angry words followed.

Doc Martin was adamant during our discussions that the soldiers in the US ambulance convoy would not do their work amid a media scrum. They would be armed and were already wary about going into a hospital controlled by a local militia. At the first sign of trouble they would call off the evacuation, and there would have to be heavy limits on the number of people present, press and otherwise.

In the middle of the afternoon we headed to Saddam City yet again, taking Steve Martin with us and hiring a driver so our car would not be left empty when we were inside the hospital.

Dr Gorea had left the hospital, perhaps not wanting to deal personally with the Americans. We were greeted in his office by the acting director of the hospital, Dr Khaldoon Khayri, who was excited but nervous about what was about to happen. Sheik Fartousi, Ali's uncle and several doctors joined us to discuss the handover, and all were as anxious as the Americans would be.

Without the English-speaking Dr Gorea I was totally dependent on Stewart's translating, and he became something of a master of ceremonies. For one thing, he suggested to Fartousi that the Americans might be more comfortable if they were not surrounded

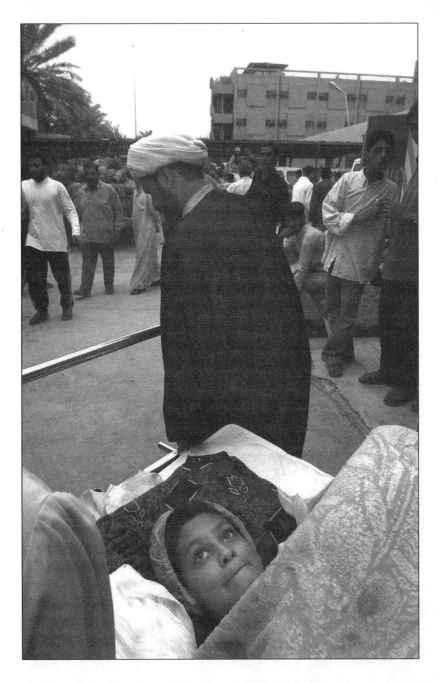

Into the sunlight. Ali is wheeled into the hospital carpark, with Sheik Fartousi helping to guide his trolley. His body is covered by a raised structure to keep the sheets off his wounds. John Feder

by locals carrying AK-47s, and arrangements were made to hide the guns when the Americans arrived. I asked Dr Khayri for Ali's medical records and he admitted that there were none. This was a hospital concentrating on warding off armed looters rather than keeping its records up to date.

The doctors were worried that they still could not get several journalists out of Ali's room. I told them that TV cameras could wait in the courtyard to watch Ali being put into the ambulance but they should not be in his room or crowding around the American troops.

One cameraman from APTN, the television service of the Associated Press news agency, pushed his way into the director's office and I urged the doctors to let him stay. AP coverage was a nice compromise as it would make footage available to any channel that wanted it without having a scrum of several cameras.

At 5.30 p.m. the Americans arrived at the front gates, with two humvees escorting a military ambulance. With all of the militia weapons out of sight as promised, Lieutenant Sean Breen, a tall blond doctor, and two other soldiers were brought to the director's office. Like most Coalition units in Iraq, Breen had no translator. His instructions had been to find me, then I introduced him to the various parties and explained that Ali was still upstairs in his room.

We had warned Dr Khayri that some form of paperwork was needed to transfer medical authority for Ali to the US military, and he now produced a blank sheet of paper and wrote the following in English.

'We are medical evacuation team from America, we receive the patient Ali Abdul Sadda [*sic*] 12 year old, with his uncle to Kuwait. For this reson [*sic*] we sign in presence of Australian press. 15/4/2003.'

Nobody noticed that Dr Khayri had got Ali's name wrong. He showed us the paper with a flourish, knocking over a glass of water which soaked the document. Everyone jumped, and another doctor helped him dry the note. Dr Khayri then signed it and asked me to sign it as 'mediating agent'. Lt Breen signed next, followed by Sheik Fartousi and Ali's uncle.

Lt Breen and his men were keen to get out of the building as quickly as possible. We marched up to Ali's room to find most reporters had left as the afternoon had ticked closer towards curfew time. The only one still there was Janine di Giovanni from *The*

Times. Doc Martin had asked if I minded him telling her about the plans and I had agreed. Now, as we gathered around Ali's bed, she appeared in his room. One of the hospital administrators asked her to leave but she refused to go. Ali was excited about leaving, biting his lip with tension, but in all the commotion and the crowd of new faces around his bed he lost sight of his uncle and began to panic.

'I want my uncle, I want my uncle,' he cried. Hamed leaned over him and reassured him that he would be going with him to Kuwait. 'There's nothing to worry about,' he said.

Lt Breen was introduced to Ali. The young American doctor smiled and ruffled Ali's hair, saying: 'I'm here to help. I'm here to take you to Kuwait.' Dr Khayri translated for Ali, then Sheik Fartousi saw an opportunity to assert himself. Standing beside Ali's stretcher he gave a brief lecture about the US having caused Ali's injuries in the first place with its bombing of civilians.

'Before starting war you should think about all the women and children who will be injured,' he said, shaking a finger at Breen who towered about twenty centimetres over him. Dr Khayri translated that into English, and Breen gave a humble response.

Lt Sean Breen, the US military doctor, shaking hands with Sheik Fartousi as the cleric urges him to look after Ali. Behind them in a checked shirt is Ali's uncle Hamed, and behind him in the ambulance is Ali's nurse, Fatim Mohsin Sharhan. Ali is finally in the ambulance. John Feder

'I'm sorry,' he said calmly. 'I assure you I'm here to help.'

Fartousi then told Breen that the Americans should accept responsibility for Ali's full medical treatment.

'We are signing this paper and giving you this boy hoping to get him back and that you will take care of him. There must be no cheating or playing games.'

Dr Khayri did not know how to translate this politely, so he hesitated and left out the reference to cheating. Breen nodded again.

'We agree to take Ali into our care, and into our hearts,' he said.

His respectful tone lanced the tension. In place of medical records the acting hospital administrator then presented Breen with the soggy sheet of paper we had all signed.

As Ali's nurse prepared the stretcher to be moved, Fartousi quietly asked Stewart in Arabic to 'tell the Lieutenant I didn't mean to be so hard about the bombing and your responsibility'.

'We realise the bombing was probably a mistake as you were probably aiming at Ba'ath Party targets and we hope there will be more of this sort of cooperation.'

Ali was then wheeled out of the room and along a grimy corridor past another stretcher covered with large patches of blowflies. He was delighted to finally be heading for care, and gave quick, bright smiles. I had not anticipated this but even in his condition Ali was especially excited about flying in a helicopter. He was, after all, a twelve-year-old boy.

Metal ridges ran across the corridor every few metres and we lifted the stretcher over them to ease the pain for Ali, who winced with the slightest bump. He was wheeled into a lift with blood-stained metal doors for the brief trip to the ground floor. An amateur cameraman had been running next to the bed recording the scene on a camcorder for Sheik Fartousi, and when we all jammed into the lift Ali excitedly asked to see his picture in the camera's viewer. Amid the tension, military organisation and fears for his survival, the big grin he came out with at the sight of his own picture was another reminder that at the centre of all this drama was a bright boy who was not yet a teenager.

Ali was anxious about leaving his gentle nurse, Fatin. As he was wheeled along a final corridor into the late afternoon light of the courtyard he began whimpering and asking her to come with him.

With her own two young sons to care for and an important job at the hospital, Fatin had already explained to him that it was out of the question. Her soldier husband Talal had not been heard from for more than a week, forcing her to take her boys to work with her each day.

Ali's stretcher would not fit into the ambulance brought by the Americans. Another ambulance was tried, with plenty of shouting and waving of arms by hospital workers, but it had a mechanical problem.

As Ali waited on his stretcher and the American soldiers were becoming visibly twitchy, the hospital gates were suddenly thrown open and a van forced its way into the yard with its horn blaring. A distraught man with a blood-soaked shirt climbed out of the front seat and a crying woman fell out of a side door. They threw open the van's back door to reveal a dead man wrapped in a blanket.

Stewart was fretting, and told me he was worried that any other surprises could lead the militia to produce their hidden guns, which might panic the Americans. As doctors, guards, clerics, soldiers and spectators jostled uncertainly in the courtyard, a cousin of Ali's, 26-year-old Karvil Ibrahim, pushed through the crowd to Steve Martin. He had recognised Steve from an earlier visit he had made to the wreckage of Ali's family home, and had brought to the hospital three singed photographs of Ali's late father, mother and brother, which had been salvaged from the wreckage.

Openly weeping, Karvil handed Steve the photos, saying: 'Please show everyone the family we have lost. Then they too will know our grief.'

A third ambulance was now being sought for Ali, and Stewart yelled over the noise in English to try to reassure the Americans about what was happening. There was some pushing and shoving around Ali's stretcher as people in the crowd tried to see what was happening. It was loud, tense and hot enough for us all to be sweating.

It was also too late now to send photos for Wednesday's papers in Australia. I swore at the delay and, thinking out loud, said to John that it might now be best to send just one or two shots for Thursday's paper and hold off a proper photo essay until the weekend papers, when there would be more space and the photos would get a bigger treatment. He looked at me with some suspicion, and we had the only real spat of our whole time in Iraq.

'Fair go! We're not here just for the *Oz*,' he said. I was stung by his implication. *The Australian* relies more heavily than any other newspaper in the country on its weekend edition, when its sales and size are much larger than during the week. That means *The Australian*'s staff often direct special features at Saturdays, so John was suggesting that I was thinking only about my own paper instead of the whole News Ltd group.

'It was the *Oz* that wanted those photos for a fucking 8 a.m. edition the other night when I missed out on the statue coming down,' he said.

He had clearly been festering for a few days on the thought that *The Australian*'s demands had contributed to his missing the fall of the statue by keeping him busy sending extra photos instead of allowing him to get into our hotel room earlier. I was offended by his suggestion that I was favouring my own paper, as we both had been trying hard to service all the papers. I made some angry response – I think it began with the words 'Fuck off ...' – then we turned our attention back to the bun-fight around Ali's stretcher, both in foul moods.

I stepped back so John could get in front of me and photograph the muddled attempts to get Ali into an ambulance, but the APTV cameraman, who was much taller and stronger than John, shouldered his way into the gap, pushing John aside. John said 'Excuse me' once, got no response, then shoved back. The term 'pointy elbows' means nothing until you have seen press photographers in a scrum, and John's jostling skills had been refined over fifteen years.

This had nothing to do with Janine di Giovanni but she chipped at John for pushing the cameraman. I told her to shut up and stay out of the way. We had never met and she demanded to know who I was working for. I ignored her a few times but when she added 'I organised this, you know!' I lost my patience.

'No, you didn't organise it. I know what you tried to do and it came to nothing. We organised it and you're only here now because of me, so if I were you I'd just shut up and watch.'

She was indignant, demanding again to know who I was working for. I said 'Rupert, like you,' as *The Australian* is part of the same Murdoch empire that owns *The Times*. She nodded in a way that suggested I was somehow going to be reported on back at HQ.

Ali was finally placed in the back of a civilian ambulance, then

Top: Sheik Fartousi farewells Ali's uncle Hamed as the 12-year-old is finally evacuated.

Bottom: The procession around Ali's ambulance, led by Sheik Fartousi and Ali's uncle. The US soldiers were getting twitchy amid the crowd. John Feder

Fartousi told Stewart to ask Breen whether the Marines minded the locals saying a prayer for Ali. Breen agreed, perhaps expecting people to quietly bow their heads. Instead Fartousi yelled out the Arabic phrases for 'Allah is Great' and 'May Allah Bless the Child' and the crowd in the courtyard responded in unison, causing flinches from the heavily armed Marines in their midst.

By the time the ambulance edged out of its parking space, the Americans had been in the hospital for more than an hour and they were more anxious than ever to get out. We ran to the Pajero to follow, while the AP cameraman and di Giovanni and her driver got into their own cars.

When the convoy got onto the main road outside the hospital we found that about two hundred people were waiting to celebrate Ali's departure. Fartousi was determined to be the leader of that celebration. He had asked Ali's uncle to get out of the ambulance for a little while, prompting a distressed Ali to again yell 'I want my uncle' as the uncle jumped down and the vehicle's rear doors were closed on him.

Fartousi now took Hamed by the hand and walked in front of the ambulance, slowing the procession to walking pace as masses of people thronged around the nervous troops. A gunshot rang out from somewhere behind the crowd, and the Marines were openly jittery.

'God is great! God bless this child!' chanted the crowd as it packed in around the humvees and ambulance, stopping them from accelerating away.

Stewart, John and I jumped from the Pajero to see what was happening. John ran to the front of the procession and pushed through the crush to photograph the scene.

The last thing the Americans wanted was to be in the middle of a chanting crowd. Scenes like this had gone wrong all over Iraq, as nervous soldiers opened fire on unruly crowds or even family cars which came too close to checkpoints. Breen was worried, and he yelled out from his vehicle to Stewart, asking him to get Fartousi out of the way so the convoy could take off. Stewart tried to get Fartousi's attention but the cleric simply grabbed his hand and kept walking, with Stewart in one hand and Hamed in the other.

Two pigeons of peace were released into the air and after what seemed fifteen minutes but must have been about five, the cleric theatrically kissed Hamed on the forehead to send him on his way with the community's best wishes. The whole performance had guaranteed that Fartousi was the centre of attention for as long as possible. Anybody in the crowd would have thought the wily cleric had triumphantly tamed the Americans and forced them to save Ali.

As Hamed clambered into the back of the ambulance we ran back to the Pajero. One second after we had jumped into the car one of the humvees roared past, smashing into the open door before John could close it. With children and cheering adults running to wave off the convoy, we broke clear of the crowd and raced after the convoy through the early dusk.

The airbase turned out to be a US Marines base in a former Iraqi secret police headquarters at Baladiyat, about ten kilometres away. We were stopped at the front gates of the base. The AP cameraman had followed us but now he gave up and headed for town to try to get back to his hotel before dark. As the light faded we waited for fifteen minutes before Lt Breen sent a soldier to the gate to admit us.

Ali was still being prepared for his flight in one of several tents housing a mobile shock trauma platoon, an eight-member team equipped to provide basic medical services in the field. Lieutenant Aaron Jacobs, a 35-year-old intensive care unit nurse from San Diego, said Ali was reasonably comfortable.

'He's not really in pain unless you move him around a bit. Most of his burns are third degree so the nerve endings are gone. It's the lesser burns on the edge of the third degree [burns] that will hurt him. He's got those second degree burns around the pelvis and shoulders, where the third degree ends.

'But this is the right time to get him out. Once the infections start, saving him becomes very hard. As soon as it becomes septic it's a big problem. He needs to get to a major burns facility fast, but with the right environment and treatment he should be OK.

'Keeping him warm during the flight is the big challenge because the skin is gone. He was complaining that he's too hot the way we have got him rugged up but there will be a lot of air flowing through the chopper and that will cool him down.'

Ali had been lifted onto a military stretcher. Four big soldiers carried it gently across open ground from the tents towards a Black Hawk chopper waiting 250 metres away. Another couple of medicos walked beside the stretcher.

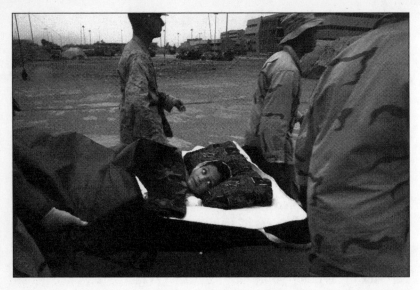

Ali being carried to the helicopter. He was excited to be going on a helicopter.
John Feder

Ali looked around excitedly, his fear once again replaced by excitement about going in a helicopter. As we walked along behind his stretcher I asked Hamed how he thought Ali kept finding such flashes of high spirits.

'He is enthusiastic to go and get treatment because he wants to be normal again,' he said. 'He wants to start eating with his hands again and playing football, playing with other children and doing ordinary things. He is very keen to get better and just wants it all to start. I have told him it will be hard, and maybe painful at first but he just wants to do whatever he has to do to get better.'

Ali whimpered with pain as his stretcher was slid into the racks of the chopper. The medic who was going to travel with him, along with two pilots and a radio operator, went to work securing the stretcher.

Hamed carried just a few possessions in his arms and was nervous about leaving Iraq for the first time in his life and dealing with the Kuwaitis. We told him we would come to Kuwait the following day to help him there. I asked if he was worried about leaving his own wife and children for what could be months and his answer was a nod towards Ali.

'What else can I do?' he asked. 'Look at this boy. What else can I do?'

As Ali called for water and the rotors began to accelerate we each embraced Hamed, who again put his open hand over his heart and nodded his head. He clambered into the back, where he leaned over Ali with a water bottle and shouted to him over the roar of the rotors. We backed away and the Black Hawk lifted off just after 7.45 p.m.

As we waved to the uncle in the gusts of wind and dust I cried for the second time over Ali, this time from relief and pleasure.

It was dark and well past curfew when we drove away but we were exhilarated. The photos of his evacuation would be appreciated by our newspapers but more importantly we had actually made a difference for Ali, who was now likely to survive and get a chance to build a decent life.

When we got back to our hotel we had a special little celebration in our room, mainly because of Ali's evacuation but also because it was our last night together. Stewart and I would leave early the next morning for Kuwait and John would spend another day in Baghdad then drive west to Jordan with Ian, Bob and Steve Martin.

Ed Martin came to our room to congratulate us and to use our phone to let the Kuwaitis know when Ali would be arriving. As we stood around having our final beers together Martin made regular calls to check the progress of Ali's trip, with each update bringing louder cheers. After a two-and-a-half-hour flight they landed at a navy and marine emergency medical base near Nasiriya in southern Iraq, where they were transferred to a C-130 for the flight to Kuwait City.

John said over a beer that he was more than ready to go. He had become increasingly nervous about leaving the hotel in the last couple of days and told me he was 'totally over it'.

I joked that I was emotionally scarred from our fight that day and he laughed, saying that a one-minute argument in the whole war was pretty good going, especially when some photographer–reporter teams around us had been at each other's throats. We all laughed as we recounted the tension in the hospital. I carried on about the striking mix of people who had been involved, impersonating a movie director using a loudspeaker to choreograph the scene.

'Could we have an American military doctor please – tall, good-looking blond guy in combat fatigues? And send in a Muslim cleric from central casting – a short guy, black beard, turban, with a fanatical look to his eyes? Now gimme a compassionate uncle, an obviously decent guy with a gentle face . . . '

There were plenty of people around but the three of us spent most of the evening together, talking about the thirty-six days I had been with John and twenty-one days we had been with Stewart. We were delighted it was over but this had been one of the most intensely 'bonding' times of our lives – being afraid together and relying on each other's friendship and humour as much as our professional skills.

What I had particularly appreciated about John and Stewart was that they had both been able to show their feelings and fears. They had made it OK for me to admit at various times that I was scared, or lost, or making it up as I went along, allowing an honesty which made it easier to deal with the hairier moments.

The huge coverage in Britain of Ali's rescue mostly attributed it to Tony Blair's supposed intervention, a self-serving myth that suggested the British media's own coverage had prodded their PM into saving the day. Several British reporters later told me that the PM's spin doctors had given background briefings claiming that Downing Street had indeed been involved.

Later in the year I asked Alastair Campbell, Blair's recently resigned communications chief, about the reports of Downing Street's involvement.

'I know that went around but I don't know where it came from. It's just bollocks,' he said. 'We weren't involved, and we didn't put it around that we were but that's what people [in the press] ran with.'

Janine di Giovanni reported in *The Times* that 'A US navy medical liaison officer, Petty Officer Ed Martin, arranged the evacuation after hearing that the Kuwaiti Ministry of Health wanted to take over the child's care and that he could be accompanied by his uncle for the treatment.'

'Not all Iraqis welcomed Ali's removal,' was her interpretation of what she had witnessed.

'As his ambulance pulled out of the hospital with American military vehicles on either side, a crowd shouted prayers from the Koran and punched their fists.

'It was believed that the Shia sheikhs now in charge of the hospital's security objected to the child being evacuated by Americans who could then claim that they were rescuing him.'

Ali landed in Kuwait City at 1.30 a.m. to a media crush organised by the Kuwaitis. He was taken by ambulance to an intensive care unit before being moved to a burns centre within the Ibn Sina medical complex on the edge of Kuwait City.

It has one of the best burns units and biggest plastic surgery centres in Europe or the Middle East. Ali was put in a private room fitted with a US$100,000 fluid bed filled with silicon and sand, minimising pressure on his burns.

I finished my report on his evacuation about 3 a.m. then called Michael Stutchbury to say it was the last story I would be filing before leaving Iraq. He said he wanted me to come back to Australia soon and to knock out a book on the war. I was pleased by his enthusiasm but still too drained to think about much beyond getting to Kuwait safely, making sure Hamed and Ali were coping and then flying home to London.

I was exhausted and needed to be up at 7 a.m. for an early start on the long drive south but I still had trouble sleeping. On our last night in Baghdad, like the first, I was sitting alone on the balcony at 3.30 a.m., looking at a skyline dotted with smoke and hearing the occasional burst of gunfire.

9

SOUTH TO KUWAIT

Just after dawn on Wednesday 16 April the driveway of the Palestine Hotel was busy with departing journalists trying to organise convoys so they would not have to drive out of Iraq on their own. We agreed to go with a few cars from CNN, knowing they were always backed up by squads of fixers and security advisers.

When the Pajero was loaded we lined up in front of it for photos with John, a mix of tired, stubbled faces. Although Stewart had been snapping away at souvenir photos for the past few weeks John and I had taken hardly any of ourselves. There were final hugs with John. It was hard to believe that the three of us had only met a few weeks earlier, and we knew that the friendships we had formed would be long-term.

Stewart and I were taking a desert route to Kuwait which was longer but, according to the CNN people, safer than the busier highway further east on which we had been driven north during the war. We knew that four-wheel drives were being attacked and robbed on Iraq's long, unprotected highways, so it would be a nervous drive lasting something like eight hours.

The fertile Mesopotamian plains soon gave way to open desert as we headed south. The sealed road ran out after a few hours and we found ourselves on a rough sandy-gravel road in sand storms which at times reduced visibility to a few metres. For some unknown reason sharp metal construction rods occasionally stuck ten centimetres out of the road to present an extra trap for the tyres of the unwary or unlucky.

Bedouin tribesmen with small herds of camels or goats waved every now and then. To avoid stopping in towns we finished off the last decent bits of our MREs while driving and we refuelled by the side of the road from our own jerry cans. During one stop we chatted with a young shepherd who said the war had not affected his life at all – he had known something was going on but nobody bothered him so he just kept taking his sheep out in the morning and putting them away at night.

An hour north of Basra the convoy was stopped and searched by a small unit of American soldiers who had spent the war guarding a bridge over a dried river bed in what looked like the middle of nowhere. They seemed to have gone feral – none wore shirts, they were all muscles and tattoos. Waiting for the cars ahead of us to be searched, we chatted with two who said they were going out of their heads with boredom.

'We were told to protect this bridge but nobody attacked the mother-fucker.'

It occurred to me that the landscape and tedium that these twenty-first-century soldiers had been stuck with was no different from that which British colonial officers had to tolerate in outposts in this part of the world in the nineteenth century. British officers sent to one early telegraphic station had such a hard time in the isolation that many went mad. The station was on a small island in a bend of the Khor ash-Sham, a rocky inlet, and being sent there gave birth to the expression 'going round the bend'.

When the bored young Americans said they hadn't had a drink in weeks I fished out the last cans of Bavarian beer, apologising that it was pretty bad stuff.

'Man, I'd sniff glue if you had some,' said one.

Held up again at another roadblock four hundred metres further on, we could see, in the rear vision mirror, half a dozen of the shirtless soldiers standing in a tight circle in the sun drinking the warm Bavarian on the spot, a thought that almost made me gag.

The children we occasionally passed seemed more aggressive than ever in running at our cars with their hands out. Instead of food or water they were now calling out for money. About forty kilometres from Kuwait we had to drop behind the convoy to fill up with petrol. A group of about eight teenage boys trotted along the side of the road to surround the Pajero, asking for money or anything else we had. We opened the rear doors to give them some water and a few packets of food but stupidly forgot to lock the doors. As we drove off they pounced, ripping open the rear doors and the right-hand back passenger door to grab a cardboard box and some plastic bags packed with food and other odds and ends.

I jumped out to run after them. At the same time a passing truck careered off the road and two middle-aged Iraqi men leapt out to join the chase. They snatched most of the food from one of the youths, then to my amazement they ran back to their truck and drove off. Instead of stopping to help us they had seized a sudden opportunity to take some of the loot stolen from the foreigners. Stewart yelled at me to let the rest of our stuff go rather than giving chase. He was right – we were less than an hour from Kuwait so we didn't need the food or any last minute conflicts.

But when we had driven about twenty metres I realised that one of the bags they had stolen contained Ali's family's last surviving photos of his parents. Steve Martin had given them to us to take to Kuwait for Ali and his uncle. Stewart spun the car around and tore off down the dirt track where the youths had disappeared. They were triumphantly dividing up their take when they heard the roar of our engine and looked up to see us coming after them. They scattered, dropping much of the loot, including the box with the photos. We were relieved to get back on the highway but rattled by this little show of hostility and by the opportunism of the men in the truck.

We detoured to Umm Qasr to see whether our tent or any of the clothes and toiletries that had been left behind might still be on the docks. As soon as we got near the town there was a nasty feeling on the road. Sullen children ran threateningly at the car and even played chicken on the road ahead of us to try to make us stop. The atmosphere was uglier than a couple of weeks earlier.

Once again we got stuck at the port gates, this time because they were manned by a Spanish soldier. He spoke no English and my Spanish lessons of the previous summer were now exposed as a total waste of time. We drove to the new port and waited an hour or so for a British officer, who took us into the old dock for a fruitless search for our things. The officer was disparaging about his Spanish allies.

'The Coalition is desperate to make out that lots of countries are involved, so the Spanish said they would come as long as they didn't have to do anything dangerous,' he said. 'They are pathetic.

All we want from them is to be here and look after themselves and they can't even manage that. They make a big deal of handing out food to [Iraqi] kids in front of the Spanish media – then we have to feed the bloody Spanish.'

At the border, Kuwaiti guards were much more diligent in searching our bags than Stewart had expected. They confiscated a bottle of Red Label whisky and one of gin. After another hour's drive to Kuwait City we were standing at the reception desk of the SAS Radisson just after 6 p.m. when John called the hotel to check that we had made it. We could not get a room in the hotel but the receptionist let us chat to John. His fears about the next day's drive to Jordan had not been helped by reports of several attacks and robberies on the road that day. One news crew had apparently arrived in Amman naked.

Stewart dropped me at the Marriott Hotel in the centre of Kuwait City. Never has a hotel room, with hot water and clean sheets, seemed so luxurious. I went online in my room and saw that the news agencies were reporting on a CNN interview in which Kiera Roche, a spokeswoman of the UK Limbless Association, gave the impression that the association had somehow been involved in getting Ali to safety. This was the start of a new competition among various charities to be involved in his rehabilitation and it was linked to efforts by half the British media to claim credit for getting him out.

The Limbless Association had been one of several British charities to form alliances with newspapers to raise money for 'Ali funds' or 'Ali appeals'. The association's 'Ali Fund', backed by the *Daily Mail* group's giveaway newspaper *Metro*, raised £350,000 which the association promised would be spent on Ali or other limbless Iraqi children. The association's problem was keeping that promise, as it had no infrastructure for operating in Iraq and did not know whether the Kuwaiti Government would choose it to provide Ali's prosthetic arms.

Using a 'poster child' who has touched public hearts to raise funds for a wider cause has become a common marketing strategy for charities around the world. In my view it is reasonable, as long as donors are not misled into believing the money will go to that particular child.

Ali was an unusually powerful marketing 'vehicle', especially in Britain, where more than a million pounds were raised in his name or using his image. Not a penny of it was involved in getting him out of the country – the US military had provided the evacuation and the Kuwaiti Government was paying for his medical care.

The *Daily Mirror*'s 'Ali Appeal' brought in more than £280,000, which went to Unicef's general work with Iraqi children. *The Mirror* at times mistakenly told its readers the money was 'for Ali' but like most of the charities and newspapers it was usually careful to say it would be for 'children like Ali'.

Two other British newspaper appeals relied heavily on Ali's story but were not named after him. One raised £133,000 for the Save the Children Fund to spend in Iraq while the other earned £304,000 for the Red Cross, which spent the money on its general activities in Baghdad like providing clean water and generators for hospitals.

I sat up until 4.30 a.m. on that first night out of Iraq answering e-mail and calling my family, deeply tired but still too wired to savour the softest bed I had ever slept in.

Three days before we left Iraq, Steve Martin had visited Salah's family to see whether there was any news of Salah. He got the news before he had even reached their house. As the driver he had hired for the day turned into the family's street Steve could hear women wailing and crying. Salah's body had been found the previous night, still sitting in his white sedan.

After searching for six days Zubaydah had learned on Saturday that several passenger cars had been shot up by American tanks in a street that had since been closed off. US troops were still forbidding access to the area but she tied a white flag to a stick and walked to the pile of wrecked cars with her son Ali. In the car with Salah's body they found food for Steve and fuel for the generator in his room at the Palestine Hotel. He was buried a few hours before Steve visited the following day.

Steve went back to see Salah's family again while Stewart and I were driving out of Iraq. He left them US$2000 to keep them going until his newspaper could organise more support for her and her four children.

Bob Graham, representing the *Daily Mail*, and David Blair of the *Daily Telegraph* had gone with him because their newspapers had also regularly used Salah's services. Salah drove for Blair for five or six weeks until the *Telegraph* pulled its man out of Baghdad the day before the war, then he worked for Ross Benson of the *Daily Mail* before moving on to his final employer, the Mirror group. The three newspaper groups eventually gave the family more money, with the Mirror giving the most.

Salah's family was disappointed with the support they received from some of his former employers. The *Sunday Telegraph*, for instance, ran a lengthy article after Salah's death in which one of its reporters explained how much she and her colleagues owed him for his courage and help over the years. But the Telegraph companies – in the headlines around that time for paying tens of millions of dollars in questionable fees to its managers, and spending millions more redecorating a private aircraft for its then chairman, Conrad Black – offered just a few thousand pounds to Salah's family. According to Zubaydah's relatives in England, the three newspaper companies gave her and her four children a total of about £11,000, but that is no longer the fortune it was in Saddam's isolated Iraq.

One year on, Zubaydah, who gave up her job as a bank worker after marrying Salah, had still not been able to find work in a Baghdad where it was dangerous simply to drive the streets. The family relied on the US$200 monthly salary that the eldest daughter Nawar earned at the Ministry of Industry.

Bob recalls that, as the three reporters drove back from visiting the family that day, they passed the Foreign Ministry, still smouldering, prompting him to regale his colleagues with my tale about groping around with Stewart amid the looters in the darkened offices. Bob and his colleagues laughed at the thought of Stewart and me staggering out, covered in ashes and sweat, and my forehead gashed by a bump in the dark, triumphantly clutching a folder with 'Australia' written on it in Arabic.

'If I was staying any longer I'd wait until the fires die down and spend a good few days in there,' said Bob, who was due to leave with John and Ian the next day.

'Good idea,' said Blair.

Six days later the *Telegraph* broke one of Britain's biggest scoops of the year. Blair had gone into the same rooms of the Foreign Ministry and struck gold in the ministry's much more expansive dossiers on

Britain – documents purporting to show that British Labour MP George Galloway had received money from the Saddam regime.

When I asked Blair about this months later he said he could not remember Bob suggesting that he go into the ministry looking for files, and could not discuss the issue because Galloway was suing the newspaper.

*

Stewart spent our first full day in Kuwait at the burns hospital helping Ali's uncle and doctors cope with the press. Our intention had been to help Hamed deal with the Kuwaitis but his most pressing problem was the flood of media requests. The doctors eventually asked Stewart for a written summary of what had happened to Ali, to make their press dealings easier, so I spent much of the day at my hotel compiling a précis.

In the afternoon I took copies of that document to the hospital, which had been staked out by ITN and other news crews. Plastic surgeon Dr Imad Al Najada was grateful for the help. A forty year old in charge of the hospital's emergency team, he had spent a year training in Adelaide as well as working in Germany and Taiwan, and was Ali's main doctor in Kuwait.

The hospital's ample stocks of anaesthetic had given Ali his first full day without pain but the evacuation could not have come much later, Dr Najada said.

'He has gone a long time without proper treatment. He's lucky he didn't get septic shock or multi-organ failure,' he said. 'The flame burn was very severe and his charring was bad.'

Dr Najada had already removed the blackened skin on Ali's third degree burns in a seventy-five-minute operation, replacing it with temporary grafts from cadavers in the hospital's skin bank to protect him from infection and stabilise his fluid levels.

'He wasn't a difficult case,' Dr Najada said. 'We treat people at this facility with up to ninety per cent burns and Ali has enough skin coverage left (on his back and legs) to provide the grafts he needs.' The doctor had found Ali to be an unusually intelligent and mature child. 'He told me he wishes no other child has to go through what he has been through,' he said.

Dr Najada was not optimistic about the prospects of Ali being able to use prosthetics, or false arms, as his arms had been left roughly like those on the broken Venus de Milo statue, both stumps extremely short, with the right slightly longer than the left.

'I think they will be more cosmetic than functional,' he said. 'He has lost his left arm from just below the shoulder and even the other arm is just a few inches longer, so he is going to find it very, very hard to do much with them.'

Several other Iraqi children had been brought to the hospital for treatment but the Kuwaitis were making a special fuss about Ali as the best-known civilian victim of the war. A procession of local charities and television cameras had headed for his bedside, and members of the Kuwaiti royal family were planning to make their own highly publicised visits.

The Kuwaitis had provided Hamed with his own room in the hospital, and that night Stewart and I took him shopping in Kuwait City. Having arrived with few possessions, he was now surrounded by well-to-do Kuwaitis and needed to buy some new trousers. Several Kuwaitis had visited Ali with gifts of toys and a CD player so Hamed also wanted a lockable suitcase.

As we walked through menswear shops in the late evening Hamed was a relieved man. Ali had been upbeat throughout the day but got tired and cranky in the evening, refusing to eat his dinner and giving his nurses a difficult time. Hamed had been summoned to impose some order. The whole performance left him feeling that Ali was coping well with his extraordinary situation.

The Kuwaitis had promised to pay both Hamed's and Ali's costs, so the money offered by Tony Trevisan was not needed to support Hamed. Standing in a dimly lit arcade I asked Hamed what was his biggest worry. I thought he might say he needed a car so Ali's family could visit him in Kuwait, or that his main concern was the longer-term challenge of paying for Ali's education and looking after his sisters.

He said the thing that was worrying him most was where his suddenly expanded family would live. Hamed lived upstairs in a two-storey home and his brother's family lived downstairs. Hamed and his wife shared their half of the house with his mother, two sons and three daughters, and they now had to squeeze in Ali, his stepmother, her son and five of her daughters – a total of sixteen people.

When I asked how much a larger home would cost he estimated that to buy land in their village and build a house would cost about 20 million dinar, at that time about US$9000. It struck me that paying for such a home would be a worthwhile project if I could build on the US$5000 that Trevisan had already offered. While being careful not to make any promises, I floated the idea with Hamed, who agreed that if I could find that money the house would be built in Ali's name.

Owning the family home might change Ali's status within the family from burden to provider, and in the longer run it could significantly improve his marital prospects. Organising it would also be relatively straightforward as it would not require complicated trust funds or any ongoing commitment through trusteeships.

That night I called Trevisan and put the idea to him. He said he was confident that some friends with whom he had made previous donations would match his US$5000 to fund the house but he couldn't contact them until the following week because we were heading into the Easter long weekend. I said I would wait for their answer rather than talk to my editors about the possibility of asking readers to come up with the money.

Happy to be getting out in one piece. Stewart Innes, Ian McPhedran, me and John Feder behind the statue that John had photographed a few days earlier standing in front of the air force headquarters in Baghdad.

The next morning, Good Friday, I flew off for London, leaving Stewart to sort out the return of the hire car. The Pajero had a crushed door, dented roof, half a dozen bent panels and a damaged electrical system. As he drove me to the airport Stewart said he had decided halfway through our travels that this media work might be his calling, or at least an interesting job for a while. He had done a beginner's photography course many years earlier and had spent the war watching John closely and asking a lot of questions. He had decided to buy himself a decent camera and a 4WD and to offer his services as a media fixer, complete with car, camera and translating skills.

He would in fact find quite a bit of work in the coming months, initially with the Associated Press agency. Each time that work took him to Baghdad he visited Ali's family and let them use his mobile sat phone, which was the only way they could speak to Ali and Hamed in Kuwait. Stewart ended up spending a lot of his own time over the next few months helping Ali and Hamed.

As we unloaded my bags at the airport Stewart produced a parting gift for John and me: two pocket knives identical to his own sturdy little Swiss blade.

I got to London late in the afternoon. After a shower and a little time at home, Pilita and I went to dinner at a restaurant on the Thames with friends who had been expecting her to arrive alone. Pilita was exhausted, having struggled to sleep for the past few weeks. Apart from the stress, she had been working full-time during the day and spending much of the night calling or e-mailing Australia, trying to find out the latest on me and keeping family and friends informed.

*

That Easter weekend a Sydney talk-back radio host and former journalist, Mike Carlton, wrote a column in the *Sydney Morning Herald* attacking News Ltd's Iraq coverage, claiming that 'all 16,475 journalists' employed by the firm had sycophantically supported the war to fit in with Rupert Murdoch's views. I thought it was an odd way to characterise my work, as I had hardly been a cheerleader for war. It was a blanket insult of thousands of journalists that did little to enlighten the real problems of diversity in a media industry of such heavily concentrated ownership as Australia's. But what particularly offended me about Carlton's column was his attack on our papers' treatment of my Ali stories.

Referring to 'gutter journalism of the most gross and tawdry cynicism, a disgusting exploitation of a child's tragedy', he feigned outrage that each News Ltd paper had identified the team involved in Ali's evacuation – John, Stewart and I – as 'their' team in Baghdad. As he and everybody else in the industry knew, we had in fact been 'their' team. What our papers did was what Fairfax's *Age* and *Sydney Morning Herald* (Carlton's employer) did in Iraq with Paul McGeough and Lindsay Murdoch – shared their costs and then described them as 'their' men.

In the same issue of the SMH, McGeough referred to the coverage of Ali's plight in the Australian media as 'the latest media stunts' surrounding the twelve year old, an apparent reference to our involvement in the boy's case. The ABC's 'Media Watch' program noted two days later that each of our newspapers had told their readers that its team had organised the evacuation. It was a cheap point but 'Media Watch's' David Marr was at least more gracious than Carlton and the SMH.

'Success has so many fathers. Yet News Ltd's men in Baghdad actually had something to be proud of here,' said Marr, noting that I had written a comment piece warning that Ali's evacuation 'does not diminish the fact that there are many more Alis in Iraq who have not caught the attention of foreigners'.

I was furious with Carlton and the SMH. I e-mailed and telephoned asking for a right of reply but not surprisingly Carlton did not allow me to discuss the issue on his radio program. The SMH published a letter of protest from the editor of *The Australian* but the damage had been done.

Tony Trevisan called me straight after the Easter break to say he had been amazed to find that his wealthy friends in Sydney wanted nothing to do with our efforts to help Ali, and that they had cited the SMH's coverage as the reason. Based in Perth, Trevisan said he had not seen the Carlton column, nor McGeough's report but his friends certainly had.

Trevisan, who by now had received some publicity for his generosity towards Ali, said he would stand by his own promise of

US$5000 and I still wanted to find the extra $5000 for a house. Bob Graham suggested that, rather than paying it myself, some of the reporters who had been in Baghdad could kick in the money, and several of my own friends offered to contribute. Michael Stutchbury eventually approached News Ltd chairman Lachlan Murdoch, who authorised the company to match Trevisan's donation to help buy Ali's home.

I began a few weeks of sleep and sloth, spending more time following the cricket in Australia than the news from Iraq. The only thing I put any work into was calling Kuwait to follow Ali's progress. I wrote a couple of updates on him in the following weeks but I was mainly keeping an eye on him out of my own curiosity.

A few days after arriving in Kuwait, Ali had a scare when he caught the hospital 'superbug' MRSA but quick treatment in his own room in the intensive care unit fended off the life-threatening infection.

Soon after a 30 April operation to complete his grafts, and just two weeks after his arrival, he was able to start spending time with the five other Iraqi children who had been taken to the hospital with war wounds. His new best friend was Ahmed Hamza, a fourteen-year-old shepherd who lost his left foot and right hand when a US missile struck his family's home. Ahmed, who had left school at nine, lived barely a kilometre from Ali's home but they had not met before the war. The missile strike on the afternoon of 1 April, less than two days after Ali's family was hit, killed Ahmed's thirteen-year-old sister Jinan, blinded his brother Saad in one eye and slightly injured their father Mohammed.

On 14 May, four weeks after arriving in Kuwait, Ali walked for the first time, taking a few shaky steps in his room as he started to regain his muscle strength. Still waiting for the swelling on the stumps of his arms to go down, several specialists worked on his burns to minimise scarring and prevent skin tears, while others began his physiotherapy treatment and taught him to do new things with his feet – to paint, write, hold a fork, even to work a camera.

'It's not just that he is clever, which he is,' Dr Najada told me a few weeks later. 'He really wants to learn and he works hard. He can already use his feet like his hands. He can take off elastic socks with his toes, he can hang up his own T-shirt, he can even write and draw with his toes.

'Ali is just so, so determined – he keeps saying he is going to go home and be normal and do things for himself.'

Ali's status as the icon of Iraqi suffering led to visits by an odd collection of foreigners vying to be part of his future. The parade by his bedside included the head of an American charity bearing a letter from Arnold Schwarzenegger, a British journalist delivering a football shirt signed by David Beckham, Kuwait's foreign minister, Britain's shadow minister for foreign aid, and cameramen and producers from two British TV networks competing to produce the first documentary about Ali.

Offers of help came from Japan, Spain, Canada and Italy. The president of the UK Limbless Association, Mr Zafar Khan, a London pharmacist who lost his own right leg above the knee, flew to Kuwait to show Ali the latest artificial arms and invite him to London to be treated with some of the money the association had raised in his name.

'It is like there is a big competition going on between some of these [groups], and Ali is the prize,' Dr Najada told me in May as the circus around the twelve year old from the village of Zafaraniya grew stranger, reflecting the ways of the global media, modern governments and the cult of celebrity.

At various times erroneous media reports declared that there would be a huge benefit concert for Ali in the US, a Hollywood film of his life, Canadian passports for him and his family and imminent flights to New York for treatment. Then he was definitely going to London. Then it was Los Angeles. Then it was Toronto.

An example of how wacky things were becoming was a widely published report in May by the news agency Agence France Presse that 'a constellation of Tinseltown stars – including Arnold Schwarzenegger, Angelina Jolie, Mariah Carey, Ashanti and Justin Timberlake – have signed on for the effort to bring Ali to Los Angeles for medical treatment.' The report continued:

'Other luminaries including Christina Aguilera are also on board and top names like George Clooney and Julia Roberts are expected to join their ranks, promoter Cheryl Shuman said.

"He needs prostheses and he is very, very badly burned and there's just no money to help him and maybe nowhere for him to go,' she said.'

Spokespeople for those stars quickly denied any knowledge of such a concert, and from London I tried to figure out what was going on.

The reports of a Hollywood extravaganza flowed from the involvement of a small US charity called the Global Medical Relief Fund, which wanted to send Ali to New York to live with the charity's founder, Elissa Montanti. Montanti had taken several other amputees into her home since 1997, creating a charity that had helped about twenty young war victims and amputees. British Airways gave her free tickets to visit Ali in Kuwait, and booked a flight to the US for Ali in the belief that he would be leaving with her.

Boro Vukadinovic, a film producer who funds the charity, told me that the fund was planning to include Ali in a documentary to promote its own activities.

'Ali is a bit afraid of America, for obvious reasons, but right now everything looks like he is coming,' he told me. 'I do not want Ali or anybody in Kuwait or Iraq to think we are bringing him here to exploit him. The aim of this mission is to make our organisation as visible as possible and bring a normal life to as many children as possible.

'Ali has become a poster child of the war in Iraq. He is the one child who is a quasi-celebrity amputee – we want to help in anyway we can.'

I then tracked down Cheryl Shuman, the spokeswoman who had been quoted talking about the concert. A former model and optician who now specialised in product placement in Hollywood movies – one of her coups was providing Arnie's sunglasses in *Terminator* – Shuman said the concert had been her idea and she was still sure that any star who was invited would take part.

Shuman said she had worked for ten months on another charity concert and album conceived by Michael Jackson after the September 11 bombings, but it had been cancelled after Jackson dangled his baby from a hotel balcony and ran into other child-related problems.

'My plan was to take the same celebrities and sponsors and do a fully-sponsored concert for Ali,' she said. 'It would be some of the same musicians from the first record and the same basic business model. We already have the sponsors in place from that concert.'

Shuman cried while telling me how moved she had been when she first saw Ali in a television news report, and said she believed such a concert 'could heal a lot of wounds'.

'I believe Ali can be a symbol for the whole world to heal all our wounds, whether they be emotional, physical or spiritual. Maybe I'm delusional but I think this kid could really have a major impact on the world.

'Ali would choose his favourite performers and would speak at the start of the concert. The thing that I envision for this little boy is to take him to Disneyland with his favourite movie star to give him hope and make him smile.'

Shuman was shocked when I told her that Ali had never seen a Hollywood movie, could not pick his favourite US pop star because he did not know any, was unlikely to know Schwarzenegger and did not speak English. I learned later that Ali had seen the *Terminator* poster on the streets of Baghdad but when Montanti visited him and read out a letter of encouragement from Schwarzenegger he could not place the name.

Shuman was also surprised to learn that Ali did not need to be urgently evacuated from his hospital in Kuwait, and that it was a different hospital from the embattled one in Baghdad that she had heard about on television.

I told Montanti and her colleagues that they were unlikely to get Ali to New York, away from his family and the support of the Kuwaiti Government, and I suggested that they might instead try to help some of the hundreds of injured Iraqi children receiving little help from foreign governments and agencies. After visiting Ali in Kuwait she went on to Iraq, and while Ali's photo did end up featuring on her group's website, she vowed to help other children.

The continuing media interest in Ali meant that his 'uncle' Hamed was receiving a crash course in British cheque-book journalism. Several newspapers and television groups were vying for exclusive access to his story and offering money for the privilege. Hamed asked Stewart and me for advice but was mainly guided by Ali's Kuwaiti doctors, who were providing much more than just medical treatment.

The *Daily Mirror* and ITN eventually bought rights to his story but at one point a British journalist asked Dr Najada whether he could borrow his camera to take copies of the doctor's undeveloped photos of Ali. According to Dr Najada the journalist left the country with both the camera and the photos.

Although I followed Ali's progress quite closely I found it hard to motivate myself to do any other work. I spent my days lounging around home while Pilita was at work, and I had no trouble sleeping. Pilita said I seemed withdrawn and I noticed that the smallest triggers, such as a nostalgic moment in a movie or a passing reference in a television news report to the death of a child, would occasionally bring a flood of sentiment, even tears.

After a few weeks of taking it easy I tried once or twice to get excited about stories but everything seemed trivial.

In Canberra, John and Ian were also struggling to get their minds back on work, although a federal government budget forced them back into action after just a couple of weeks off.

*

At the end of May, Pilita and I returned to Australia for ten days. It was my mother's birthday – I had been stuck in Baghdad for my parent's fiftieth wedding anniversary – and News Ltd was holding a dinner with the company's editors in Canberra for our team from Iraq.

It may not be a coincidence that it was during this trip, when I was talking a lot to friends and family about the war, that I began having trouble sleeping. I would go to bed tired but wake around midnight with a racing heart and anxious breathing. I could not remember having had stressful dreams but I still lay wide awake until just before dawn.

News Ltd offers counselling to journalists returning from con-flict zones and I decided to see somebody if these anxiety attacks continued. They stopped after a couple of weeks so I didn't bother. John had one session with a counsellor at his home in Canberra but decided it wasn't worth continuing. He told me over a few beers at the end of the year that he probably should have kept on with the counselling, and he was thinking about doing so.

Dr Anthony Feinstein, a Canadian psychiatrist who is a world expert on post-traumatic stress among journalists, interviewed eighty reporters who covered the Iraq war and found that just seven per cent had received counselling at some point in their careers for war-related stress. In a 2003 study of war reporters, Dr Feinstein found that twenty-eight per cent of reporters with significant experience covering conflicts had at some point suffered from post-traumatic stress disorder and 'a slightly smaller number had developed clinically significant depression', rates well above 'those in journalists who had never been in zones of conflict'.

In his research on the Iraq conflict Dr Feinstein asked journalists several months after the war whether they had experienced certain symptoms over the previous week. Almost a quarter said they had experienced the following: 'thinking about a traumatic event in Iraq even when they didn't mean to; trouble staying asleep; traumatic dreams; images of a traumatic event unexpectedly popping into their minds; and reminders of events triggering waves of strong emotion'.

'During the previous two weeks between a quarter and a half of all journalists reported feeling the following: sad much of the time; discouraged about the future; a sense of failure; less enjoyment of life; guilt; restless and wound up; a loss of interest in people; difficulty making decisions; lack of energy; and a loss of interest in sex,' Dr Feinstein reported.

'Of concern was the fact that eleven per cent of journalists had had thoughts of suicide during this fortnight, although none was planning on acting on them.'

The dinner with News Ltd editors was an old-fashioned counselling session, with plenty of alcohol and congratulatory speeches, and it was greatly appreciated by Ian, John, Rory and me.

I used my speech to exhort the News Ltd editors, who between them produce something like seventy per cent of the daily newspapers sold in Australia, to be deeply sceptical about embedding reporters in future conflicts, saying that I expected the Australian military to follow the Pentagon and decide that the embedding in Iraq was the template for future coverage of conflicts.

Embedding gave the media unprecedented access to the frontlines and could be a useful innovation if paired with liberal access for journalists travelling independently. One obvious trade-off was that the embeds had to sign agreements banning off-the-record interviews with military personnel and forbidding the press to use their own transport. They also had to promise not to describe battles until they were over, report missing aircraft while search and rescue was underway, or visit medical centres without prior approval.

But there were much greater problems in the embedding system – primarily the temptation for military planners to use it exclusively, keeping independent or 'unilateral' reporters away from the conflict zone.

Not only did the Coalition try to close Iraq's borders to unilaterals, it refused to accept any responsibility for its own attacks on non-embedded journalists, like those in the Palestine Hotel. Many unilateral reporters felt that the military had treated embedded journalists as a protected species but declared open season on unilaterals.

Robert Menard, the head of the international press watchdog Reporters Sans Frontières, insisted that Coalition forces displayed 'contempt' for unilaterals.

'Many journalists have come under fire, others have been detained and questioned for several hours and some have been mistreated, beaten and humiliated by Coalition forces,' he said.

The numbers are stark. Of the fourteen journalists who died while the embedding system was in full flight – from the start of the war on 20 March until the fall of Saddam's statue on 9 April – only four were embedded, even though the embeds heavily outnumbered their unilateral colleagues within Iraq. Among the 700-plus embeds Michael Kelly of the *Washington Post* died in a car accident, fellow American David Bloom of NBC suffered a blood clot on the lung, and there were just two combat deaths – Julio Anguita Parrado of the Spanish newspaper *El Mundo*, and Christian Liebig of Germany's *Focus* magazine – who were killed on 6 April in a 'lucky strike' by an Iraqi missile on a US field base. Another seven news workers died after the fall of the statue, of whom just one, the 27-year-old Australian television soundman Jeremy Little of NBC, was embedded. Little died on 6 July from injuries suffered a week earlier in an attack by a rocket-propelled grenade in the town of Falluja. That means that sixteen of the twenty-one media workers killed by the end of 2003 were unilaterals and only five were embeds.

Aidan White, the general secretary of the International Federation of Journalists, has said that the imbalance was at least partly caused by the embedding system making non-embedded journalists more vulnerable.

Overall this was probably the worst war ever in terms of the rate at which journalists were killed – fourteen in the twenty days of 'major hostilities' and seven more in the turbulence after the fall of Saddam's statue. In contrast, the first Gulf War killed only four foreign journalists – a German photographer and three members of a British agency team working for the BBC; while the Afghan War in 2001–02 killed nine media workers.

Any analysis of the 2003 media fatalities showed that the greatest killer of Western journalists was the Coalition. Of the fourteen killed during the war, just two, Liebig and Parrado, were killed by Saddam's forces. Five died from 'neutral' causes, including Kelly's car accident, Bloom's blood clot and British TV reporter Gaby Rado's fall from a hotel roof in northern Iraq. Paul Moran was killed by an Islamic extremist whose group was at war with both Saddam and the US, while experts say the landmine that claimed BBC cameraman Kaveh Golestan could have been planted a decade earlier during the Iraq–Iran war. Seven were killed by the Coalition. Terry Lloyd and his two colleagues were either shot by the Coalition or died in crossfire started by Coalition forces, John Simpson's BBC translator Kamaran Abdurazaq Muhamed was hit by a missile fired from a US plane on 6 April, and US forces 'took out' three television workers in Baghdad within a few hours on 8 April – Taras Protsyuk, Jose Couso and Tareq Ayyoub.

A unilateral-free war would obviously have been safer for media workers but it would have seen the media paying even more attention to 'the soldiers' war' and the Coalition's gee-whiz feats of military derring-do, and less attention to Iraqi casualties, especially civilian deaths, which even in the first Gulf War were hidden behind the euphemism 'collateral damage'.

While numbers and estimates were quickly provided for almost every other aspect of the war, in both Gulf Wars civilian deaths were never quantified and only grudgingly even admitted by the Coalition. The Pentagon's tight control of information in the 1991 war led to the wide acceptance of the myth that the Coalition had mostly used new-fangled 'smart bombs' to ensure that they hit only their desired targets, rather than civilians. In fact fewer than ten per cent of munitions dropped in that war used 'smart bomb' targeting technology.

The Pentagon openly admitted before the 2003 war that it would rather there were no Western journalists in Baghdad at all, and the result of its pressure on the US networks and other organisations to leave Baghdad was a drastically reduced focus on what the war was doing to Iraqi civilians. Even in the south the footage and reports sent home by embedded reporters of happy Iraqis greeting US tanks gave a strikingly different impression from the experience of teams like ours, which were able to hang around longer and talk to locals.

Jeff Gralnick, a CBS reporter during the Vietnam War who became a senior figure in the US television industry, pointed to another danger of embedding in a warning he offered to embeds before the war.

'Once you get into a unit, you are going to be coopted. It is not a purposeful thing, it will just happen. It's a little like the Stockholm Syndrome,' he wrote in a US magazine article.

'You will fall in with a bunch of grunts, experience and share their hardships and fears and then you will feel for them and care about them. You will wind up loving them and hating their officers and commanders and the administration that put them (and you) in harm's way . . . I loved mine. And as we all know, love blinds and in blinding it will alter the reporting you thought you were going to do. Trust me. It happens, and it will happen no matter how much you guard against it.

'Remember also, you are not being embedded because that sweet old Pentagon wants to be nice. You are being embedded so you can be controlled and in a way isolated.'

The danger of reporters identifying too strongly with 'their' units is obviously greatest with less experienced reporters. Chris Ayres, a business reporter for *The Times* of London with no war reporting experience, was embedded with a US Marines artillery unit but was honest enough to admit later that the threat of being killed by the Iraqis had led him to wish for a swift victory for the US troops who were protecting him.

'My objectivity was shot to bits. All I wanted was for the Americans to win quickly: for my own safety, rather than any political reasons,' Ayres wrote in the *Times* on 11 April. 'I was no better than the [American] reporters with their [US] flags. One US writer, a pale, bespectacled and rather geeky figure like me, kept saying: "Let's giddyup, motherfucker!",' Ayres wrote.

Australia was fortunate that its only embedded print reporter in Iraq was the *Age*'s Lindsay Murdoch, an experienced and hard-headed journalist who was always likely to keep a mental distance from 'his' troops.

But experience itself was no guarantee that objectivity would be maintained. CNN's 'Senior International Correspondent' Walter Rodgers went to Iraq with thirty-six years of broadcasting experience but if he had been any more deeply embedded in the US Army's 7th Cavalry he would have had to be surgically removed.

With the wind blowing through his hair as he roared through the desert in a US armoured column, Rodgers enthused that he was part of a giant 'wave of steel' rolling towards Baghdad.

'It's more than a little exciting to see this armored force rolling through the desert in a classical cavalry manner,' he said, adding proudly that he had been allowed to sit 'in the gunner seat on a rolling M1A1 Abrams. It's like riding in the stomach of a dragon.'

If the column came across any Iraqi troops 'We'll simply kill them, we'll find the enemy and grab him by the nose,' he said.

We?

Boston Herald reporter Jules Crittenden actually lived out the action that Rodgers seemed to be fantasising about. Crittenden was travelling through Baghdad in a lightly armoured M113 armoured personnel carrier with the rear crew hatch open. Beside him were a lieutenant and a psychological operations soldier armed with M-4 rifles and in front of them was another soldier with a .50-calibre machine gun.

The vehicle became involved in a gunfight. With the US soldiers concentrating on fire coming from the sides, Crittenden noticed a group of Iraqi soldiers preparing to fire rocket-propelled grenades from only seven metres to his left. He told the soldier on the machine gun, who swung his weapon around and fired where the reporter was pointing, killing three Iraqis. When other reporters raised ethical questions Crittenden's answer was blunt:

'I'll keep the argument short,' he wrote in his newspaper. 'Screw them, they weren't there. But they are welcome to join me next time if they care to test their professionalism.'

Professor Ulf Hannerz, a Swedish academic who has studied the attitudes of foreign correspondents, cites the work of CNN's Rodgers as proof that even veteran reporters could identify too strongly with their hosts when embedded. A professor of social anthropology at Stockholm University who has interviewed hundreds of foreign correspondents in his research, Hannerz told me the attitudes of many embeds were coloured by the fact that 'embedded came to mean encapsulated'.

'They did not move about much on their own or have much independent interaction with people outside their military units. I am not sure that they should even really be considered *foreign* correspondents any more because they were living with the boys from home, in an insular, "domestic" social environment.'

When combined with an almost blanket refusal to release real information at the official briefing centre in Qatar, the embedding system's presentation of hundreds of small slices of action often made it harder to get a coherent overview of the war's progress. Some of the biggest mistakes in the reporting of the war originated with embeds who received incorrect information from officers in 'their' units, and who may have applied less than their usual levels of scepticism to what they were being told.

Britain's *Daily Telegraph* ran a front-page headline in the first few days of the war declaring 'Saddam sends out his tanks'. It was based on a spurious report by CNN's Rodgers that a thousand Republican Guard vehicles were charging south from Baghdad under cover of a sand storm to confront Coalition forces in what would supposedly be the decisive battle of the war. There was no such column.

The non-existent uprising in Basra was first 'fed' to journalists working in the field with British forces, and it was a *Jerusalem Post* reporter embedded with the US 3rd Infantry Division who broke a story claiming incorrectly that an Iraqi chemical weapons factory had been found in Najaf a few days into the war.

A longer-term problem with embedding that was shown up in Iraq in 2003 was that it gave the impression of a 'Reality TV' war when it was actually presenting a heavily sanitised version of the battlefield. Viewers watching real-time tank charges and clean missile strikes were led to believe that was what the twenty-first century war really looked like.

It was not.

The cameramen and editors of the Western media were never going to show soldiers, let alone civilians and children, having their arms burned to the bone, their abdomens sliced open or their brains squeezed out of their skulls.

The result was an impression of war that was even less violent and less honest than that shown in the movie *Saving Private Ryan*.

10

RETURN TO IRAQ

On 1 May, standing in front of a huge sign declaring 'Mission Accomplished' on the deck of the aircraft carrier USS *Abraham Lincoln*, George W. Bush declared an end to 'major hostilities' in Iraq.

Ten weeks later I returned to an Iraq in which hostilities were not exactly over to find out just what Bush's mission had accomplished. I also wanted to see what had happened to the Iraqis I had come across during the war, like the family in Basra I was interviewing when we were arrested, the brother and sister who had been searching for their missing brothers at Saddam's prison, and perhaps even the Fedayeen and Ba'ath Party officials who had arrested us.

Coalition troops had been killed almost every day since Bush's declaration of victory. Despite the Coalition's optimistic noises the insurgency campaign was not only persisting, it was gaining in intensity, with about a dozen attacks a day on Coalition forces. Some 162 US military personnel died during the war but another sixty-five US troops and six British military police had been killed in the ten weeks since Bush's 'Mission Accomplished'. The US military toll would eventually top 600 by the first anniversary of Saddam's fall. By 7 April 2004, 636 members of the US military would be dead, along with 103 troops from other Coalition countries – 59 British, 17 Italians, 11 Spaniards, five Bulgarians, three Ukranians, two each from Poland and Thailand, one Dane, an Estonian and a Salvadoran.

Some 374 of the US fatalities were killed by hostile action after Bush declared 'Mission Accomplished'. By contrast, there was not a single US combat death in Germany after the Nazi surrender in May 1945.

The Pentagon and the Coalition refused to put any estimates on Iraqi casualties but independent observers estimated that perhaps 6000 Iraqi fighters had been killed. The Iraq Body Count, a research group of Left-leaning academics and peace activists that monitored media reports of specific civilian deaths, calculated that by the first anniversary of Saddam's fall somewhere between 8850 and 10,720 civilians had been killed by combat, the breakdown in law and order, or the collapse of the health and sanitation systems due to the war. In Baghdad alone in the first four months after the war the civilian death toll reported at city morgues was 1500 higher than the pre-war rate.

Amid this relentless death toll one particular death grabbed my selfish attention just as I was preparing to return to Baghdad. A young British journalist was shot in the back of the head while standing in a crowd outside the Baghdad Museum. If journalists were now being deliberately targeted I did not really want to go back. I eventually decided that the reporter, Richard Wild, had probably been mistaken for a soldier. He had recently done a year's military service, was tall and well-built, had a fresh, short haircut and was wearing military-style pants and a white T-shirt. I was forty-two, short-ish, overweight and bald, and I packed my bag with the loudest pink and yellow shirts I owned, topping off my ensemble with a multi-coloured 'Malcolm X' cap I had picked up in Washington DC many years before.

I travelled in from Jordan with Bob Graham, Stuart Clarke, and a young American freelance journalist, Jill Carroll. Like the unfortunate Richard Wild she was one of many young reporters attracted to Baghdad to try to build their journalism credentials. Stewart Innes was going to drive in from Kuwait in his new 4WD and meet us in Baghdad.

Dawn saw us waiting at the Iraqi border crossing and provided enough light for me to notice that my side of our car had six bullet holes in it. The driver Abdul laughed that they were from an encounter with 'Ali Babas' near the town of Fallujah on a trip along the same road a few weeks earlier. One bullet hole in my door in the back seat could be lined up with another in the metal frame of the driver's door, showing that the bullet had passed five centimetres in front of Abdul's face.

I pulled my flak jacket into two and leaned it against the doors as home-made armour plating. Abdul had photos of his three sons jammed into his rear-view mirror, reminding him why he was doing such risky but lucrative work. The six-hour drive from the border in a six-vehicle convoy was tense, and we later learned that seven other cars were attacked on that road that day, in some cases with mortars.

The fear of being attacked led to dangerous speeding. The greatest killer of reporters, after the Coalition, had turned out to be road accidents. In addition to the American Michael Kelly who died during the war, on 14 April two Argentinian journalists died after their car blew a tyre on the road we were now using. An injured survivor said the Jordanian driver was scared and speeding to get to Baghdad before dark.

A reporter and translator from the *Boston Globe* died in a similar accident driving from Tikrit to Baghdad on 9 May. Jerome Delay, the French photographer who had tried to save Taras, would break his back but survive an accident on the same road later in the year.

*

The first signs of change and new economic life in Baghdad came before we had even reached the outer suburbs. Trucks and buses were heading into the city crammed with cardboard boxes holding washing machines, air conditioners, fans and other appliances which had been scarce during the sanctions. Stalls had been set up along the highway selling beer and whisky in a country where Saddam had cracked down on alcohol to try to bolster his Islamic credentials. We were soon driving along shopping streets, their footpaths lined with long-banned television satellite dishes, which already dotted the city's skyline.

The Coalition had set up a mobile phone network for its own staff, aid groups and private contractors, and the once-banned Thurayas were on sale everywhere. Dozens of Internet cafés had sprung up. The unshackling of the economy and the sudden flood of imports with the end of sanctions were unmistakable, and the first expatriate Iraqis were already in town to set up businesses.

Buildings were no longer burning but the office blocks all over the city had not been repaired. If you lined up the holes in each side

Angry Iraqis being restrained outside the Palestine Hotel. John Feder

you could often see straight through the middle of a ten-storey building. Power and basic services were still patchy, and the scarred bitumen and flattened highway rails left by the marauding US tanks had not been repaired, giving the streets a smash-up derby feel.

Disrupted fuel supplies had left the streets clogged by enormous queues for petrol, which locals said were worse than the queues after the first Gulf War. Drivers had a choice: they could queue for two or three hours to buy 'benzine' for just one US cent a litre, or avoid the wait by paying higher prices to one of the freelance operators who stood patiently in the gutter, each with a few plastic containers of fuel.

During the day the noises of war and looting had been replaced by the wail of car anti-theft sirens and the occasional reversing signal on trucks, which for some unknown reason seemed always to play the tune of the Lambada.

The other striking difference was the heat. The desert swelter that Saddam had claimed would melt his enemies had come too late to save him but it had certainly arrived. It was uncomfortable as early as 10 a.m. and often reached 50 degrees Celsius in the after-noon. Hot dry winds meant that standing in the open between

1 p.m. and 3 p.m. felt like standing in front of a blow dryer, and the city basically shut down for those hours.

Some crucial things had not changed. Saddam had still not been caught, and there was no sign of the Iraqi weapons of mass destruction promised by Coalition leaders.

The attacks on Coalition forces and their new Iraqi allies did not seem to be centrally coordinated but they were gaining in confidence and sophistication, and in the past week they had begun using mortars to back up their roadside booby traps and remote-control landmines, or what the Coalition called IEDs – Improvised Explosive Devices.

Iraq had already been a heavily armed country where hundreds of thousands of homes contained at least one weapon, and Saddam's regime had left caches of weapons and money to sustain the insurgency. In the exasperated words of Lieutenant-General Ricardo Sanchez, the senior Coalition commander on the ground in Iraq, 'This country was a huge ammo dump – there's ammo all over the country.'

The US military was hitting back with impressively named campaigns like Operation Ivy Serpent and Operation Sidewinder, issuing daily updates on how many houses had been raided, guns seized and militants arrested.

Caught in the middle were the ordinary Iraqis, the great majority of whom were happy to see the back of Saddam but were already tiring of the US presence. As we drove through Firdos Square, the roundabout we had looked down on from our room in the Palestine Hotel, we could see that the plinth from which the Saddam statue had been torn down now had a bold piece of graffiti with a clear if poorly spelled message for the Americans: 'All donne [sic]. Go home.'

It was 46 degrees at 1 p.m. when we arrived at the Flower Lands Hotel, just south of the city centre. The hotel was an improvement on the Palestine but its biggest attraction was that it was directly across the road from the more desirable Al Hamra Hotel, which was fully booked with reporters drawn by its Internet café, Chinese restaurant and – most alluringly – its swimming pool. We lugged the crates of food and drink we had brought from Jordan up to our rooms. Bob and Stuart were sharing a two-bedroom suite and I would share another with Stewart.

Bob went off to negotiate with some minders and drivers and I tried out my Thuraya phone in the room. To get a clear line at the satellite I had to go up on the roof. A few minutes there, even standing in the shade of the hotel's liftwell, left me dripping with sweat. I spent the next couple of hours trying to call Australia's diplomatic office, one of the few that were functioning in Baghdad, to find out where it was. It took me two days to discover that in this broadly spread city of five million people it was just four hundred metres from my hotel room – I had actually been looking at it while frying on the roof trying to call it.

The mission was in a villa which had housed Australia's ambassador in the 1980s. Next to it was a half-finished apartment building now occupied by a contingent of Australian troops protecting the mission. Britain also had a diplomatic office in Baghdad but Washington was in a more delicate situation. Given that sovereignty actually resided with the occupation chief, US diplomat Paul Bremer, the State Department would in effect be appointing an ambassador to itself if it opened an embassy.

Over the next few days we got our bearings. All thirty-four police stations in Baghdad had reopened but a curfew would be needed for another three months because of the violence at night, when gunfire still sounded off regularly. The hospitals were crammed with fresh casualties, as the victims of war and the initial wave of looting had given way to people hurt in robberies, kidnaps and attacks by opponents of the invasion on Iraqis who had thrown in their lot with the Coalition. Life in Baghad and the rest of the Ba'ath Party's stronghold, the so-called 'Sunni triangle' of towns to its north-west, was much more grim than in the south and north of Iraq, where conditions were already much better than before the war.

The British troops in Basra had an easier task and they had proved to be more astute and culturally aware than the Americans, who strutted the streets in wrap-around sunglasses and helmets with a heavy-handed weapons-ready posture which brought a sour reaction from Iraqis.

While everyone cited Northern Ireland as having taught the British military the subtleties of urban warfare and policing, they were actually benefiting from their broader colonial history. The British military learned centuries ago that they could not always overwhelm or outnumber 'the natives', so they had to understand and deal with local cultures and power structures to get their way. The American troops, on the other hand, seemed bewildered and threatened by the society around them. They were generally tired, desperate to go home and often inadequately trained and equipped for their new role in the middle of this Iraqi muddle. Soldiers, including armoured divisions, had gone straight from battle to police work and they did not like it one bit.

The soldiers who frisked us as we waited to enter one of the new Coalition centres, a convention centre near the Al-Rashid Hotel, were much more surly than they had been even during the war. Many were reservists who had day jobs waiting for them back home and they had all had their tours of duty extended indefinitely by the Pentagon.

The front of the convention centre was shielded by concrete barriers and coils of barbed wire, which forced visitors to approach on foot over a hundred metres of open road, giving the US sentries and machine-gun posts plenty of time to take down any attackers. There would still be more than one deadly car bomb attack at this entrance, and the Al-Rashid Hotel across the road, which housed senior Coalition officials, would be hit by missiles.

When Bob and I visited the new UN headquarters in what had previously been the Canal Hotel it was the bustling base of a string of humanitarian groups working with the UN. The former hotel had been freshly painted in the blue and white of the UN, and an elaborate system of passes and security checks slowed down visitors at a front gatehouse. None of that would save the building and its occupants a few weeks after our visit when a suicide bomber drove a truck packed with explosives up to the side of the main building. Local UN chief Sergio de Mello was among the twenty-three dead.

Even Assassin's Gate, the huge arch which was the entrance to the headquarters of the occupation administration, in Saddam's old palace compound, would be hit by a suicide bomber in January 2004, killing eighteen Iraqis and two American private contractors.

The 'Coalition Provisional Authority' (CPA) had set up its headquarters in the grand palace we had toured after the war, which still had Saddam's four busts on its roof. That huge building was now the centre of absolute power and home to hundreds of overwhelmed foreign bureaucrats trying to govern a country of twenty-five million. They were struggling to rebuild systems for schools, prisons and dozens of other services. For a new court system alone they needed to screen 860 judges and prosecutors in just four months. To get the electricity working they had to cope with dilapidated generators while thieves were still pulling down cables across the country to steal the copper. Every one of these problems had been made much worse by the outbreak of crime when the old regime dissolved, and by the Iraqi public's anger at the Coalition's failure to maintain security and basic public services as promised.

The fundamental question that I was still grappling with was how the Coalition had managed to get it so wrong. How had they failed to anticipate or respond to a regime collapse that they had planned and brought about? The US Government was hardly blind to the importance of public opinion, so how had it managed so comprehensively to ignore Iraqi public opinion?

This was the same US military that had produced General Douglas Macarthur sixty years earlier, as one of history's most successful Occupation leaders. Macarthur was so aware of the need to win the goodwill of the occupied population that he persuaded the Allies to whitewash Emperor Hirohito of his obvious war crime guilt in order to use him as a stabilising factor in Japanese society. The sanitising of Hirohito was an historic lie but it was a deliberate strategy to calm and coopt the Japanese and ultimately to save American lives.

According to senior members of the CPA whom I interviewed over the next few weeks, the basic problem in Iraq was that the Americans had banked on a coup being launched against Saddam either just before or just after the start of its invasion. They thought they would be taking control of a functioning state apparatus. All they would need to do was cleanse the top echelons of Saddam supporters and a new Iraq would be born on its feet.

President Bush had wasted the State Department's elaborate planning for the occupation by belatedly giving the Pentagon control of post-war strategy. With little cultural or political expertise on Iraq, the Pentagon then placed ideology above practical knowledge by relying on the supposedly expert exiles like Ahmed Chalabi, who claimed that US soldiers would be welcomed with flowers and candy and that Saddam would be overthrown by his own military. Chalabi had not been to Iraq for decades, and the other exiles who enjoyed influence in the Pentagon proved to be equally out of touch with the situation in Iraq. Now, four months after the invasion began, the CPA was still shocked that things had not panned out that way, and that the state's machinery, weakened as it was by a decade of sanctions, had collapsed in the face of the Coalition onslaught and the following wave of looting.

Having sent few real experts on Iraq to Baghdad to run the new administration, the White House compounded its problems by failing to win the active involvement of the UN and major powers like France, Germany and Russia because of Washington's continuing stand-off with those nations about its decision to go to war in the first place. A White House that had mocked the concept of nation-building as 'foreign policy by social work' now found itself stuck with the biggest nation-building intervention in half a century.

The first occupation chief, retired US general Jay Garner, quickly proved a disaster. Before arriving in Baghdad he suggested that the Coalition could hand power back to the Iraqis in as little as three months, a timeframe that ignored its lack of peace and security, let alone a constitution, election rules or even acceptable records of who was entitled to vote. According to one senior Coalition official, Garner began more than one internal meeting at his new headquarters with the query, 'So how are my little brown buddies today?'

He was sacked by the White House within a month and replaced by Bremer, a hawkish former diplomat who exuded much more confidence and competence but once again knew precious little about Iraq. His most important credentials seemed to be that his conservative views and diplomatic background made him acceptable to both the State Department and the neo-conservatives in charge of policy at the Pentagon. Senior CPA insiders told me that Bremer tended to make decisions on the fly, often getting off the phone from Washington to demand that drastic changes with serious long-term effects be prepared within an hour or two.

One of his first decisions was the ridiculous idea of sacking the entire Iraqi military and retraining a new, much smaller force. This brainwave threw 400,000 armed and trained fighters onto the streets with a personal grievance against the new regime. Another of

Bremer's early decisions was to sack senior bureaucrats with strong links to the Ba'ath Party. After three decades of the Ba'ath Party running Iraq as a one-party state and making membership almost essential for professional advancement, Bremer's order meant sacking many of the country's senior technocrats. There was clearly a need to remove some Saddam supporters but too wide a purge threatened to cripple the bureaucracy. It also ignored the history and nature of the Ba'ath Party. Founded in Syria as an Arab nationalist movement, it had originally attracted many idealistic Arabs, only to be perverted over time by Saddam and his clique. Many decent people found themselves belonging to the party. Bremer was particularly keen on selling state assets and opening up the economy to foreign investors as quickly as possible, an especially delicate issue in Iraq when it comes to oil, the centre of the nationalist agenda.

For months the gaping hole in Bremer's 'can-do' strategy for change was a clear timetable or openly explained plan for handing power back to Iraqis. Even a vague schedule for drafting a constitution and electing a new government would have given Iraqis a sense that the occupation was temporary but Bremer kept fudging those issues, fuelling Iraqi cynicism and the growing belief on the streets that the Americans were self-interested invaders who wanted to stay.

The reality was that the CPA was scared of what early elections might produce, fearful that Shi'ite clerics would impose an Iranian-style government. Saddam had certainly been ruthless in crushing most forms of civil society or alternative power centres, so that there were no obvious alternative leaders. That left the clerics as a potent social force but the fears of a hardline Islamic government, and some Islamic version of the domino theory, ignored the strong secular streak in Iraq, a very different society from Iran. Islamist candidates were indeed likely to do well in Iraqi elections but they were unlikely to retain any monopoly on power.

The rise of fundamentalism that the Americans had feared was nowhere to be seen. In fact the Shi'ite clerics had almost all been patient and reasonable, stepping into the vacuum of law and order to maintain security, making their suburbs and towns some of the most peaceful in the country. It would take a few more months of a rising Coalition death toll, and the approach of a US election year, before the White House would order Bremer to speed up the transition and announce a timetable for handing power back to Iraqis by June 2004, with a new constitution, elections and government by December 2005.

On Sunday 13 July 2003, a few days after we returned to Baghdad, Bremer appointed an Iraqi Governing Council, a group of twenty-five prominent Iraqis that was described as 'the most representative' body ever to hold authority in Iraq. The Orwellian language masters were hard at work. The 'Governing Council' would not actually govern nor hold real authority, which was in Bremer's hands. The CPA even refused to acknowledge that it was an 'occupation' administration. The council members did come from most of the leading social and religious groups but they did not legitimately 'represent' anybody as they had been hand-picked by Bremer. That process was the only way the CPA could get away with including a large number of exile leaders, who had been shipped in by the Americans but held little support among the Iraqi population.

Bremer retained a veto over the council's decisions but knew that openly over-ruling the council would fatally undermine its authority. The council's first actions did not encourage optimism that they would work effectively on the huge problems confronting Iraq. Their immediate priorities were ensuring decent salaries, security, cars and offices for themselves, and in the next few months they moved extremely slowly on challenges like drawing up a process to create a constitution. The best news was that the members of the council had agreed to work together at all. The Shi'ite majority had so far been positive and peaceful, and there had been nothing like the civil wars between Kurds, Shia and Sunni that had been predicted by many pundits.

Outside the convention centre after the announcement of the council I ran into Ahmad Al-Rikabi, the Iraqi exile journalist who had told us on my Hostile Environment training course in February about his detention long ago in Lebanon. Over a beer at Heckfield Place he had confided to a few of us that he had just been offered a job by the Pentagon helping to set up a new state broadcaster for a liberated Iraq. He had obviously taken the job and we met that night in his room at the Al-Rashid Hotel to talk about his experiences. He had made the first radio broadcast of the new Iraqi Media Network from a tent at Baghdad airport just two days after the fall of Saddam and went on to run a 360-staff television operation, training new reporters and finding journalists untainted by Ba'ath Party links.

When he aired a Shi'ite call to prayer as well as the usual Sunni one it sparked celebrations in Saddam City. Rikabi also found himself changing some of the nation's symbols.

'For the early radio broadcasts I couldn't play the national anthem because it praises the Ba'ath Party. So I chose an old Iraqi song I liked called "My Homeland".'

At the first post-war concert by the national symphony orchestra, he was stunned to find it played in place of the national anthem, with men listening in tears. He became a hate figure for supporters of the old regime, reviled as a collaborator. Death threats appeared in graffiti around Baghdad and at one point he had to appear on television to rebut rumours that he had been assassinated.

The network's crews initially went out only with US military escorts, which did not exactly facilitate interviews with ordinary Iraqis, and some of its news crews got into the habit of carrying their own weapons for protection. The Iraqi Media Network (IMN) led a media explosion, as more than a hundred local newspapers were soon being published. But as we sat drinking and chatting it became clear that Rikabi was disenchanted with his US employers, who had not kept their promise of allowing independent journalism. Senior US officials had interfered in the network's affairs to the extent that it was seen by Iraqis as a mouthpiece for the Americans.

Rikabi believed the CPA had been hampered by cronyism, incompetent leadership and a contempt for independent journalism. The result was that the free-to-air IMN had larger audiences than the small Arabic satellite broadcasters like Al-Jazeera and Al-Arabiya but among Iraqis who had satellite access, and therefore a choice, the satellite broadcasters were much more trusted and much more watched than IMN.

The bad feeling between Rikabi and his employers was apparently mutual. We did not know it but he had just finished his last full day in the job. The next day he flew to England for his first break since January, and he was sacked while he was away. By the time we had finished talking I had missed the curfew and was forced to stay overnight at Rikabi's hotel. I shared a room with a consultant at the network, veteran Canadian journalist Don North, who slept with a handgun beside his bed.

The next morning, when I got back to my own hotel room I finally found an address for the Australian diplomatic office. I was driving towards it in a local taxi at 11 a.m. when I had a taste of the US military treatment that Iraqis were complaining about. We were approaching a US armoured vehicle parked by the road in heavy traffic when a soldier suddenly stood up in the back of the vehicle and pointed his automatic weapon straight at my face and that of my driver.

We instinctively leant back and threw our hands up. As the driver jabbed his hands back at the wheel the soldier waved his left hand, telling us to stop. We could not brake until we had passed his armoured vehicle but the car behind us did manage to stop.

The armoured vehicle then pulled out behind us and I realised that the soldier had simply wanted to create a break in the traffic. Holding up a hand would have achieved the same thing, or he could have just waited for a gap in the traffic. That brief, frightening experience left me furious at such a display of arrogance.

I had similar experiences twice more over the next two weeks while passing US convoys on major highways. Each time I got a sense of the humiliation and anger that ordinary Iraqis were feeling when they were treated this way in their own streets and often in their own homes.

Later that day Bob's fixer, Mahmood, translated for me as I chatted with several Iraqis whom we approached in the street. Their society was still in a state of shock and dislocation, and one of their main responses was to resort to fabulous conspiracy theories. Some were adamant that the Americans were somehow in league with Saddam and would bring him back to power. Others blamed Iranians, Israelis and even Kuwaitis for the looting and crime wave, despite clear evidence that Iraqis were inflicting violence on each other.

Drivers, shopkeepers, even a casualty ward doctor insisted that they had it on good authority that Kuwaitis had come over the border to vandalise, loot and rape to avenge Saddam's invasion of their own country. Even Mahmood was convinced that Kuwaitis were doing much of the looting. Coalition officials told me they had caught Syrians, Saudis and even Chechens but not a single Kuwaiti looter. The claims about the Kuwaitis led some cynics to argue that the Kuwaitis, who import foreigners to do menial work, were far too wealthy, comfortable and lazy to do their own looting.

I had spoken to many looters and they were generally polite, well-armed Iraqis. The urban myth about Kuwaiti looters, and the refusal to accept the obvious fact that it was Iraqis who were vandalising their own country, pointed to an ingrained sense of victimhood and a denial of uncomfortable truths, traits which were not going to help Iraq in its recovery. The sourest attitudes were among the middle-class and professionals, who had fared best under Saddam.

Living conditions for many of the country's poorest had already improved. The electricity system, for instance, was still a shambles but the CPA had been able to improve conditions sharply in areas like Saddam City simply by delivering power fairly to all suburbs rather than favouring wealthy Sunni areas as Saddam had done.

The middle-class had lost privileges without any marked improvements yet in their material living standards. Many had hoped that the end of Saddam and sanctions would somehow make them rich, free and able to travel the world. The reality of a hot and dusty Baghdad with unreliable electricity and rising crime often left only bitterness.

Stewart arrived on the weekend. On Tuesday 15 July, he and I drove out to the Saddam City Hospital. The director, Dr Gorea, had a day off and assistant director Mohammed Khudeir, the hospital's lawyer, was in charge. The air of crisis had passed, as other hospitals had reopened and supplies of oxygen and drugs had been restored. Only about two hundred of its three hundred beds were now being used.

Renamed the 'Al Thawra Public Hospital', which was a popular name for the area, it was receiving only one or two victims of violence a day, as the calls by the clerics for an end to violence had made it one of the safest parts of Baghdad. The clerics had left the hospital and disbanded their volunteer militia three weeks earlier when the CPA had provided security guards.

I joked with Khudeir that the cleric, Sheik Fartousi, seemed to have appointed himself as hospital director when we were working on Ali's case, and he rolled his eyes. Fartousi had subsequently fallen into a heated power struggle with Dr Gorea. According to Khudeir, Fartousi had begun to intervene in the administration of the hospital, even taking a large amount of cash for 'safe keeping'.

'He was supposed to be overseeing security but he was interfering in everything.'

At one point during their confrontation Fartousi had put a gun to Dr Gorea's head. Dr Gorea appealed to more senior clerics in Najaf, who replaced Fartousi. Their power struggle had been given an extra edge by the fact that Dr Gorea was a Christian, but most of the locals had eventually backed him. After his efforts to keep their hospital open during the war, the locals had given him the popular nickname of Wahab al Nasrani, a Christian who had fought alongside Shi'ite founder Imam Hussein.

Relaxing in his office, Khudeir made it clear that the US military's efforts to help Ali had not significantly improved the Americans' popularity at the hospital.

'They hurt him in the first place,' he said with open cynicism. 'They were like a crocodile that grabs its prey and cries about it.'

Stewart and I left the hospital to visit Ali's family so we could deliver two large suitcases of gifts and appliances that Hamed had asked Stewart to bring to Baghdad. Ali's half-sisters and half-brother Hamza were staying at Hamed's home, being cared for by their mother Layla and Hamed's wife and mother. In the courtyard outside their small brick house we lent them my satellite phone to call Ali and Hamed in Kuwait.

After the phone had been passed around for half an hour, Ali told Stewart that he wanted to talk to his grandfather, Ali Thaher Jassam, and we agreed to take the phone to his house, a few kilometres away. A teenage cousin came along with us as a guide.

A wizened 71-year-old in traditional dishdasha, his grandfather cried while talking to Ali, affectionately chiding him to 'behave yourself, you little pup'. Ali's married sister, Asma'a, who was now nineteen, lived in the grandfather's house as she was married to a cousin. Instantly recognisable as Ali's sister, she was heavily pregnant.

When he eventually surrendered the phone to Asma'a, the grandfather told me that he was especially relieved at Ali's progress because he had been the one who had authorised the amputation of Ali's arms.

'God is generous so we seem to have done the right thing,' he said in Arabic. 'He sounds much better – he is healthier and happier. But I won't be happy until I can see him again. He is going to have to struggle to look after his family, and with ten or eleven people to look after I'm worried that that will cause him extra stress.

'As the oldest male he is the head of his family, and only one of his sisters is married so he is the guardian of the other five and the decisions will fall on him.

'His uncles and I will help him but Ali is now in control of his sisters, and they will have to wait until he decides what he wants to do and where he wants to live. This area will be difficult for him. These people are all peasants. If they see him walking down the street without arms they will clap and taunt him. He could end up killing himself around here. I just hope that he can live somewhere where people are more understanding of life.'

We went to see the family's bombed home. After fifteen weeks cement blocks still lay around in a mess but the shape of the walls could be made out. A fallen palm tree had not yet been removed, and a separate pile of rubble indicated where two cows killed in the explosion had been buried.

Karim Jassim Ahmed, the neighbour who dragged Ali clear of the rubble, showed me the scars on his left shin from power cables which had been alive in the wreckage.

As I spoke to the neighbours I noticed a young boy of about Ali's age. Thirteen-year-old Nabil Sabah Eidan was a distant cousin and playmate of Ali's. He was not injured but had lost all six members of his immediate family in the missile blast and now lived in the hamlet with an uncle.

The next day I was determined to find the Salehs, the brother and sister we had met just after the fall of Saddam, when they had been searching for their missing brothers at one of Saddam's prisons. By now Kasim Finjan Saleh and his sister Jamila might have found some answers to the most horrible mystery of their lives – their twelve-year quest to resolve the fate of their brothers, Amer and Jassim, who had been arrested by Saddam's thugs.

All we knew of their whereabouts was that they lived in the large Shi'ite suburb of Shu'ala in the north-west of the city. More than 70,000 people live in Shu'ala's densely packed mud-brick homes and we did not even have an address for the Salehs but the tight social networks allowed us to find them within ten minutes of driving into the area, a tangle of honking, beaten-up cars and horse-drawn carts. The owner of a car parts store pointed us to a cousin of the Salehs, who got into our car to take us to the family's bakery.

Kasim invited us to their home in a nearby dirt street, where we were welcomed into a living room to sit on carpets on a cool, tiled floor and drink sweet black tea. Like most Shi'ite homes this one was adorned with portraits of the Shi'ite founders – Imam Hussein, the grandson of the prophet Mohammed; and Imam Ali, the prophet's son-in-law.

With no air conditioning I gulped down a Pepsi, then a glass of cold water, while Kasim explained that the prison where we had met had yielded no survivors and no records.

'For the next month we went to other prisons and travelled to several mass graves looking for any sign of them,' he said. 'Some time after the fall, a woman working in the market at Mansour [a Baghdad suburb] told people that she had seen regime officials hiding a large amount of files in a cellar under the market.'

The basement contained security files listing the fates of thousands. A volunteer society of relatives of the missing began posting the lists outside its office according to the dates on which people were arrested. On 12 May, Kasim was checking a list when he saw his own name and those of his brothers near the bottom of the sheet. 'Next to my name it said "still available". Next to my brothers' names it said "executed 8/5/1992".'

That meant his brothers had been kept alive and no doubt tortured for fourteen months. Kasim showed me a tattered photocopy of the list, which carried eighteen names, fourteen of which were marked 'executed'.

'It opened the wound again,' he said. 'We would have been happier if we were able to find some sort of remains, but at least we finally knew what happened. We held a group funeral in the neighbourhood, with three or four token coffins and about four hundred people carrying photographs of their [deceased] relatives.'

He seemed more relaxed than when we had first met but his

sister Jamila clearly drew no relief from the concept of 'closure'. Her brothers' tragedy had ruined her life, she told me, and the pain and frustration were almost visible on her face.

'This has made it worse. It would have been much better if we could have continued living in the hope that they were still alive,' she said. 'This has just removed any hope. We are happy with the fall of the regime but we are not happy with what we found on that piece of paper.'

Mass graves were still being excavated across Iraq but Kasim said his family had stopped searching. He knew his brothers were stripped of their identification papers because he was still with them in jail when that happened, and he believed there would be no way to identify their bodies. The family's bakery shop was draped with a black banner covered in gold and white writing announcing the martyrdom of the brothers. The whole suburb was dotted with similar banners.

The next morning, when we returned with Stuart Clarke to take photos of the Salehs, Kasim took us on a tour, pointing out homes that had lost three, four or even more people to Saddam's murderers. One house was covered by banners for sixteen dead relatives. Teenagers who gathered around us in the streets were quick to show their view of Saddam, saying 'Saddam Horse, Saddam Dog' or acting out the punches and kicks they would give the fallen dictator if they caught him.

When I asked Kasim and Jamila what they thought should happen to Saddam Jamila shrugged as if his fate was almost irrelevant.

Kasim said Saddam and his accomplices would meet justice 'in the next life'.

'There is no justice on earth, justice is in God's hands. And there is not enough vengeance in this world to deal with Saddam,' he added. 'If you took a small pinch of him at a time you would still not quench the thirst, the need to avenge the pain he has caused.'

A few days later Ali's guardian Hamed arrived in Baghdad for his first visit since going to Kuwait three months earlier. He came to my hotel room, where we discussed his negotiations with the British newspapers offering to buy Ali's story. The money would certainly not be enough to support Ali and his sisters for life, and Ali was already thinking of ways to earn a living without his arms. Ali had decided, Hamed said, that he should learn English and become a translator. At that stage they were thinking that he should go to the UK for treatment and then take up an offer of sponsorship to Canada, where he could study.

Much would depend on whether Ali's family could go with him, as it was unthinkable that he and his uncle would leave the family behind. They might still stay in Baghdad, and Hamed said he was not as worried as Ali's grandfather about the prospect of him getting a hard time from his neighbours – 'He will have his family to support him and he will have new arms by then'.

*

Stewart and I set off at 8 a.m. on Saturday 19 July for Basra. My plan was to retrace our steps from our first visits to Basra and Umm Qasr and try to find out what had happened to the people we had met. Just after 9 a.m. we had another uncomfortable encounter with the arrogance of US soldiers. As we overtook a small convoy a soldier with a mounted machine gun spun around to point his weapon straight at Stewart's face from just a few metres away. Stewart was furious and I had to persuade him it was not a good idea to go back and protest.

We stopped at a mass grave at Hilla, near Babylon, where 3000 bodies had been found and something like 10,000 more might be buried. The farmer who owned the surrounding corn and wheat fields, Sayyed Jaber Mohsin Al Hussini, told us that after the uprisings of 1991 he had watched government officials and local thugs bring truckloads of people here, make them stand blindfolded in trenches, then shoot them.

By early afternoon we could see the ancient Ziggurat squatting on the horizon like a blunt pyramid and fifteen minutes later we were at its base. Six thousand years ago this site was the centre of Ur, the world's earliest recorded civilisation. The first known city, it was the home of Abraham and the place where irrigation was first used in what was then a lush landscape.

Today the Ziggurat stands almost alone in a desert, stranded by climate change amid hundreds of kilometres of sand which has been baked into a crust. That crust was now crisscrossed by the tracks of

US military vehicles, and helicopters from a nearby US airbase occasionally flew directly over the top of it. Three US humvees sat in front of the Ziggurat, their crews apparently taking a break. Each day two vendors drove from Nasiriya to sell iced Coca-Cola and home-made tourist trinkets at the foot of the temple but their only clientele since the war had been American soldiers. The Ziggurat has been dated at 2113 BC but only its top viewing platform is original. Most of the outer layer is made up of clumsy brick restorations ordered by Saddam's regime.

Stewart and I climbed to the top of the temple, where we had a Coke in the hot silence as we looked at Nasiriya on the horizon and watched US military vehicles crawling over the desert in half a dozen directions. Archaeologists estimate that Ur may once have been home to 500,000 people but today the only residents are the twenty-five members of the extended family of Dhief Muhsen, the guide and guard of the temple, who live in two mud-brick homes a few hundred metres from its base.

A few kilometres away, on the road leading to both the Ziggurat and the US airbase, Iraqi entrepreneurs had already opened tiny shops with names and products aimed at the US military. 'Fast Freddie's Laundry' cleaned uniforms for $2. 'Uncle Sam's Choice' and the 'New York Restaurant' sold hamburgers and hot dogs, while the 'Supermarket Indiana' was a three-metres-square white-washed hut selling Coke, Pepsi and ice.

Back on the main highway, we regularly passed cars with coffins on the roof, taking them to be buried in the Shi'ite holy city of Najaf, and the petrol station in Nasiriya had a sign offering free petrol to cars carrying coffins. We filled our tank here with eighty litres of fuel for 1750 dinar, or about US$1.15. The poor quality of the fuel could immediately be felt in the lack of power in the car.

Basra, which we reached at 6 p.m., was dominated by raw concrete rather than the sandy-brown palette of Baghdad. Within a few minutes we had found our way to its southern edge and the spot where we had been arrested.

Abdul Razzak Oraibi Hashim, one of the residents who saw our arrest, came out into the street greeting us as if we were old friends. He said he had assumed we were dead. He and his wife, Nisreen, ushered us into their carpeted lounge, where they seated us on a couch under an air conditioner, while their two children fetched orange juice and water. As usual a portrait of Imam Ali smiled down from one wall but another wall had a large photo of Elvis Presley.

A lot of windows in their house had been broken during the war, they said, but nobody had been injured. Several other houses had been hit by Coalition shells, and one neighbour in a nearby street was killed on his roof. A house nearby had been used by Iraqi Fedayeen and foreign volunteer fighters, including young men from Palestine, Syria and Tunis, he said.

'One of the young foreigners told us he was not here to fight, he was here to become a martyr. We used to send them water and food if they asked for it. They never moved in with families until after the fall of Baghdad, when the survivors were trying to get back to their own countries. After the war they were in a daze, depressed and really surprised to have lost.'

He said we had been spotted by a Ba'ath Party checkpoint and had been lucky to end up at the local office of the Ba'ath Party militia rather than being taken by the Fedayeen.

'They would probably have slit your throats straight away.

'When you were taken away everyone in the street said you might be killed and the men who arrested you would get a reward and probably keep your car. We believed you really were journalists because of your questions and the fact that you did not have a military escort but everyone was too scared to express any sympathy for you.'

He was quite sour on the invasion, saying that living conditions had deteriorated, and playing down the political benefits of the fall of Saddam. The most important impact on him, Hashim said, was that he used to sell clothes in a market but his supplies had been cut since the war.

'You say it is freedom but I am not happy because I have no income. Feed me first, then ask if I appreciate freedom. I can't vote when I'm hungry and my children are hungry. Yes, as Shia we were oppressed but we could still work and we could come and go in safety.'

It was 7.45 p.m. but we thought we would try to find the Ba'ath Party office before heading to one of the city's few functioning hotels. Stewart found the office within minutes. It was in a row of single-story mud-brick and cement houses, mostly white-washed and with blue doors. The Arabic script for the names of the Ba'ath Party and Saddam had been half scrubbed off its front wall.

As usual, a crowd formed the moment we pulled up. Two middle-aged neighbours stepped forward to say they recognised us from our previous visit and they too had thought we were dead.

'A lot of people were arrested and brought here then sent to the Mukhabarat and never seen again,' said one. To be 'sent to Baghdad' had become a local euphemism for disappearing.

'They were like gangsters and they were right in the middle of us,' he said, almost spitting the words.

I asked about the man in command of the office, and the neighbour raised a laugh from the crowd by mimicking the captain's peculiar smoking style, holding an imaginary cigarette to his mouth between two horizontal fingers.

The captain's name was Abdul Mun'im Abdul Majid, they said. Like most of his colleagues he had run off as soon as the regime had fallen, although there were rumours that he had been sighted in Fallujah. Mustafa, the large man who had arrived to take us to the Sheraton, was from the secret police, they said. The Ba'ath Party lawyer who spoke English was named Yahya Al Muheisin but he too had run away.

The party office had originally been a private house and it had now been taken over by squatters, a Shi'ite family. We arranged to return the next day, when they said we could look through the offices.

We headed off to find a hotel, ending up in a place with rooms that were tiny, covered in dust and blighted by air conditioners that produced more noise than cool air. A more religious city than Baghdad, Basra had much tighter restrictions on alcohol. Muslim extremists had driven the alcohol trade underground by attacking alcohol vendors but Stewart had visited Basra with other news crews and knew how to find a beer.

The operation felt like we were buying heroin. We drove down a darkened shopping street and pulled over near a small group of men in their twenties loitering on a corner. Stewart had a quick conversation through the window then our 'dealer' disappeared down a laneway. Five minutes later he returned, carrying a plastic bag containing a dozen cans of Turkish beer.

Stewart had bought a laptop which allowed him to store and transmit photos, and it also allowed him to download and play hundreds of songs. He had developed a routine for making the best of evenings in uncomfortable hotel rooms, which revolved around the music on his laptop and the bottle of whisky among our supplies.

The next morning Stewart and I drove to the riverfront. All but one of the statues of martyrs from the war with Iran had been cut down by looters and removed for scrap, their now-bare white granite pedestals still lining the waterfront.

After all this time the Sheraton was still being looted. As we drove up to the front steps two men were carrying an almost worthless two-metre-long hunk of twisted metal down the front steps. Inside we saw that the entire building had been burned out and picked clean by thieves. Two looters offered to keep an eye on our car for us, touting for a reward.

The hotel's huge covered courtyard was an empty cavern, its caved-in roof letting in the only light. Pieces of metal and pipes hung from the ceilings, and underfoot there was about fifteen centimetres of ash, ceiling insulation and wallpaper. The reception desk where we were forced to check in had totally disappeared. A dozen looters were still picking the bones bare, pulling wire from the walls and sifting through the rubble for pieces of metal.

We picked our way up the dark stairs to the top floor and our old room, which was just a shell. The doors, even the door frames, were gone. Somebody had tried to steal the toilet bowl we had used but they had broken it and left it outside the bathroom. Only the bathtub remained, too heavy and too firmly attached to budge.

The glass doors and windows onto the balcony had gone, leaving the room open to the elements. From the balcony we quietly took in the same view of the palms across the river that we had seen in rather more fearful conditions seventeen weeks earlier. A kilometre to the left Saddam's large private yacht lay on its side, having been hit by Coalition missiles.

When we came downstairs in 48-degree heat the self-appointed guardians of our car lied that they had warded off a gang of looters trying to steal the car, and they were unhappy with the amount of cash Stewart gave them. Later we discovered they had stolen the decal from the front of the car.

Over the next few days we tried to track down the Ba'athist lawyer, Yahya Al Muheisin. We made several visits to a local law firm, where we chatted for hours to idle lawyers – the courts were closed – and businessmen about life in Basra. We explained that we wanted to contact Muheisin because he had helped us during our arrest.

One lawyer who tried to deny his rather obvious Ba'ath Party sympathies eventually acted as a go-between and took us to meet Muheisin amid much mystery about our meeting place. He had insisted that Muheisin had fled for his life but the lawyer who had laughed throughout our interrogation back in March was actually at his own home, awaiting our visit.

Muheisin greeted us in his front yard, smiling broadly and wearing a white dishdasha. He kissed and hugged Stewart, and shook my hand heartily, then led us into a tiled reception room. There was no air conditioning but the house was large, well furnished and in good order.

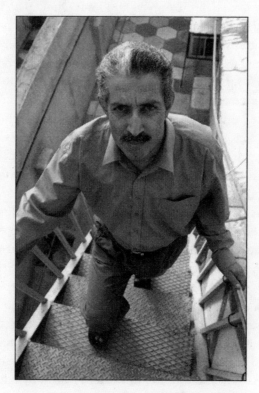

Yahya Al Muheisin. Stuart Clarke

We waited in large armchairs while he disappeared, emerging a few minutes later in a grey shirt and trousers over sandals. He asked after John Feder, saying he had noticed that our friend was very afraid during our interrogation. I told him we had all been afraid, and Stewart filled him in on our drive to Baghdad and experiences there.

Muheisin's English was not perfect and he often asked Stewart to translate my comments into Arabic. He smiled confidently as if our first meeting had been a fond experience for all of us, and after a few minutes of small talk got down to the reason why he had agreed to meet us. He was desperate to get out of the country and hoped that I could help him emigrate to Australia.

'You have done a humanitarian thing if you can help,' he said, explaining that he wanted to flee with his wife, sister and six children, who were aged from one to seventeen.

The daughter of his first cousin lived in Australia and had said life was good there. More to the point, dozens of his Ba'ath Party colleagues had already been killed by anti-Saddam vigilantes in recent weeks, he said, 'and they will kill me, too, if I stay'.

We had told our go-between that Muheisin had helped us during our interrogation, and that seemed to be how Muheisin himself remembered things.

'Your friend's hand was shaking and you were [all] worried. That's why I was talking to you in English, to put you at ease.'

His interventions had not seemed particularly reassuring at the time. I reminded him that he had gone on at some length about how Saddam was going to win the war, and asked him if he had believed those claims.

'No, I expected Iraq to lose the war. I had to say that stuff about how we would win.'

His boasts had actually been made in English so they were not to convince his listening colleagues of his loyalty but I now found myself questioning my own memory of Muheisin's unhelpful role in our interrogation. He had not spoken up in our defence but by the same token he had not exactly denounced us and in the circumstances he could hardly have argued that we should be released. And the longer we talked now, the more I realised that his regular bursts of laughter had been an annoying mannerism rather than a deliberate taunt or a sign of indifference to our fate.

I still did not feel any particular gratitude for his behaviour during our interrogation but I was increasingly and uncomfortably aware that we had swapped roles, and he was now in just as much fear as we had been when last we met. The difference was that Muheisin was also afraid for his whole family.

'The situation here is not stable,' he said. 'It is chaos. The nation is on the brink of civil war and the Americans are encouraging dangerous splits between ethnic and religious groups.' The armed resistance to the Coalition was just beginning, he said, and it would spread – much violence lay ahead.

'The trouble will increase because the American handling of Iraq so far shows a surprising lack of understanding. For example, they have fired all the senior Ba'ath Party and military people from their jobs. Multiply that number by an average of five for their family members and ask yourself what the attitude will be of all those people who have lost their incomes.

'The problem in the party was not its ideology but the behaviour (and abuse of power) of its leadership and yet the Americans are treating everybody in the party the same as the leadership.

'I can no longer work as a lawyer and at any moment people could attack me and my family. I am scared of going out.'

I asked him how he came to be at the party headquarters when we were arrested.

'We used to go there every day because of the fighting – we would go to fight. There were a lot of Ba'ath Party members in the room with you including some heads of divisions.

'Everybody there thought you were quite brave for coming into the war zone. We believed that you were reporters. It was obvious from your demeanour, the way you looked, the cameras in the car, your logic when you tried to talk your way out of it. When you are honest about what you are saying people can tell.

'That's why you got full respect. I don't think anything was stolen from you – I locked your car to make sure that not even a bottle of water was taken.'

We did lose a few items but it was indeed striking that we did not lose the rest of our equipment, including potentially life-saving flak jackets.

'The British tanks used to come in and make incursions and

leave, so there was always shooting. At one point I was hiding in a dug-out in a muddy clay area and a missile landed four metres away. I only survived because it went into the mud.'

A few hours after we were taken away one of the men in the room, Nasser al A'amiri, was killed in a fight with the British, he said.

'Nasser had snuck up to two hundred metres from the tanks and fired off an RPG but they fired back and killed him.

'The next day at about 4 p.m. the tanks came in and reached the building you were sitting in, so we had to run away. Our RPGs were just ricocheting off the Challenger tanks so we ran away. I just got away.'

The office commander, Majid, was a party division head. 'He's OK – he got away but I don't know what's happened to the others who were there because since the fall the party has disintegrated.'

Mustafa, the large man who took us to the Sheraton, had been a Mukhabarat agent named Sa'ad. 'Nobody knew the full names of the Mukhabarat people. He came because the Mukhabarat were responsible for foreigners.'

The driver Mohammed was also Mukhabarat, not Fedayeen as he had claimed, and was not from Basra. The young uniformed man, Ali, was a local policeman and 'a genuinely nice young man'.

I told him that Ali had indeed been sympathetic to our plight.

'All Iraqis are like that – you have to provoke them to get a violent response. Nobody is killing the British now because they are not provoking people. The Americans are throwing people to the ground and putting their boots on their heads in front of their wives and families.'

The tall, handsome young man in the dishdasha who had held a gun to our faces as we were taken to the party office was the son of a tribal leader who had been killed in a clash with a tank. He agreed 'to some extent' with the opinion of witnesses that we were lucky we were not held by Fedayeen.

'There was no order to kill journalists but there was not much control over people either. The Fedayeen were young and enthusiastic and were not educated, so you don't know what they could have done. But you were brought to the proper authorities so you were OK.

'We had been ordered to seize any vehicle with 'TV' written on it because there were Kuwaitis coming into Iraq to cause sabotage.

There were a lot of people with binoculars looking at the tanks and watching the road and they would have known you were there.'

His role after our arrest, he said, was 'to prepare the way for a decision to be made about what to do with you'.

'I told them it was an infiltration case, a breach of Article 24 of the criminal code. It carries a sentence of up to seven years but unless there is any suspicion about the motive of the entry you get one year. They don't usually enforce it, and people get a suspended sentence.'

We spoke for three hours. He seemed to be talking candidly and I was intrigued to hear what such an active party member really thought of Saddam, and his rationale for the regime's behaviour. I asked him what he thought of the Ba'ath Party now.

'Everybody is attacking the party because defending it now can get you killed. The problem of the party was not its ideology but the dominance of Saddam's close supporters from Tikrit and Ramadi. But that was not exclusive to our party. The problem is that there is no way democracy can be applied in Iraq. Look at Chalabi and [Kurdish leaders] Barazani and Talabani – they are all from dynasties, not true democrats.

'And it's not just Iraq. The president of Egypt is lining his son up to replace him. Iran, Kuwait, the Saudis – even Lebanon once had democracy but Iran and Syria ruined it.

'My personal opinion is that the problem is outside interference. If any party grows with support from the people then outside influences create problems for them. In the Cold War the Americans and Russians never even thought about democracy in the Middle East.

'The US conspiracies and campaigns against Iraq over the years created a security situation through which the Tikritis were able to grow and dominate the party. They increased the security apparatus under the cover of defending the revolution until many of their behaviours were hurting ordinary people and were individual actions not known by the leadership.

'People could abuse their power. If you complained you got justice, as long as you reached the right person in the government. But the problem was reaching the right person.'

Most killings in detention were crimes by regime members rather than acts of policy, he insisted. Remarkably, he admitted that

LIBRARY

MEMBERSHIP

APPLICATION FORM

 LONDON BOROUGH OF
RICHMOND UPON THAMES
Education, Arts & Leisure

For official use only

● ●

PROOF OF ADDRESS IS NEEDED

Please show your driving licence or pension book or bank/credit card statement or any official bill such as a gas bill, or a letter from an official body such as a tax office or local council. This document should show your name and address.

Please complete on BLOCK CAPITALS

Please tick   Mr ☐   Mrs ☐   Miss ☐   Ms ☐   Other, please state ....

Surname ....

Forenames ....

Address ....

Postcode ....   Tel ....   email ....

Date of Birth (if you are under 18)   /   /

If you are aged 60 or over you can pay a reduced reservation fee.   Tick here to claim ☐

If you are a non-resident, please also complete this section:

Name of college or workplace

Address ....

                                                             Postcode ....

I accept responsibility for books and items borrowed on this ticket

I agree to observe the Library Regulations

Please sign   **Print name**

(If you are under 18 please ask your parent or guardian to sign and print their name.)

Address

Borrower ticket number   ☐ ☐ ☐ ☐ ☐ ☐

If you would like a copy of this leaflet in Braille, large print, on audio tape, or in a community language, please contact us on 020 8891 7500; Minicom number: 020 8891 7539.

his own wife's brother was killed while being interrogated after the 1991 uprisings.

'He had been involved in the uprising but at that time almost everybody in Basra was. It was chaos. He was arrested in the recriminations later but it was not the regime that killed him, it was a few individuals.

'The regime did not say "Kill them", it said "Arrest them and interrogate them". Yes, the regime often turned a blind eye to such crimes but the person who did it would be punished if caught. If a citizen lodged a complaint he would be protected but there was always the fear that sometimes the person you were accusing would get you.'

Muheisin raised the issue of the mass graves now being uncovered.

'In 1991 as our troops were withdrawing from Kuwait the Americans were bombing them and infiltrators were coming from Iran to cause trouble. Bodies were lying everywhere so they were buried together.

'That's what is in those graves, not [the victims of] government mass murders.'

When I told him what the farmer at Hilla had told us he had seen, Muheisin was unconvinced. 'He is saying that to win favour,' he said with a shrug.

He said many had joined the party 'for personal advancement' but he had been attracted by its vision of a united, nationalist Iraq. He studied law from 1993 to 1997 and had specialised in major criminal cases. He had been studying English literature at night, and had recently been working on *Macbeth* and sixteenth-century poetry.

Muheisin said he had already learned that he would not be accepted into Australia as a political refugee, as Australia now considered Iraq to be free and democratic. Instead he wanted to know about the normal immigration system. I explained to him that applicants were given points for various factors such as family connections in Australia and having job skills Australia desired, and they could also apply under investment or business categories.

He wanted to go with his own family and his 39-year-old unmarried sister, an assistant professor who had been teaching life sciences at university for sixteen years. They could raise about US$200,000 between them.

I promised to go to an Internet café to look at the emigration rules and get some sense of his prospects of emigrating.

We returned to Muheisin's house the next day with Stuart Clarke, who had just arrived from Baghdad, and with the results of my Internet research. I told him that the eligibility rules on the website suggested he had little hope of entering Australia.

He reflected for a few seconds then said, with that disconcerting laugh: 'So it is Syria for me or they will kill me.' Some forty to fifty Ba'ath Party members in Basra had already been killed since the fall of the government, he said, and they had no protection. He asked whether he could work for my newspaper, or at least have a piece of paper which said he did. I told him I could not do that. Stuart took some photographs, then I lent Muheisin my satellite phone for a few calls. He smiled with some disappointment but no bitterness as we left him to his fate.

Stewart and I had earlier made the forty-five-minute drive to Umm Qasr, through 48-degree heat and a sand storm. The town was even uglier than it had been, with rubbish blowing around the streets in the sand storm. One striking difference was that most of the trees lining the main road and dotted through the arid patches of land around the houses had been chopped down about a metre above the ground.

Poking around town we found that the Ba'ath Party office had met the same fate as the one we visited in Basra and was now home to a family of squatters.

My main interest was to see what had become of the town's experiment in local democracy. As far back as April, when we were trapped in the Palestine Hotel in Baghdad, I had heard BBC reports that the British forces in Umm Qasr had created the first town council in post-Saddam Iraq, appointing a local school teacher as mayor. I had been pretty confident that this would have been Najim Abd Mahdi, the school teacher we met outside the British head-quarters as one of the first locals to offer assistance to the Coalition. The British military had since made great play of the Umm Qasr council, holding it up as an example of how civil society might be kick-started without relying on the traditional power structures based on religious, ethnic and tribal divisions.

A few conversations with locals quickly confirmed that Mahdi was indeed the mayor, and we soon found our way to his home, a run-down single-storey mud-brick house in a storm-blown, dirty street.

Mahdi remembered us from the early days of the British occupation and welcomed us warmly, sending his two sons to fetch water and tea. School teachers were paid notoriously poorly in Saddam's Iraq and his home was one of the most humble we had visited. Plastic flowers sat on a table, and alongside a portrait of a Shi'ite Imam was a poorly framed photograph of the Mona Lisa which seemed to have been cut out of a magazine.

During the war Mahdi's wife, two sons and four daughters had all gone to stay with family in Basra, and several friends had moved into his house to protect him in the first weeks after he had approached the British, with an offer to name the local Ba'ath Party leaders. He had rejected lucrative offers of translating work from foreign reporters and the World Food Program in order to stay and help in Umm Qasr.

'I have never liked Umm Qasr but after the war I felt obliged to say here and try to promote democracy in this town.'

Mahdi had first been sent from Basra to the relative backwater of Umm Qasr for a one-year teaching stint after his graduation in 1975. For the next twenty-eight years he was refused permission to move back to Basra or another big city, banished because of his one-time membership of the Communist Party and his lack of enthusiasm for teaching Saddam's view of the world. Stranded in a town he considered a cultural desert, he wrote and published short stories but gave up in the late 1970s because 'writing could lead to death' under Saddam.

'I was the first one to cooperate with the British, not because I loved the British or American armies. I felt obliged to cooperate with them because I think they were coming to liberate us. I wish Iraqis were able to liberate Iraq by themselves but the authority of the Ba'athists was very, very crude against us.

'Six of my friends who were my students many years ago co-operated with me, and the British officers suggested that we should do a town council. I had no idea about that because we had no experience of town councils. We have read about it in books or newspapers but had never had it.

'I formed the first town council in Iraq. First we dealt with electricity. All the lines were cut and we depended on the grain silo because there were eight generators there. The batteries had been stolen and we did not get them back so the Coalition brought new ones from Kuwait and we provided the town with electricity from 31 March.'

But the progress had not been sustained. Mahdi said that most municipal services collapsed when the British withdrew their support too hastily. 'This town is now a hellhole of garbage, worse than it has ever been.'

The British stopped collecting garbage in May. 'We had no equipment or money to pay sanitation workers so we asked people to help us clean the streets as volunteers.'

The council was expanded to fifteen but ran into conflict with Shi'ite leaders who thought they should run the council. The clerics discouraged volunteers from doing the council's work, and after two weeks Mahdi's volunteer force collapsed.

An early attempt at a town election – with the British reserving the right to reject the results – produced a voter turnout of just ten per cent and allegations of cheating. Infighting and resistance from Muslim clerics had since crippled the council, marginalising Mahdi, who was about to be replaced by the British and was bitterly disillusioned about his brief political career.

While most Iraqis were insisting that the Coalition should hand power back to Iraqis as soon as possible, Mahdi said his experience showed that the handover should not be too quick. However much the British and Americans wanted to leave Iraq, Iraqis were simply not ready to be thrown straight into a democracy, he said, making his point with a joke.

'An Egyptian, a Kuwaiti and an Iraqi are all asked, "What is your opinion of the shortage of meat?" The Egyptian says, "What is meat?" The Kuwaiti says, "What is a shortage?" And the Iraqi says, "What is an opinion?"

'I think the Coalition should stay until we are ready. We wish we could be able to run everything but now we are not and we depend on them. They should stay until we are ready.' Having once risked his life to try to democratise his town, Mahdi now simply wanted to leave. 'I am in exile here. I wish I could leave but I do not have the money. Teachers are the poorest paid people in Iraq. The

Saddam Government did not respect education or educated people. A teaboy in an oil company earned three times a teacher's salary.'

We left Mahdi mid-afternoon and drove around town chatting to people for some time before dropping in on the house of the Lazem brothers, whom we had seen being arrested in March.

Their younger brother Hussein came to the front gate and insisted that the pair who had been arrested, Ali and Hadi, had both moved away two months earlier. A nosey neighbour who overheard this conversation interrupted to say that was nonsense, and told Hussein to go and get Ali. Ali emerged reluctantly and unsmiling, saying there must have been a mix-up about him having moved away.

We then had a less than comfortable conversation in the street, with Ali saying the Coalition had released him and his brother because their only offence was to have a weapon. Their eldest brother Fadhil, who we knew was a senior party member accused of extortion and executions, had certainly left town.

Others had told us that the neighbours were no longer afraid of the Lazems, and proof of that was played out in front of us. As we talked about conditions in Umm Qasr, Ali complained about the shortage of jobs and public services, adding that the presence of the British had done nothing for the local people. He was cut off by a neighbour, Amir Hadi Thijeel, a truck driver wearing a singlet in the late afternoon heat.

'What do you mean they haven't done us any good?' he asked, challenging Ali aggressively. 'Do you see anybody getting shot around here now? Do you see any of us being arrested and tortured or robbed by Saddam's people? We can all sleep at night now without worrying what will happen to us in the morning.'

There was a surly silence from Ali.

As we headed out of town we saw a vivid demonstration of the desperate times in Umm Qasr. About four hundred metres along the road we passed a young man chopping down one of the town's few remaining trees, a straggly specimen some four metres high. The heat was still stifling at 5.30 p.m., and he was sweating heavily as he went about the job, with a hand trolley waiting ten metres away to carry home his spoils.

When we stopped our car, Haidar Abdul Satter, twenty, leaned on his axe to explain what he was doing. Yes, he agreed, it was a pity to destroy the trees which provided the only shade in town. But a breakdown in the British distribution of cooking gas had left people short of firewood for their kitchens, with prices now ten times the usual rate.

'It's bad to ruin the environment but how else can we cook?' The tree he was sweating over would fuel his family's kitchen for one or two weeks, he said.

He agreed to be photographed. Hearing Stewart's camera clicking away, he tried to accommodate him by keeping up his swings until Stewart had the shot he was after. He didn't know that Stewart's camera style was to keep shooting with a machine-gun shutter technique, then select the best photo later. When Haidar began to turn red I had to intervene.

'God, Stewart, stop shooting – you are going to kill the poor guy.'

Given the terrible things we had seen in Iraq I was surprised at how troubled I was to see people chopping down their few trees. They were not just vandalising their own town, they were cannibalising it in front of us.

The next day, Monday 21 July, when we returned with Stuart to photograph Mahdi, we saw six young men pulling down a metal power pole on the road into town. They looked at us cautiously, then decided we were no threat and gave the pole the final yank to the ground. Looters across Iraq had for some time been tearing down power transmission lines for scrap; now they were attacking the actual power poles.

We took photos of Mahdi amid the street rubbish which symbolised the failure of his council, then returned to Basra to photograph the former Ba'ath Party office and the Sheraton. The party office had been stripped of its furniture and Saddam portraits – even the plaster portraits had been chipped away, leaving just the outline of Saddam's head.

It was 7.30 p.m. by the time we showed Stuart up to 'our' gutted room at the Sheraton, and as the daylight faded and the lights came on across the river it was pretty much the view we had contemplated the first time we were here.

While Stewart wandered around the hotel and Stuart photographed the room, I spent some time on the balcony remembering just how scared I had been on the last night of March. The same fishing boats were lined up along the waterfront but two British Scorpion tanks rattled past to remind me there had been a few changes. I was uneasy with the knowledge that Muheisin was now feeling like we had.

The next morning we made one final visit – to Abu Nashwan, the storeman we had been interviewing when we were arrested. He greeted us warmly at his gate at 6.30 a.m. and laughed when Stewart translated my first words: 'As I was saying before I was so rudely interrupted . . . '

While his full name was Sabeh Abdullah Zuwir, the 54-year-old storeman adopted the common practice of calling himself the father of his eldest son, so he was 'Abu Nashwan' or Nashwan's father. He was wearing a nightshirt and invited us into the house, where his family was just getting up. But first we stood talking for a short while on the footpath, in the same spot where we had been arrested.

I told Abu Nashwan that I had heard that some Fedayeen had been based nearby and he corrected me to say that they had been staying in the house right next door – 'Palestinians, Syrians, Tunisians and Iraqis'. 'We felt like human shields in our own homes.'

Within two minutes, we were interrupted again. A neighbour ran up, distraught, saying that armed men had just burst into his home, beaten him and stolen his car and life savings, US$1500.

Over the wailing of his neighbour's wife, Abu Nashwan said the collapse of law and order had been the biggest hardship in their neighbourhood. 'That makes everything hard. We can't go out at night and it could be us robbed next – tonight, tomorrow, any time.'

The family insisted that we share their breakfast of flat bread, marmalade, scrambled eggs and tea. When we were seated in the lounge room, Abu Nashwan said his second-eldest son, Arkan, a 27-year-old tailor, had had to close his store and bring his equipment home to stop it being stolen. While his neighbour had told us that crime was so bad he would prefer to live under the Saddam regime, Abu Nashwan disagreed, saying he was delighted that the Coalition has ended 'this nightmare for all Iraqis'.

'We're happy that the Americans were so persistent about removing him from power. And most people think like this.

'Every family was oppressed. Most families lost one or two members to that regime. We just kept our heads down to survive.'

He had certainly been keeping his head down when I interviewed him in March, spouting pro-Saddam rhetoric about the public support for the old regime. Now he snorted at the memory. 'I would have been arrested and taken away if I said anything else.'

His home was hit several times by shrapnel but nobody was hurt. In fact, he gained a grandson, Hussein, the day after our arrest when Nashwan's wife had her delayed Caesarean operation and Abu Nashwan's fourth grandchild, Fatima, was delivered on 5 June.

He was optimistic about Iraq's future, saying the daily attacks on the Coalition had little public support. 'These are people attached to the old regime so it won't last long or spread.'

Abu Nashwan said he was confident that even the economic disruption would soon pass. The end of UN trade sanctions would lift the supply of goods and stimulate the economy, and 'with a good government in place we should be able to control inflation so living standards will rise quickly'.

'If the Americans restore order, then leave, we should be able to handle things well. I prefer a short invasion to the old regime.'

He said the tall man in the white dishdasha who arrested us had been from a town called Ashar, and had been killed three days after our arrest when he and other Fedayeen were caught by British tanks in the open land across the road from the Ba'ath Party office.

'There was a lot of fighting there and many people were killed – that's where he died.'

After breakfast we accompanied Abu Nashwan to the silos where he had worked for more than thirty-one years, then we packed up to leave. Stuart Clarke hired a car for the drive back to Baghdad, while Stewart and I made the short drive south into Kuwait.

A four-wheel drive carrying a Red Cross worker had just been attacked on the same road we had taken past Hilla. The driver was killed and we were keen to keep our time on the road to a minimum.

That night in Kuwait City I turned on CNN in my hotel room to discover that, as we had been driving out of Iraq, American troops had trapped Saddam's sons Uday and Qusay in a house in the northern city of Mosul and killed them in a drawn-out firefight.

I had been planning to spend the night writing a magazine article but instead I sat up watching interviews by Paul Bremer and US military officers so I could pull together a news report – cushy work sitting in a hotel room with Internet access and several news channels.

The death of Saddam's sons was a morale boost for the Coalition and raised the confidence of ordinary Iraqis that the old regime was finished. Saddam's rule had been so long and oppressive that he had managed to turn himself into a dynasty in the eyes of his people. The death of his sons left him as just a single-generation tyrant.

'These guys mattered a lot because they symbolised the forlorn hope of a lot of Iraqi Ba'athist types that Saddam is somehow going to come back,' said Paul Bremer. 'This is really a great day for Iraqis.'

But there was no reason to believe that it would stop the terror attacks, and it did not.

I had long been convinced by many Iraqis that even the capture of Saddam might actually increase the number of attacks, by allowing Iraqis who opposed both Saddam and the Americans to tackle the occupiers without having to worry that Saddam might return if the Americans left.

*

Two weeks after I returned to London, Ali and his friend Ahmed, who had lost a hand and a foot, finally flew to the UK for prosthetics and further treatment by the Limbless Association. The Kuwaiti Government put on one of its private jets and plenty of publicity for the 8 August flight, on which the boys were accompanied by Hamed, Ahmed's father and a team of Kuwaiti doctors and government officials.

The other injured Iraqi children who had been treated in Kuwait had been sent back to Iraq without this level of follow-up care but the Kuwaitis promised at a press conference before the flight to London that they would keep paying for the treatment of Ali and Ahmed until they reached adulthood.

I was now worried that Ali might become a political tool, fears that were stoked when three US military officers who had visited Ali in hospital placed American army hats on the boys for smiling photographs at their farewell press conference. 'No hard feelings' was the implied message in those rather tacky photos and there was no guarantee that that was how Ali would feel when he was old enough to weigh up the US military's impact on his life.

In London the *Daily Mirror* got its money's worth from Ali, organising a double-decker bus to take him on a tour of London, and publishing 'Ali comes to London' photos of him doing things like wearing a bobby's hat outside Buckingham Palace.

The two boys and their guardians were put up in a house near Wimbledon in London's south-western suburbs, rented with some of the funds raised by the Limbless Association in Ali's name. From there they could attend the Queen Mary's Hospital Rehabilitation Centre in nearby Roehampton for rehabilitation while work was done on their prosthetics and Ali's burns were treated. He would have to wear a pressure suit until the middle of 2004 to try to minimise the scarring on his torso and legs.

When they had been there for a few weeks Hamed, who spoke almost no English, called me with the help of the boys' English tutor, Zainab Hashim, to ask me to visit. This was the first time I had really met Ali, who wanted me to tell him everything about his rescue – his memories were patchy and he had not really understood what was going on around him. I became a regular visitor to their home, a decent-sized, two-storey house with a large backyard equipped with a miniature soccer goal for the boys.

Ali was shy but unusually bright and surprisingly happy and mischievous. On my second or third visit I was talking to Zainab and Hamed when Ali picked up my mobile phone under his chin and disappeared under the table. A few minutes later Hamed raced into the next room to answer the phone, where he stood for some time saying 'Hello?' Each time he was about to hang up Ali, who had dialled with his toes, teased him from under the table with a whispered 'Hello!'

I was struck by the fact that Ali was now at that juncture reached by every adolescent, when they slip back and forward between being a child and something more mature. That is always a difficult time but Ali's situation was something else. Apart from his injuries and the horrors he had been through, he was living in a foreign culture and, most importantly, was constantly being reminded that he had responsibilities as the head of his family.

Hamed and Ahmed's father cooked and maintained their all-male household. On the lounge-room mantle was a David Beckham doll and a signed photo of Robin Gibb of the Bee Gees, a celebrity they had never heard of until he took an interest in Ali's plight.

Satellite TV gave them access to Arabic cable television stations, and this allowed Hamed to avoid British and US movies, which tended to show the boys a little too much female flesh for their guardians' liking.

Apart from doing daily English lessons with Zainab, Ali and Ahmed eventually attended a normal English school near their home for several hours a day, mainly to play with other children but also to take some lessons conducted in English.

By early October I had the sense that Ali understood much of what was said to him in English, although he did not have the confidence to attempt sentences. In November he made a fair effort of his first 'translation job', being the go-between, amid much giggling, in a conversation between Hamed and me.

In October, six and a half months after the missile attack, Ali was fitted for the first time with prosthetic arms and began the lengthy process of learning how to use them. On his shorter left arm the prosthetic would be largely cosmetic until some new technology was invented but his new right arm could eventually give him quite a degree of independence. An electrode attached to the muscle in his arm would allow him to open and close the hand, while he could lock the elbow in three positions and use a strap across his chest to operate the wrist. Getting new arms and 'looking whole again' was the first in a long list of goals he had set himself, which still included eating with a spoon, brushing his teeth and driving a car.

The new limbs would need to be replaced every year while he was growing and every three or four years after that, which the Limbless Association had promised to fund. Foreigners notoriously have difficulty opening bank accounts in Britain and it was not until late November that Hamed was able to open an account in Ali's name. I sent the account details to Tony Trevisan in Perth, along with my estimation of how Ali and his family were placed financially. He and his uncle were not penniless, I said, but they still faced a challenge supporting their combined household of fourteen women and children including Ali, and then helping Ali over the rest of his life.

The Limbless Association had no intention of handing over the money raised in Ali's name, and was instead considering spending any money left over after Ali's treatment to set up a centre for amputees in Iraq. The Kuwait Government had bought clothes and accessories for Ali and his uncle, and private donors in Kuwait had given him some money. The *Daily Mirror* had paid for his story, and HarperCollins would publish a book on him in April 2004, with royalties going to Ali.

Trevisan e-mailed me back saying he now thought his money could be better spent on more needy cases.

'Recent TV images of Ali and his uncle clearly show a very significant change in their circumstances. Ali, thankfully, looks extremely healthy – in fact he looks decidedly overweight; whilst his uncle looked more like a successful London-based businessman than a refugee, in his tailored suit and fashionable tie.'

Disappointed, I e-mailed Trevisan that I thought Ali had 'a lot more than many Iraqi kids but a lot less than I would want if I was in his situation'. At the same time, I understood his decision.

In March 2004 the British Home Office granted Ali and Hamed 'indefinite leave to remain', meaning they could apply for British passports without giving up their Iraqi citizenship. Ali was keen to go to university in Britain, and Hamed would be allowed to work. They would not have stayed in Britain without their family but their family was now almost certain to be allowed to join them.

Ali's half-sister Asma'a had had a daughter in December, making Ali an uncle. To his delight the baby was named Azhar, after his mother. He returned to Baghdad over the Christmas holidays to visit his family, although the trip was kept secret because of fears that he could be a kidnap target in Baghdad.

I was there at the same time, having rushed to Iraq because of the capture of Saddam in a hole on a farm not far from his home town, Tikrit. Once again I arrived in Baghdad without my satellite phone or clothes. This time the culprit was not the Mukhabarat but Lufthansa airline, which managed to lose my luggage on the way to Jordan and then repeated the fiasco a week later on my way back to London.

Iraq had avoided the most pessimistic predictions of civil war, and was moving with cautious optimism into what was finally a future free of any involvement by Saddam Hussein.

Unemployment was painfully high, the petrol queues were longer than ever and electricity supplies were still patchy. There had been little improvement in public security, with a continuing campaign of often audacious attacks on the Coalition and its Iraqi allies.

But there were also undeniable signs of an improving economy. Wages had increased dramatically since the fall of Saddam, property prices had soared and an extra 250,000 cars were on the streets of Baghdad. The imported goods which had been flooding into the country since the lifting of UN sanctions had also helped to control inflation while making available an enormous new range of consumer products.

I found myself being more optimistic than most Western journalists about Iraq's fate. While enormous political challenges and security dangers lay ahead, the most important fact was that the overwhelming majority of Iraqis were happy to see the back of Saddam and would support a Coalition presence that was not open-ended.

Their country also had more natural assets and a better-educated workforce than any other nation with such a weak economy, meaning there was enormous scope for the sort of sustained economic growth that could make Iraqis feel that they and their families were winners rather than losers from the painful transition they have begun.

*

After Saddam's arrest it was still dangerous to move about in Baghdad after dark but that did not stop people celebrating his capture. When I returned to the Shi'ite suburb of Shu'ala a few days after the dictator's capture, the Saleh family, including the brother and sister Kasim and Jamila whose brothers were killed in Saddam's prisons, were planning to mark the event with a party outside their bakery.

'Lots of people have put in money for the party and we will give the whole neighbourhood food and drink to celebrate,' said Mohammed, the son of one of the dead brothers. 'And we will have a party every year to celebrate his capture. It was the best day of our lives.'

They invited me to be the only outsider at the neighbourhood party but my new 'fixer' and several other Iraqis who I consulted insisted that it would be too dangerous for a foreigner to attend a party in the open after dark. As I was driven back into central Baghdad I knew I was missing out on a special night, as I felt an empathy for this family, for their pain and now their triumph, that surprised me.

I was still just a reporter doing a story, after all, but I had to keep reminding myself that I had not known any of these people for that long. Not the Saleh family, celebrating at last after all those years of pain; not the thugs of the old regime whose crimes we saw time and again; not the fugitive Ba'ath Party lawyer Muheisin whose uncertain fate had made me so uneasy. Not Taras, Salah the driver, or Ali and his family. Not even John Feder and Stewart Innes.

It was Taras who best articulated the strange intensity of what I felt, good and bad, for the people I had come to know during what now seemed like one long, haphazard drive through Iraq's war.

Hundreds attended his funeral in downtown Kiev on 13 April, and the next day Ukraine's leading commercial television channel broadcast an extraordinary interview with him. The station had done the interview while making a documentary on war reporters in 1997, and to help him speak freely about his job it was recorded on the understanding that it would not be aired unless Taras was killed or until he had left Reuters.

In a war zone, Taras had said, 'there is different psychology, different laws, different behaviour'.

'There are many conventions in our life – we smile at other people, wear clean clothes . . . obey traffic rules. In war all these conventions slip into the background. A good person can be clearly seen as a good one and a bad person is clearly seen as a bad one.

'The person is exposed, uncovered, without a mask. I think it is very interesting from a psychological point of view because there is an opportunity to get to know a person much better.'